Praise for *Running Up the Mountain*

"I regularly raced against tough NAU runners during my career at UCLA. With so many outstanding programs out west, NAU still stands out as a special dynasty for its location and history. NAU and Flagstaff represent our sport at its best. This book chronicles the journey."

Meb Keflezighi, 2014 Boston Marathon winner, 2009 New York City Marathon winner, Olympic silver medalist

"I've lived in Flagstaff since 2010. At that time, I was just a fan of my college alma mater. But after living and training in this community for over ten years, I can't help but become an immense fan of the NAU men's and women's program. *Running Up the Mountain* is a rich history that details both teams' work ethic, dedication, camaraderie, and pride. I'm a converted Lumberjack fan. As much as the men have seen success in recent years, as a female runner it's been exciting to see the rise and prominence of the women's team."

Stephanie Bruce, three-time U.S. national champion; three-time mom; co-founder, Picky Bars

"NAU has been inspirational to runners for more than fifty years. My fellow Kiwis know that well; there has been at least one New Zealander on NAU's top seven for four of their six national titles. Matt Baxter and Ron Mann bring to life how an upstart school on the road to the Grand Canyon came to beat the best through friendship, mutual trust, hard work, and building a shared tradition second to none."

Rod Dixon, 1983 New York City Marathon winner

"I used Flagstaff for my base training in summer 2011 leading up to my second-place finish at the Chicago Marathon (2:06:13 PR) and my Boston Marathon win in 2012. The running conditions and community are the best around. Flagstaff is a town for champions."

Wesley Korir, 2012 Boston Marathon winner

"*Running Up the Mountain* is an inspirational and intimate story well told. Matt and Ron provide an insider's guide to the fifty-year ascent of Northern Arizona University to the pinnacle of U.S. collegiate distance running. The book reveals how thoughtful and innovative coaching, dedicated student-athletes, a strong team culture, and the unique Flagstaff training environment converged to build the dynasty that NAU has become. A highly enjoyable read!"

Pete Pfitzinger, two-time Olympian, author of *Advanced Marathoning*

"More than a history of a college running program, more than a celebration of a running mecca, *Running Up the Mountain* is a blueprint for how to have success in the sport of running, with lessons that are surprisingly universal in their appeal."

— **Matt Fitzgerald**, author, *Running the Dream: One Summer Living, Training, and Racing with a Team of World-Class Runners Half My Age*

"My fondest memory of Flagstaff is one of extreme gratitude to the community at large. It welcomed us Olympic hopefuls with open arms. The salvation of the USA distance running team from complete disaster at the 1968 Mexico City Olympics was due in large part to Dr. Jack Daniels and the Flagstaff community."

— **Jim Ryun,** former mile world-record holder, Olympic silver medalist

"Flagstaff became an annual, then bi-annual, four-week, altitude training pilgrimage in my career. The trails, the open community of elite runners, and the thin air made the perfect retreat before the intensity of the Olympics. The various coaching staff at NAU were always welcoming and encouraging as I utilized their world-class indoor and outdoor track facilities."

— **Nick Willis**, two-time Olympic 1500m medalist

"The high altitude training under the supervision of Dr. Jack Daniels is the only reason this farm boy from Kansas made the 1968 Olympic team. Jim Ryun, George Young, Billy Mills, and I could not have had that training experience without the generous support and facilities of NAU and the Flagstaff community. My hat's off to all those Arizonans who played such an important role in that mentorship."

— **Dr. Conrad Nightingale**, 1968 Olympian

"In the thin mountain air of the western United States, generations of collegiate distance running greats have been nurtured at institutions big and small, from CU-Boulder to BYU to Alamosa's Adams State College. No star has shined brighter in recent years than that of Northern Arizona University in Flagstaff. What a treat it is to read this book and learn about the personalities that built one of America's great running programs in one of our treasured running communities."

— **Chris Lear**, author, *Running with the Buffaloes*

RUNNING UP THE MOUNTAIN

Lumberjacks Nico Young (699) and Drew Bosley (690) guide Stanford's Charles Hicks (770) and the rest of the field up the hill at the Greiner Family OSU Cross Country Course in Stillwater, Oklahoma, at the NCAA Men's Cross Country Championships on November 19, 2022.

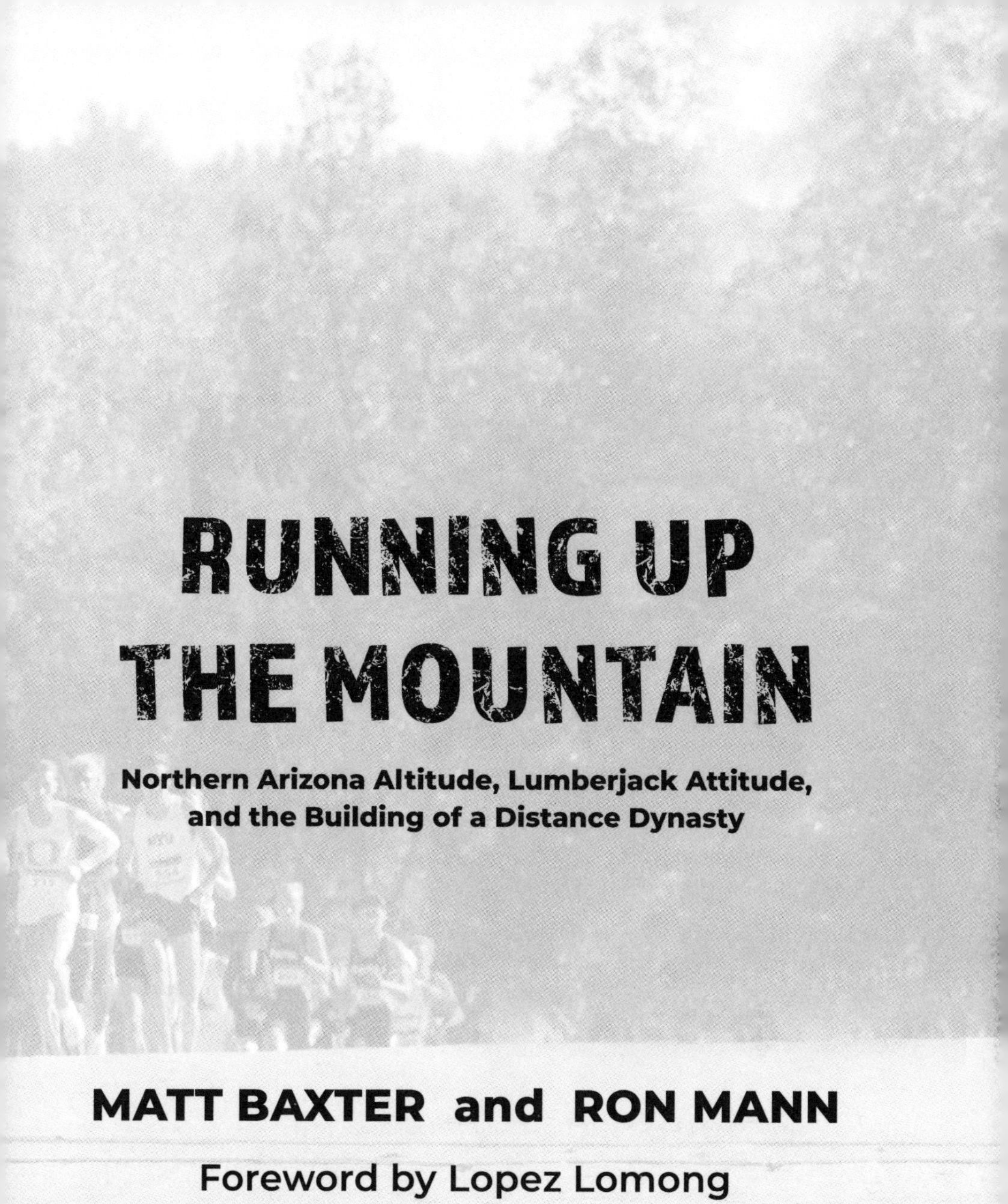

RUNNING UP THE MOUNTAIN

Northern Arizona Altitude, Lumberjack Attitude, and the Building of a Distance Dynasty

MATT BAXTER and RON MANN

Foreword by Lopez Lomong

Soulstice PUBLISHING
books with *soul* • Flagstaff, AZ

Running Up the Mountain: Northern Arizona Altitude, Lumberjack Attitude, and the Building of a Distance Dynasty

ISBN: 978-1-7349899-6-0 (hardback)
ISBN: 978-1-7349899-7-7 (e-book)
Library of Congress Control Number: 2022920615

Graphic design by Dariusz Janczewski
Editorial Services by Catherine Bell, Julie Hammonds, Myles Schrag, and Claudine Taillac
Proofreading by Marci Madsen Martinez

Printed in the USA by Versa Press

Cover montage designed by Dariusz Janczewski. Runners photo: © Colin Schultz. NAU men at the starting line of the 2021 NCAA Cross Country Championships, held in Tallahassee, Florida, on November 20, 2021. Mountain photo: Bob Blasi/Coconino National Forest.

Text font: Minion Pro
Display fonts: Almaq, Montserrat, Futura PT, and Times New Roman

Soulstice PUBLISHING
books with *soul* • Flagstaff, AZ

Soulstice Publishing
PO Box 791
Flagstaff, AZ 86002
(928) 814-8943
connect@soulsticepublishing.com
www.soulsticepublishing.com
9 8 7 6 5 4 3

To my wonderful grandma, Val Eliason.
Matt Baxter

To my three sons, Steven, Ryun,
and Brandon. Thank you for your sacrificial love
and support throughout my coaching career.
Ron Mann

Grand Canyon
Provo
"The Peaks
I
II
Grand Canyon
79 Miles
Snowbowl Road
180
Elks Lodge
Flag Staff
Lowell
Observatory
"Dwarf" planet Pluto
discovered
A-1 Mountain Rd
" The Lollipop Loop"
Train Station
Biff's
Bagels
NAU
ROUTE
US
66
2
1
Milton Rd
Woody Mountain Rd
5
Kiltie
Woody Mountain Rd
INTERSTATE
40
Kiltie Ln
"Down the hill"
To Sedona–Phoenix–
Tucson
INTERSTATE
17
Lake Mary Road
Fort Tuthill
County Park
"Mailboxes"

Welcome to
FLAG!
You're in Lumberjack Country...
(elevation 6,909')
III
IV
Mt. Elden
Buffalo Park
ROUTE US 66
KEY
San Francisco Peaks
I. Humphreys (12,633 ft.) Arizona's highest peak!
II. Agassiz
III. Fremont
IV. Doyle
4
Boulder-Madison-Terre Haute-Louisville
Albuquerque-Stillwater
3
Northern Arizona University (NAU)
1. Fieldhouse (formerly, Student Activity Center)
2. Lumberjack Stadium
3. Student-Athlete High Performance Center
4. Cardinal Field
5. Skydome
INTERSTATE ARIZONA 40
Foxglenn Park
N
W
E
S
COCONINO National Forest
Lake Mary
Lake Mary

Contents

Foreword

WHEN I THINK ABOUT NORTHERN ARIZONA UNIVERSITY, I REMEMBER the people.

This is a program with a proud history that goes back more than fifty years, but ultimately the success of the track and cross country teams is centered on the humble idea of brotherhood and sisterhood. Competing toe-to-toe with much older and more celebrated universities, NAU's Lumberjacks have always shown fierce determination to reach the summit of their sport.

Greatness is not a given. It is developed through hard work and a team-first spirit at this small school nestled at the base of the San Francisco Peaks.

In 2005, I took a leap of faith and visited Flagstaff, Arizona. I believed NAU could help me achieve my academic and athletic goals. Being at altitude and running among the ponderosa pines, I realized this was more than a campus. NAU was where I would climb the mountain toward my Olympic dream.

For me, this dream began decades before, continents away. In 1991, I was kidnapped from my family at gunpoint to become a child soldier in the civil war in South Sudan. I was left to die at a rebel training camp before being rescued by three older boys who became my angels. After ten years spent in Kakuma refugee camp, I was adopted by a family in upstate New York and given the opportunity to go to school for the first time, at age sixteen. A Lost Boy, without a country or a family, I was embraced by the American people and given a second chance at life.

I started my first semester as a Lumberjack in fall 2005. Cross country began with a team retreat at Lake Mary, where I met the men who would become my brothers. At this camp we set goals for the year: win the Big Sky Conference championship, compete strongly at regionals, make the NCAA Championships, and get on the podium. At the same time, the team held each other accountable to work as hard in the classroom as we did on the track. This was an eye-opening experience for me. Wearing the NAU uniform was not something to be taken for granted. The goals of the team became our doctrine. The trails became our temple.

We forged our identity on Soldiers Trail, Woody Mountain Road, and many other routes surrounding the town. Every year, the initiation of the NAU cross country team happens in the heartbeat of the Flagstaff community. At the George Kyte Classic, locals line the two-mile loop at Buffalo Park, cheering as the team surges over the crest toward the finish line. Adopted into this special family, all of us are united through a deep-rooted love for the sport of running and an enduring respect for one another.

It is not the name of the school or the size of its budget that makes a champion. It is the deep devotion of professors, coaching staff, and most importantly, teammates committed to a common goal. I remember the long hours of mentorship from Professor Jon Hales as vividly as I remember Coach John Hayes timing mile repeats at Fort Tuthill. The big, blue track of NAU made me a better man and unlocked my potential as a leader. The people there taught me the responsibility to lead and make a difference. The uniform made us ambassadors for the school and the community. When we stood on the podium at the NCAA Cross Country Championships in 2007, it was as trailblazers for the next generation of athletes who would follow in our shoes.

Success at NAU elevated my story to the international stage, and in 2007, HBO came to Flagstaff to take me on a life-changing journey to reconnect with my family in southern Sudan (after decades of civil war in Sudan, South Sudan wouldn't officially become a country until 2011). Still wearing the blue and gold of NAU, I traveled back to Africa for the first time in the six years since I came to the United States. I reunited with my mother, father, and younger brothers. I was no longer the six-year-old boy who had been kidnapped, but a young man driven to find a way to give hope to those in greatest need.

I felt empowered by my reunion. I returned to NAU and managed to win the NCAA 1500m title in Sacramento, California. From this launching pad, I went on to make my first Olympic team in 2008 and was honored by my fellow Olympians to be selected as the U.S. flagbearer. I am one of a long line of NAU athletes from across the United States and all over the world who have come through the proud program, which is the topic of this long-overdue book.

Lopez Lomong and NAU setting the pace.

I continue to run today in thanks to my adoptive country, my family, and the communities that give me the opportunity to chase my dream. Every year, I return to NAU to elevate my training as a professional runner.

Flagstaff and the facilities at NAU have become a mecca for runners, but for me the pilgrimage brings me back to my roots.

This is the soil where I was sown. These are the mountains where I proved my mettle. When I look up at the Peaks, I remember deep in my bones what it takes to make the climb.

Lopez Lomong
NAU alumnus, 2011
Two-time U.S. Olympian and 2008 U.S. Olympic Team flagbearer
Author of *Running for My Life: One Lost Boy's Journey from the Killing Fields of Sudan to the Olympic Games*

Preface and Acknowledgments

WHEN LEO "RED" HABERLACK PASSED AWAY IN 2017, I KNEW THIS BOOK must be written.

In the mid-1960s, Red was the first coach of Northern Arizona University's cross country program, and he revived the track and field program as the college soon transitioned to the NCAA. He also was my mentor and a major influence on my life.

I realized that with Red gone, I was the only person who had intimate insight into the NAU running story from its origin up to the present—including how the school's athletes and the local running community have always been supportive and intertwined, knowing they are fortunate to live and train in one of the most perfect places on Earth for their sport.

I knew the early history personally through my time as an athlete and coach. I had also kept an eye on things as my immediate successors, J.W. Hardy and Eric Heins, and the current director, Mike Smith, further developed the program. Although I no longer live in Flagstaff, I'm grateful that the school and NAU Athletics welcome me back and encourage my input. I will be a Lumberjack forever.

With Red's widow, Shirley Haberlack, and legendary Arizona runner George Young in their eighties, and me and my early teammates in our seventies, the time had come for a thorough history of our prestigious program and running community to be written.

I looked for someone who had current knowledge of the program and an ability to put my vision and ideas into words.

Matt Baxter was my choice for this project, and what a great job he has done with it. A fantastic runner and writer, Matt provided a link to the past half-decade of the program, sharing his insider's perspective on the dynamic recent years of the program's run up the mountain that no other co-author could have given.

The result is a book we're very proud of. It is the account of a distinctive, rags-to-riches collegiate program as well as a profile of a unique running town. This is the celebration of a dynasty in the making and an entertaining look back at more than fifty years of ups and downs. While the focus is on a men's team rewriting the record books even as we go to print, it's also about a women's team whose incredible athletes and team performances helped shape the storied Lumberjack history.

No book is written in a vacuum. The basis for this book comes from people who love northern Arizona, the city of Flagstaff—or "Flag," as the locals like to say—and Northern Arizona University. Tales abound by the thousands of how our little town came to be a vital force as a running community and treasured specifically by the athletes of NAU.

This book could not have been written without the help of many people who shared their experiences and special moments. In these pages, you will read how the running program at this great university was formed, and how Flagstaff and surrounding areas of northern Arizona became a mecca for altitude training. This project strengthened my belief that the people mentioned in these pages, as well as many more who are not, were strong-willed, hardworking, and dedicated to their vision of making Flagstaff the seat of NAU's distance dynasty. With the help of NAU Athletics as a whole, NAU Licensing and Marketing, as well as Northern Arizona University Advancement, this book has taken a life and vibrancy beyond my wildest dreams.

I interviewed many people who helped frame this book through their passion in sharing their memories. A special thanks to Shirley Haberlack, who provided much information about how the program started at NAU.

Other interviewees included Lumberjack alumni Henrik Ahnström, Chris Bray, Steve Cross, Kristy Klinnert, Joe Lange, Mark Lomeland, Jennifer Martin, Jeff Matthews, Richard Sliney, Matt Smith, Leonard Suarez, Milfred Tewawina, and Larah Treadwell.

I also learned from discussions with Sean Anthony, founder and CEO of HYPO2 Sport; Scott Baxter, NAU running enthusiast; Ed Eyestone, Brigham Young University cross country coach; Al Flitcraft, former NAU baseball coach; Mike Nesbitt, former NAU athletic trainer; Bill O'Neil, Casa Grande High School runner; Dusty Sullivan, former Flagstaff High School track coach; Nat White, Flagstaff running enthusiast; and George Young, 1968 Olympic bronze medalist. Anne Ryun graciously helped us obtain insights from her record-setting husband as well as Dr. Conrad Nightingale from their 1968 training sessions in Flagstaff.

Young passed away in November 2022, just months after we spoke, as the manuscript was nearing completion. It was another reminder of how important it was to record this history while those who helped shape it are still living.

In addition, Matt Baxter interviewed these recent NAU athletes: Drew Bosley, Tyler Day, Blaise Ferro, Luis Grijalva, Brodey Hasty, David McNeill, Miranda Myers, Abdihamid Nur, Taryn O'Neill, Theo Quax, Ryan Raff, and Nico Young, plus NAU assistant coach Jarred Cornfield and HOKA NAZ Elite executive director Ben Rosario. Interviews conducted by Shannon Thompson with recent NAU athletes were vital to filling in some gaps in the story.

J.W. Hardy, Eric Heins, and Mike Smith were especially helpful to us in capturing the recent history of the running program.

Myles Schrag and Julie Hammonds from Soulstice Publishing have been invaluable. They believed in this project from the outset and provided direction and guidance from start to finish.

Matt Baxter spent countless hours writing, editing, and bringing *Running Up the Mountain* to life. To him I will be forever grateful.

Ron Mann,
Louisville, Kentucky
January 2023

up the mountain [uhp thuh moun-tn]
phrase (colloquial)

1. Used by Arizonans to indicate the quick rise in elevation ascending the Mogollon Rim onto the Colorado Plateau from the central part of the state into northern Arizona. Traveling to Flagstaff itself is not a literal trip up the mountain, as the town sits high on the southern edge of the Colorado Plateau and at the base of San Francisco Mountain, aka the San Francisco Peaks, the highest point in the state.

Example: "The temperature dropped 25 degrees in my two-hour drive up the mountain from Phoenix to Flagstaff on I-17."

Alternative: up the hill.

2. Running. Reference to Flagstaff and its rugged terrain at approximately 7,000-foot elevation that is considered ideal for the sport's altitude training possibilities. Example: "I came up the hill after my track workout in Sedona on Saturday to get altitude training on Woody Mountain Road in Flag."

3. Aspirational. Used figuratively for the pursuit of a difficult or improbable goal, especially in athletics. Example: "The NAU cross country team is running up the mountain in pursuit of a legacy unmatched in the sport."

Prologue
Expectations

"HEY NAU!"

Amid the chaos of the finish chute, the Northern Arizona University women's cross country team heard a ringing shout. The seven-foot, blacked-out fence stood no chance against their excited head coach, Mike Smith. He had to share the news immediately.

"You got fourteenth. Fourteenth!"

The women were overcome with a mixture of disbelief and uncontrollable joy, similar to the emotions felt by their coach when he first heard the result. For a team with a goal of finishing in the top twenty, this was a sweet surprise. The 2019 women's program at NAU had finally ended its ten-year streak of not qualifying for the National Collegiate Athletic Association Division I Cross Country Championships. Their efforts in Terre Haute, Indiana, deserved a rowdy celebration.

"Let's act like we won," said Taryn O'Neill.

"We did," replied Mikayla Malaspina.

Success is a subjective thing; its measurement depends on the team being asked to define it. For these athletes, finally making it to nationals fit their criteria, while taking fourteenth would reset the bar for NAU's next generation of women runners. They knew the happiness they'd just created would reverberate with Lumberjacks for years to come.

The 2019 season's joyful conclusion had been fueled by disappointments endured in years past. Heartache has a way of contributing to positive growth if it happens to the right group of people. These women had dealt with the pain of several near-misses. Most recently, in 2017 and 2018, the team had headed into the NCAA Mountain Regional Championship the week before nationals with high hopes of qualifying. On both occasions, the Lumberjacks hadn't done quite enough during the regular season to clinch their spot at nationals. Coming up short at regionals had confirmed them as another good team that wasn't quite ready for the next level.

Left: Bryn Morley (309), Pipi Eitel, and Miranda Myers (310) move their way through the pack in the early going of the 2019 NCAA Championships. Right: Shannon Molvin in the closing stretch as the NAU women finished fourteenth in their return to the national stage.

Now, the Lumberjacks were in no rush to exit the finish chute after Smith's big announcement. Surrounded by the elation and devastation of the teams around them, the women huddled together, shivering as their bodies cooled down. Senior athlete Miranda Myers relished a moment she never thought possible when she was recruited to NAU in 2015. Her successful collegiate career now ensured that future recruits would feel very differently.

A crowd of supporters waited outside the chute, eager to congratulate this team on their amazing performance. The love they received made the hike back to the team tent feel more like a victory parade.

"It was a good walk back," recalls Myers.

Mike Smith, NAU Director of Cross Country and Track and Field, talks with the women's team on the day of their strong showing at the 2019 NCAA national cross country meet.

Nervous tension made for a quiet team tent as the NAU men's cross country team completed final pre-race preparations. A burst of excitement shattered the silence as the women rushed in to share their good news. The men were quick to congratulate this fourteenth-place effort, while their minds never left the task still at hand.

It was a hectic scene as the women raced around the tent trying to find something warm to wear. A trash bag, used to collect their extra layers at the starting line, was unceremoniously dumped onto the tarpaulin floor. The women sifted through the pile of identical warm-ups, sorting out what belonged to whom.

While the struggle against the wintry chill commenced for the women, the challenge of staying relaxed continued for the men. Drew Bosley's hands shook as he drew in deep breaths while tying his shoelaces. On this occasion, the shaking wasn't from the cold.

Coach Smith tempered his joy over the women's performance, shifting to focus on the men. "It's time to head to the start," he quietly announced.

This instruction made Geordie Beamish visibly uncomfortable. It was a déjà vu moment for the senior preparing for his final cross country race as a Lumberjack. The last time he lined up for nationals in Terre Haute was 2016, when NAU won its first NCAA team title for any sport. The squad went on to win in 2017 and 2018, with Beamish running in each championship. But this year was different. The team had been more dominant throughout the season than ever before. They had not lost a cross country race since fall 2015. The Lumberjacks were not just hoping to win; they were expected to.

Beamish stood in the team's starting box ready to do one last pre-race stride, his gaze on the 800-meter stretch of grass in front of him. With a deep breath and a bounce to his step, he drove out of the box with the kind of power and determination he intended to call upon in a little over ten minutes.

With every step, his three-quarter-inch spikes shredded the Earth. They collected mud like the bristles of a brush, painting the back of his jacket. The uneven terrain played no role in altering the smoothness of his stride. For those fortunate enough to catch a glimpse of the NCAA Indoor Track and Field mile champion, it looked like he was running on the track. In reality, his body was working twice as hard to maintain form as it navigated every divot. He took no notice of the eyes on him. If they wanted to look, then let them look. His eyes were focused on the challenge ahead.

Pumping the brakes, Beamish rolled to a gradual stop just shy of a hundred meters from where the stride began. Smith's incessant advice of "Gas, gas, gas!" did not apply just yet. It was OK to test a different pedal.

Standing on the spot where his stride concluded, Beamish took a deep breath. Other runners flew past in every direction. Some came close to bumping his shoulder. It was important for Beamish to have this time to himself, to reflect on an amazing season with guys he had come to know as family. His biological family was 7,000 miles away and feeling even farther in this moment. With an exaggerated exhale, Beamish left every ounce of calm on this spot and jogged back to his teammates.

Congregating just fifty meters up from their starting box, the Lumberjacks came together—arm in arm—to share one last moment with the whole team. Everyone was either bouncing up and down or swaying side to side in a desperate effort to stay warm. What had been a frigid but light rain during the women's race was now a deluge, soaking through the guys' warm-ups before they had an opportunity to discard them.

The Lumberjacks' team chant shot through like thunder from the storm above. "Jacks on me, Jacks on three. One. Two. Three." Then every mouth roared, "Jacks!"

The guys broke from their huddle to take turns hugging one another. "It was like a hug you were going to give someone if you were never going to see them again, like your best friend moving away," said Beau Prince, who would be supporting his teammates from the sidelines.

The warmth of each embrace was soon lost as the runners stripped down to their racing kits. A sense of guilt washed over their teammates who were standing in big jackets—still cold—while the top seven shivered in thirty-seven degrees Fahrenheit temperatures, wearing shorts and singlets and maybe arm sleeves.

Geordie Beamish focuses early in the 2019 NCAA national meet.

From a safe position behind the starting line, the team watched as the gun went off and their best friends disappeared into the fog.

The start of a cross country race is frightening. Athletes run on pure adrenaline, doing everything they can to stay on their feet while they jockey for position. Elbows are used like shields to protect the little space a runner has. Getting too close to the back kick of the person in front can result in being sliced by their spikes. Falling is every runner's worst nightmare. It exposes them to being trampled by people who have nowhere else to plant their feet other than on a curled-up torso below. All runners—253 of them on this day—think it won't happen to them as they navigate the slippery conditions underfoot.

The LaVern Gibson Championship Cross Country Course begins with a long, wide starting stretch before sweeping into a right-hand turn that bottlenecks the field before passing the first kilometer sign. It was vital that the Lumberjacks establish their position by this point. The day's race would be run more conservatively because of the conditions, which would make it difficult to move through a dense pack once the course narrowed.

NAU's biggest rivals heading into these championships had devised a cunning plan to ensure they held their position toward the front of the field. "We had box forty-two to the far right, and I told the guys we have to get out well," said Brigham Young University head coach Ed Eyestone. "I put a strong steepler on the outside of our group to keep the guys on our left out of the way." The field naturally veers to the right in anticipation of the first corner, and Eyestone didn't want his guys to get cut off before they got there.

As they came through the first kilometer, the advice being shouted at every NAU runner by their coaches was, "We gotta move up!" Blue BYU singlets littered the front of the pack, yet only specks of gold from the NAU singlets could be seen. Instead of fighting their way into the right position, the guys had allowed themselves to get swallowed by the pack.

The NAU women crisscrossed the course trying to catch a glimpse of their teammates when they came by. This doubled as their cooldown and a way to keep warm. The temperature had dropped significantly for the men's race, with the rain being to blame. Nothing was waterproof at this point. Multiple layers, double gloves—it all got soaked.

Smith had often challenged his team at practices, "How fast can you run while staying relaxed?" Strain in any part of an athlete's body signals the brain that something is wrong. During the regular season, the Lumberjacks had run relaxed. They won every race with ease, and knowing they were going to win from early on in a race helped alleviate physical stress. In Terre Haute, on that cold, wet day when they didn't get out well, tension started to consume their bodies. Their minds would soon follow.

At three kilometers, NAU was down by fifty-seven points to BYU, but it wasn't until a few kilometers later that the team could really see the writing on the wall. "At six or seven kilometers I knew we were losing," admitted Luis Grijalva. His conclusion was drawn from contrasting the urgency in Smith's voice every time he told Grijalva to keep moving up with the excitement radiating from BYU supporters.

Smith, along with his assistant coaches Jarred Cornfield and Becca DeLoache, hastily made his way to the finishing straight as their athletes entered the last kilometer of the race. A film crew from FloTrack trailed them closely. The cameras had been there all season, capturing NAU's attempt to win its fourth consecutive national title. Instead, they were witnessing one of the greatest upsets in collegiate cross country history.

The jumbotron updated the team results in real time as each runner came across the line. BYU popped up first, then the University of Colorado squeezed into the top spot with two runners placing in the top ten. BYU recaptured the lead with three runners in the top twenty as NAU finally joined the leaders with three in the top thirty-two.

The quest for a four-peat came to a sudden end for the Lumberjacks as BYU's fourth and fifth runners crossed the finish line. The NAU team finished fifty-four points back in second place, just one point ahead of Colorado.

Cheers erupted from the BYU team camp. The chant "family hug" echoed through the finish chute as the Cougars embraced each other, celebrating their first national title for the men's program.

"Ninety miles for twelve weeks. All of that work, and I knew we lost the moment I crossed the line," said a frustrated Grijalva. Everything that happened during the season had pointed to a different outcome on this day. That expectation ended up being one of the nails in the coffin for this team. "I try to avoid predictions, but I thought on paper we were supposed to win, and that might have been what got us," reflected Smith.

Losing was never an outcome the Lumberjacks contemplated, and there's a risk to that, since it's always a possibility. But the only way this team could be successful was if they never gave energy to the possibility. They had channeled all their effort into winning. When they lost, their minds weren't ready for it.

Back at the tent, the team went into survival mode. All the runners scrambled to get out of their wet clothes and into something dry. Their hands were so cold it became impossible to untie the laces on their spikes. Wearing gloves was futile. Smith grabbed a pair of scissors from athletic trainer Jamie Spicuzza and cut through the laces of Bosley's shoes.

Nobody knew the pain these young men were feeling more than Smith. He understood the toll this loss was taking on each athlete. As much as he may have wanted to join them on their level, as he had done with the women before the men's race, he couldn't. He had to be the leader this team desperately needed.

In the weeks and months to come, Smith would learn about every emotion swirling through his athletes' brains after this race, but for the next hour before the bus left, his role was to preserve the dignity of his team. That's why he made sure they got dressed and headed to the awards ceremony promptly. Any team can look good when celebrating a win, but it was important for the Lumberjacks to learn how to hold their heads high in defeat. Smith, along with his four predecessors as NAU head coach, had always preached that the program is bigger than one race. Now, he wanted to ensure his guys practiced it.

On their walk to the awards ceremony, alternate runner Cade Burks turned to his teammates and expressed what they were all feeling. "I appreciate having the opportunity to be bummed as shit for not four-peating."

Although the Lumberjacks were beaten to the mountaintop in 2019, their motivation to get back there would soon return. They knew how beautiful the view was.

What they didn't know was exactly how many miles it had taken to get the program to the top, or that the journey began here: with just one man taking the first step to develop a path that would eventually transform NAU into a distance powerhouse and Flagstaff, Arizona, into one of the premier running locations in the world. △

Part 1 – The First Steps (1964 – 1982)

Chapter 1
"When Do I Start?"

IN THE SMALL TOWN OF MINOT, NORTH DAKOTA, LEO "RED" HABERLACK and his wife, Shirley, were enjoying a relaxing afternoon when the phone rang. Shirley answered. "It's Ted Keck," she told her husband, her hand covering the receiver. Red slowly got up from his chair in the living room and made his way into the kitchen. Shirley handed him the phone and left Red to talk with his previous boss.

Red had been hired to work as the assistant football and head track coach at Minot State University by Keck, who was the school's athletic director in 1962. A year later, Keck accepted an athletic director position at Arizona State College at Flagstaff. Red was disappointed to see Keck move on, as the two had built a strong working relationship.

Now, Keck was calling the Haberlack home to discuss an open coaching position. ASC President, Dr. J. Lawrence Walkup, wanted to take the track program to the next level, in hopes of earning an invite to join the NCAA's Big Sky Conference. He tasked Keck with finding someone to make it a reality. Impressed with Red's dedication as a football and track coach during their short time overlapping at Minot State, Keck decided to reach out to Red and extend the offer.

There was hesitation in Red's voice as he asked for more details. Keck explained that if Red were to accept the position, he would begin working as an assistant football coach in fall 1964, and his track program would begin competing in spring

1965. Walkup, Keck assured Red, was determined to see this track program become a rival to other schools within the state, and he was willing to allocate the necessary funds to make it happen.

Red still wasn't convinced. Flagstaff was more than a thousand miles away from where he and Shirley called home. Living in the desert did not sound like an appealing lifestyle to either of them. Keck was quick to reassure Red that Flagstaff wasn't like most of Arizona. It was a beautiful town nestled in the middle of the world's largest ponderosa pine forest. The San Francisco Peaks provided a picturesque backdrop in distinct contrast to the saguaro and prickly pear cacti of the Sonoran Desert in the southern part of the state.

Keck explained that at 6,909 feet above sea level—or 7,000 feet as the widely accepted round number—the town's thin air brings cooler temperatures, although dryness is inescapable. The area benefitted from a heavy monsoon season to cool things off in late summer, while winter snows were strong enough to white-out the city. It rarely got too hot or too cold. Flagstaff boasted a cozy population of around 20,000, which would make for an easy transition from quiet Minot.

Needing a moment to think, Red ended the conversation to speak with Shirley. Was this something they could both be happy with? The two spent some time going back and forth before Red called Keck back.

"When do I start?"

It was the summer of 1964 when Red packed the car in preparation for his and Shirley's big move to Flagstaff. Although Shirley still had doubts about whether this move was the right decision, a level-headed Red helped keep her concerns at bay. Being eight years older than Shirley, Red was a little more well-traveled.

After his first two years as a student at Minot State from 1952 to 1954, Red joined the United States Army and was stationed in Stuttgart, Germany, as a Morse code operator. He then returned for his final two years at Minot State, where he captained the football team his senior year. A broken leg during the 1957 season dashed his hopes of a strong track showing in the spring.

Following graduation, Red worked as athletic director at Harvey High School in North Dakota before returning to Minot State to coach in 1962. That same year he married the love of his life.

Although she trusted his judgment, Shirley struggled to hold back tears as Red started the car and pulled out of their driveway. This was the last time they would call this place home. Shirley hoped one day Flagstaff would become deserving of that name, but upon leaving Minot it seemed unlikely.

The San Francisco Peaks started out as a blur in the distance as the Haberlacks neared Flagstaff. Shirley was flipping through an encyclopedia to find out more about their mysterious destination.

"It's an old railroad town named after a tall flagpole," Shirley wryly observed to her husband.

Flagstaff never would have boomed the way it did in the early 1900s if not for the railroad. The famed Route 66 ran alongside the tracks through the city, bringing tourists from all over the country. Flagstaff's proximity to the South Rim of the Grand Canyon, a ninety-plus-minute drive, made it an ideal gateway location for exploring one of the Seven Natural Wonders of the World. With the construction of Interstate 40 already underway as the Haberlacks drove, there would soon be even more opportunities for people to discover the mountain town.

The Haberlacks arrived in Flagstaff on Route 66 heading west toward downtown. Shirley took a deep breath, noting how the thin air seemed to fill only a portion of her lungs. It was clear she wasn't in Minot anymore.

On the right was a sign for the Mt. Elden Drive-In Theatre. For sixty-five cents, patrons could pull up with five hundred other cars to catch a film. The Haberlacks drove past a large sign for the Texaco gas station and the Grand Canyon Cafe. On their left, hugging the railroad track, was the 1889 train depot, built to replace its predecessor ruined in a fire. Much of the young Arizona Territory settlement had been threatened or eliminated by fires in 1886 and 1888 before new structures were built from stone or brick. Those buildings could still be seen by the Haberlacks as they took a quick detour through the heart of downtown.

Driving up San Francisco Street, they came across the Babbitt Brothers Building. It had stood since 1888 and operated as a department store. Across the street was the Hotel Monte Vista, catering to guests for almost four decades. Red took a left onto Aspen Avenue to avoid traveling too far north of the city. There wasn't much up that way except high mountains, towering pines, and a new wildlife park, opened a few months before the Haberlacks arrived.

Buffalo Park, a 163-acre site on the McMillan Mesa, had been turned into a drive-through Wild West theme park. The tourist attraction featured eight buffalo—give or take a couple based on which ones decided to stay in the park—some mule deer from the Grand Canyon, elk from Yellowstone, rams, geese, and waterfowl. At fifty cents a car, visitors to Buffalo Park could enjoy the wildlife while being escorted around the grounds in a stagecoach.

Shirley looked up at the Weatherford Hotel that dominated the corner of Aspen Avenue and Leroux Street. It first opened in January 1900 and was one of two ventures by John Weatherford on this block. The second was the Orpheum Theater, where the Haberlacks could catch a movie indoors if they didn't fancy staying in their car. Downtown Flagstaff in 1964 was small, but it had enough amenities to suit its residents and visitors.

Red got back on Route 66 and drove toward ASC, where he and Shirley glimpsed the enormous Lumberjack statue outside The Lumberjack Cafe. Later in the decade, the twenty-five-foot-tall fiberglass figure would make a brief cameo in the film *Easy Rider* before eventually finding a new home on campus.

The Haberlacks passed an imposing building they would soon learn was called Old Main. Built in 1894, the same year Flagstaff became an incorporated town, Old Main was the first building of the Northern Arizona Normal School, which opened for lessons in September 1899. The school's name would change two more times before becoming Arizona State College at Flagstaff in 1945. The student population had grown steadily since its origins to boast 4,003 students for the 1964–1965 school year.

After an exhausting drive from North Dakota, the Haberlacks finally arrived at their accommodation. Keck had arranged for Red to be the head resident at the newly built men's dorm, Tinsley Hall.

The transition to life in Flagstaff wasn't as daunting as the Haberlacks had anticipated. With the help of the Keck and Gibler families, Shirley and Red were soon introduced to the whole city. When they wanted to explore more of northern Arizona, it was a pleasant drive to Sedona or Oak Creek Canyon. Less than an hour away from downtown Flagstaff, Sedona is home to some of the most breathtaking views in all of Arizona. Its remarkable red rock buttes would one day become a drawing card to tourists from all over the world.

After a short settling-in period, head football coach Max Spilsbury put Red to work. The home of the Arizona State-Flagstaff Lumberjacks was Lumberjack Stadium, its field surrounded by what Red described as a "pathetic excuse for a running track." The uneven dirt oval was certainly not going to entice any students Red would try to recruit for his track team. On the west side of the field were bleachers, while the east side offered an empty lot where fans could drive up, park, and honk their horns during home football games.

As Red stood on the sidelines giving directions to his football players, he knew that, come spring, this would be his track and field battleground; the dirt beneath his feet would be the place where he would push his guys to their limits. When he closed his eyes, he could picture a squad of athletes running quarter-mile repeats on the track while his throwers hurled weights on the infield and his jumpers practiced in a pit that—in his mind—had already been dug.

This place could be something truly special he believed. Then Red would open his eyes and his stomach would drop; a dream this big would take years of hard work. The towering San Francisco Peaks to the north were dwarfed by the figurative mountain Red still had to climb to turn his vision into reality.

Trying to recruit athletes to come to a new program—at a no-name school, at altitude, without any decent facilities, to train under an unknown coach—was a hard sell. The athletic department had only one athletic trainer, who primarily worked with football, so Red did everything with the help of a part-time student assistant. Red spent hours on the road, sometimes arriving home at four in the morning. Shirley accepted this as just part of the job, but being the wife of a track coach, especially one as dedicated as Red, wasn't easy. The difficulty of spending so much time apart from her husband was a job in itself for Shirley.

When Red wasn't on the road recruiting in-state athletes, he was writing letters to out-of-state prospects. There was no easy way to go about this, and communications by mail were slow. Red had to be proactive when it came to recruiting because all the best athletes in-state would end up at either Arizona State University in Tempe or the University of Arizona in Tucson. ASC might never get the best recruits in the state, but Red would do everything he could to develop the athletes he did get.

Red Haberlack surveys his squad at Lumberjack Stadium in the mid-1960s.

Red drew most of the athletes that first year from the state's large cities, including Phoenix, Yuma, and Tucson. The kids who committed were looking to escape scorching desert heat for the holiday destination that was Flagstaff's reputation.

It was a place Arizonans would take their kids to go skiing in the winter and play outdoors in the summer, instead of hiding away when temperatures hit 120 degrees. Flagstaff was the cool place to be.

With Keck's help, Red came up with a budget for costs necessary to get this new program moving forward. The two presented the budget to President Walkup for approval. Even though Walkup was the one who wanted to start the track program in the first place, he had not accounted for just how high the costs would be. Thankfully, Walkup was usually obliging in giving Red the funds he needed for his team. The university president's support would become a common theme in years to come.

A significant investment in ASC's track program came in 1965 when the school installed a 220-yard indoor track at the Activity Center, which Red's athletes broke in during the 1966 indoor season.

Installing a new track wasn't the only exciting change coming to ASC. The Arizona Board of Regents, pleased with the wide range of academic programs the university offered and its steadily growing student population, believed a name change was in order. On the first of May 1966, ASC officially changed its name to Northern Arizona University. Then, beginning in fall 1966 with the help of student Glenn Mayle, a men's cross country program was added to the list of varsity sports at the newly named NAU.

In 1965, Red was an unknown coach starting a program that realistically might never be good enough to progress beyond its NAIA (National Association of Intercollegiate Athletics) status. The stars would have to align for the track program at NAU to develop into something people wanted to be a part of, not only within the state of Arizona but one day nationally and internationally.

Perhaps the Lowell Observatory, perched above the original townsite since 1894, could have predicted the stars would come together the way they did for Red. The city where Pluto was discovered was itself about to be found by runners from around the world. △

Chapter 2
Altitude Training Takes Center Stage

AS STORM CLOUDS DARKENED THE SKY, RED HABERLACK GOT NERVOUS, thinking back to his first year at NAU. During the 1964–1965 winter, 167 inches of snow fell across the city. Such a dumping was perfect for those who loved to ski on the slopes of the San Francisco Peaks or for kids who scoured the city for the steepest sledding hill. It was less ideal for a track coach who needed to shovel an area for his team to practice.

Winter in Flagstaff removes any last indicator that the city is located in a desert—albeit a high one. Snow covers city streets quicker than they can be cleared, soon melting into a muddy slush spraying anything within ten feet of a tire. The branches of sixty-foot pine trees that stand over downtown and wrap the city like a blanket strain under the mounting weight of snow.

Lone runners navigating the sidewalks make split-second decisions on where their feet go; a wrong step can spell disaster if ice lurks below the freshly powdered surface. Winter adds a cold bite to the already-dry Flagstaff air, burning the lungs with each inhalation. With temperatures occasionally dipping below ten degrees, winter isn't a comfortable time to be training as an endurance athlete. But you can't beat the view.

Red was right to be nervous as he looked through his living room window to watch the first flakes. It was two weeks out from Christmas 1967 when the snow began to fall, and the storm didn't stop for eight days. A total of 84 inches of snow covered Flagstaff during that time. The sheer volume of snow paralyzed northern Arizona as the "storm of the century" engulfed the area.

A story in the *Arizona Daily Sun* detailed the difficulties those within the city faced. Grocery store shelves emptied as families stockpiled necessities, unsure how long they would be stuck inside. Mounting snow collapsed roofs and stacked higher than first-floor windows. Some residents of north Flagstaff also had to deal with unwanted wildlife roaming their yards.

The fences keeping animals inside their home at Buffalo Park had been damaged by the pressure of seven feet of snow on the wooden posts. Several buffalo took this opportunity to explore the yards of residents. As a result of the damage caused during this storm and ongoing financial difficulties, Buffalo Park would close its gates in 1969.

NAU freshman Steve Cross was one of the few people in Flagstaff who was excited about the enormous dumping of snow. With teachers unable to get to campus, an extended Christmas break began for all students within the city. "There was no online learning at that time, so we were basically on vacation." Cross chuckled as he qualified his statement, "Except training—that was still two a day."

The NAU track team was fortunate to have the use of an indoor track at the Activity Center during inclement weather, but there were plenty of times when they had to endure the elements to get in their mileage. Without ample gear to bundle up in, these runs were more like survival challenges. Cross remembers the standard-issue pair of shoes, sweatpants, and a sweatshirt he received when he first arrived in fall 1967. "That's all we got, and that's all we needed," he said.

For an athlete who couldn't afford to eat anywhere off campus during his time at NAU, Cross's appreciation for what the university gave him was genuine, even if the kit paled in comparison to what a current-day athlete may receive.

What the NAU athletes missed when it came to gear was made up by the environment they trained in, although that environment wasn't yet fully appreciated. How training at 7,000 feet affects the human body had not been adequately documented. Not until the chosen host city for the biggest sporting event in the world was a location at a similarly high elevation did the need to study altitude training gain a sense of urgency.

When the International Olympic Committee convened in Baden-Baden, West Germany, on October 18, 1963, people from around the world anxiously awaited news of where the XIX Olympic Games would be held in five years. Four cities were in the running—Buenos Aires, Argentina; Detroit, USA; Lyon, France; and Mexico City, Mexico—and the last one had the global sports community on edge.

At 7,350 feet above sea level, Mexico City would be by far the highest elevation yet for a Summer Olympics location. Research into how altitude affects the body was still in its infancy. Aside from some research studies conducted on mountain climbers, only personal anecdotes could attest to the effects of running at altitude. There was growing concern over the unnecessary risk that holding the Olympics in Mexico City might create for athletes, particularly those in the endurance events.

With a collective holding of breath around the globe, IOC President Avery Brundage stepped up to the podium and made the announcement. The host for the nineteenth Olympic Games would be Mexico City. Winning the bidding process with thirty votes over Detroit's fourteen, Mexico City became the first Latin American site to host the games—and the first over an elevation of 466 feet. Nobody knew what an Olympics at this kind of elevation would look like. Even worse, few knew how to prepare for one.

"There will be those that will die," remarked Finnish trainer Onnie Niskanen.

Throughout history, people have speculated about how much stress the human body can endure. Sir Edmund Hillary had to ignore concerns for his health as he and Tenzing Norgay made the grueling climb in 1953 to be the first people to officially summit 29,032-foot-high Mount Everest. Roger Bannister had to block out similar concerns as he attempted to break the four-minute-mile barrier the following year. In the same decade, Murray Halberg was warned his heart might explode as his coach, Arthur Lydiard, used him to trial his innovative hundred-miles-a-week training method.

The human heart, as well as the whole body, mind, and spirit, was apparently capable of far more than the masses thought. Each of these mid-century milestones was achieved through extensive preparation. Everest wasn't Hillary's first mountaineering expedition, 1954 wasn't the first time Bannister ran a fast mile, and Halberg didn't hit a hundred miles in a single week after covering only twenty the week before. In a similar vein, distance runners preparing for the 1968 Olympic Games didn't want to take their first breath at 7,350 feet the day before their race.

With emerging Kenya and Ethiopia expected to make a strong showing, some athletes were concerned that these formidable competitors who were born and raised at altitude would have an advantage. George Young, the former University of Arizona star who had represented the United States at the previous two Olympics in the steeplechase, voiced this sentiment. "Obviously, I think it's ridiculous to hold the Olympic Games at altitude, which gives certain countries a head start."

There was no handbook or expert that athletes like Young could call upon to understand how to prepare their bodies for what awaited them in Mexico City. The general consensus was that spending time at elevation before competing in Mexico City was a good idea; for how long, well, that was another point of debate.

No matter how much time and effort someone like Young put into his preparations for Mexico City, if he didn't commit to preparing for elevation, he was actively placing himself at a disadvantage. The Olympics were going to be held in Mexico City—that was a given. Athletes could either accept that fact and prepare the best they could for the difficult climate, or they could stay at home and cheer from the couch. Young was certainly opposed to the latter option. He wanted to be an Olympic champion, and if it took spending time at altitude to keep his dream alive, then the challenge was worth it.

Once Young determined some altitude training was essential, he had to decide where to go. The United States Olympic Committee had set up a base in Lake Tahoe, California, to allow the team to acclimate before Mexico City. The main training site for athletes who chose this option was Echo Summit, located fifteen miles from south Lake Tahoe at an elevation of 7,300 feet. This was the perfect spot to mimic the elevation awaiting the U.S. track and field team in Mexico City.

One of the draws to this spot was the track. Built in the middle of the forest with enormous pine trees towering over the back straight and into the final bend, this temporary track was worth every penny to the athletes fortunate enough to train on it. When the U.S. Forest Service permitted the track to be built, it required installation methods that preserved as much of the forest as possible. All the trees that didn't need to be cut down in the infield were left standing.

Echo Summit was a stunning place for athletes to base themselves prior to the Olympics. It also doubled as the 1968 U.S. Olympic Track and Field Trials location, to ensure the team selected for Mexico City would be those best prepared to handle the elevation.

It seemed illogical for an American athlete to train anywhere other than Lake Tahoe during their buildup to Mexico City, but that wasn't how Young looked at it. The problem he had with the camp in Lake Tahoe was the commotion.

If he joined the rest of the U.S. team, he would have training partners and a per diem, and he would be at an appropriate elevation to replicate what he would feel running in Mexico City. However, the stress of being in that bubble and the constant media attention on the athletes there far outweighed the benefits. Journalists would be on site, not just because track and field was a marquee Olympic sport but also because of rumors of a possible boycott by African American athletes. Young needed to find somewhere else to train for his potential third Olympics, and it needed to be somewhere nobody would bother him.

Young arrived in Flagstaff at the conclusion of the teaching semester in late May 1968. A conversation with Red had motivated his decision to come to northern Arizona. Red was persuasive, highlighting everything Flagstaff had to offer. He told Young the city was located at an elevation close to that of Mexico City, it had countless running trails, and NAU had recently put down a rubberized track at Lumberjack Stadium. Everything an Olympic runner would need, Red said, Flagstaff could provide.

The outdoor track was a significant piece to convincing a runner of Young's caliber to consider Flagstaff as a training site. Red had asked NAU President J. Lawrence Walkup to have it installed because his athletes needed somewhere adequate to train. However, not everyone was happy about the money invested in the project. *Arizona Daily Sun* reporter Larry Green summarized locals' excitement and concerns about the track:

> Mixed opinions are being voiced about the new, rubberized asphalt track that has been installed in Lumberjack Stadium. Tradition lovers and budget hawks are calling it one of the greatest rooks in the history of NAU sports. Many more disagree. The fast new track could be the shot in the arm for promotional consideration of what should be considered a major sport at NAU [. . .] I hate to break it to you tradition lovers, but cry as you will, they are not going to rip up the track and sell it back to whoever we got it from [. . .] To the athletic money lenders: I sure hope things happen to make this investment worth it.

It wasn't surprising that Red was the one to lure Young to Flagstaff. The ambitious Lumberjack coach had begun making a name for himself within the national and international running community. After a modest 1966 track season for the NAU program, the team set sixteen individual and school records and six district records during the 1967 season. They would win the District 7 NAIA crown at Adams State before finishing fifteenth at nationals in Sioux Falls, South Dakota.

At the end of that season, as Red concluded his time as an assistant football coach at NAU, the U.S. Department of State asked him to conduct coaching clinics overseas. He spent summer 1967 as a track and field consultant to the Panamanian coaches and athletes in their Olympics preparation.

Among the many changes and upgrades Red was beginning to bring to NAU as a coach, his invitation to Young to train in Flagstaff over the summer of 1968 stands out as one of the most important moments of the city's running history. Had the Olympics not been awarded to Mexico City and had Red not been hired as track coach at NAU, Flagstaff's running history may not have developed until years later.

Holding the Olympics at elevation highlighted Flagstaff's single biggest draw as a training environment. While Mexico City set the stage, Red brought out the opening act. From there, Young recruited the rest of the cast. Flagstaff began the year as a quiet spot in the mountains of northern Arizona, but it would finish 1968 as one of the best training locales in the country. △

Chapter 3
Putting Flagstaff on the Map

SITTING AT A TABLE IN THE MORMON LAKE LODGE STEAKHOUSE, George Young thought back to a time when his father drove the family from their home in New Mexico to the Grand Canyon. Instead of stopping in Flagstaff for something to eat on their way through, the Youngs continued on to Williams, just thirty minutes closer to the Canyon.

A steakhouse on the side of the road caught their eye, so they all piled out of the car and went inside. After a quick look over the menu, the family went back to the car and continued their journey. The cost of a steak in Williams was outside their price range. With a collective grumbling of stomachs, the Youngs left Williams hungrier than when they arrived.

Nearly two decades later, with a similar grumbling in his stomach, Young now sat patiently waiting for his free steak at this restaurant thirty miles southeast of Flagstaff. Cooked over an open fire, this was widely touted as the best steak around. When Young said the people in and around Flagstaff were good to him during the summer of 1968, he was referencing folks like the owner of the Mormon Lake Lodge, among many others, who generously offered exemplary hospitality to him and his fellow runners.

After Young decided to come to Flagstaff during the break from his teaching and coaching job in Casa Grande, Arizona, for his Olympics buildup, he called a couple of guys in search of summer training partners. Olympic hopefuls themselves, the three who agreed were convinced by Young and exercise physiologist Jack Daniels that Flagstaff was the right place to prepare for the elevation awaiting them in Mexico City.

Sitting across from Young at the table was Billy Mills, the most decorated Olympian among them and a man Young described as "a really good human being." Mills came to Flagstaff looking to qualify for his second Olympic team. His first time representing the United States would be hard to top—a golden performance in the 10,000m at Tokyo in 1964 that was arguably the most riveting upset ever in a major distance event. His powerful kick down the home straight continues to captivate sports fans now just as it did back then. The black-and-white footage that still circulates is highlighted by the ecstatic commentator shouting, "Look at . . . Look at Mills! Look at Mills!" as he came flying toward the line.

Mills was happy to be enjoying a steak with his training partners in Flagstaff, but he was less impressed with the gnawing discomfort in his back. After a poor chiropractic adjustment, back pain was seriously inhibiting his ability to train. He cut some workouts short when the pain became unbearable. This wasn't an ideal way to kick off the summer for the reigning Olympic champion, but with the U.S. Olympic Trials only a couple months away, he didn't have much choice other than to push through.

In the chair next to Mills sat Young's fellow steeplechaser Conrad Nightingale. Looking to make his first Olympic team, twenty-three-year-old Nightingale brought a youthful edge to the group. However, that brashness occasionally shone in ways that irked Young. On easy runs, Nightingale would increase the pace to a near-tempo effort. This is a risky move at sea level; at altitude it can be devastating.

It takes the body longer to recover at 7,000 feet, so turning easy runs into workouts can compound stress on the body and risk putting athletes into a hole in their training they can't climb out of. Young didn't always take issue with Nightingale's eagerness, however. That drive and excitement was generally good for the group, he thought. Ideally, though, he preferred reserving intensity for workout days.

Rounding out the athletes at this table was someone who had both youth and experience on his side. Twenty-one-year-old running phenomenon Jim Ryun came to Flagstaff looking to qualify for his first Olympic team, much like Nightingale. The key difference between the two, respectfully, was that Ryun had a real shot at winning in Mexico City.

Olympians Billy Mills (left) and George Young training on the Lumberjack Stadium track in 1968.

The world record holder in the mile (3:51.1) and the 1500m (3:33.1), Ryun would speculate with Young about the time it might take to win gold in the 1500m at Mexico City. Accounting for the difficulty of running a fast time at 7,350 feet, the two agreed: just under 3:40 should do it. It was a fair assessment based on what Ryun thought he could run and him being the favorite for the event. Neither of them could know that 3:40 was wishful thinking.

You couldn't count on both hands how many American and world records the athletes sitting at that table would accumulate over their careers. Their caliber was something Flagstaff—and certainly this small table at the Mormon Lake Lodge—had never before accommodated.

Relaxing in his dorm room at Sechrist Hall was incoming NAU freshman Ron Mann, the 1968 Arizona state 880-yard champion from Sunnyslope High in north Phoenix. His high school track rival, Billy O'Neil, had assured Mann that he wouldn't want to miss this special summer up the mountain. O'Neil, much like everybody else, had been invited to Flagstaff by Young, his coach at Casa Grande High. Young and Mills stayed off campus with their families, which meant the teenagers got to bunk together with Ryun and Nightingale in the dorm room beside them.

Since Red Haberlack had already recruited Mann to start in the fall, early arrival gave him extra time to adjust to the elevation before the semester began. And no way was he going to miss the opportunity to train with Young, Ryun, Mills, and Nightingale over the summer.

The head of the Chamber of Commerce arranged for Young to live at Clark Homes during his time in Flagstaff. This free housing option helped alleviate the strain on Young and his family, since he would not be receiving the USOC per diem during his training camp. Young also worked as a coach for a senior citizens aerobic training group that met at the Activity Center. His primary role was to improve their physical condition through walking and jogging.

While the two-time Olympian was working a minimum-wage job just to get by, the world record holder—Ryun—was employed as a staff photographer for the *Arizona Daily Sun*, and Nightingale as a sales and stocking clerk at the Babbitts department store. "All four of us were amateurs," explained Ryun. "This job not only provided income, but allowed me the time to train in the morning and to participate in afternoon workouts."

Nightingale's time in Flagstaff ended up being fruitful for his post-running career as a veterinarian. "I'm not sure how much money the Babbitts may have lost due to my inexperience at that job, but the family took me under its wing. They even invited me back in the fall to go on an elk hunt and camping trip with the family. This love for Arizona led to a veterinary summer internship with Dr. Tom Schrimsher in Kingman the year following the Olympics. His family allowed me to stay in their home and fed me that summer at no charge."

As for O'Neil and Mann, they were just happy to keep Young company while running a seven-mile loop west of campus out toward A-1 Mountain Road and back. Interstate 40 was still being constructed, so most of the run could be completed on dirt before a major road would soon transform south Flagstaff. Hanging with Young on easy runs was possible for O'Neil and Mann on occasion, but as Young got fitter and better acclimated to the altitude, his "easy" days started to dip below six-minute pace, leaving the teenagers in the dust.

The I-40 loop was a convenient run to do from the front door, but it was far from Young's favorite route in Flagstaff. That honor was reserved for a stunning dirt road nestled among ponderosa pine trees at the base of the San Francisco Peaks. Beginning on U.S. 180 and continuing out along U.S. 89, Schultz Pass was the perfect out-and-back for Young when he was looking for an eighteen-to-twenty-miler.

Between easy days and Schultz Pass long runs, Young put his body through hell at Lumberjack Stadium. A staple workout as he prepared for the steeplechase in Mexico City was a set of 12x400m on sixty seconds recovery, aiming for each rep to be at or below sixty seconds.

Mann was tasked with holding the watch and giving Young his splits. On his tenth rep, Young dropped to his knees and began to suck in as much oxygen as Flagstaff would allow his lungs to have. His legs were burning, his mouth was dry, and the sixty-second recovery felt like the shortest minute of his life. Then Young turned to Mann and from his knees said, "Let me know when it's fifty-five seconds." Mann did exactly that and, on cue, Young got to his feet, took a deep breath, and began the next rep from a standing start.

"That was a fifty-nine," Mann shouted as Young came hurtling across the line.

The time only mildly registered with Young as, once again, he found himself on his hands and knees just past the finish line. The idea of another rep seemed impossible in the immediate aftermath of every previous effort. This is when altitude really starts to bully everyone who dares challenge it.

A visceral battle is waged between athlete and environment. The former's internal fight bubbles to the surface for everyone to see. It takes guts to get back on the line and grind through one more rep, not knowing if the body can handle it, only trusting that it will. If anything was going to steel Young for the final barriers of the steeplechase in Mexico City, it would be this last rep. Young's career was forged on his willingness to be ready for that kind of hurt.

Mann gave the fifty-five-second call and Young rose to his feet. Seemingly without hesitation, he drove off the line and began the grueling quarter mile that would round out a great day of training. As Young came roaring around the bend into the home straight, those hanging around the finish line could tell this rep was fast. His stride had completely opened up, and the reason why he held the American record in the steeplechase became obvious. With a burn throughout his entire body—a feeling that can't be replicated at sea level—Young came flying through the line and for one last time dropped to his knees.

Mann looked down at his watch with amazement. "That was a fifty-six," he said to O'Neil. The two looked at each other with stunned expressions. Watching one of the greatest runners of their time, they were starting to comprehend why he deserved such a title.

The main reason that Young and his training partners felt comfortable pushing their bodies to the limits at Flagstaff's elevation was Daniels. "Jack was a forerunner in understanding the hazards that altitude would cause, especially to distance runners," said Ryun. "We four runners were listening and trusting Jack to prepare us."

Daniels and his assistant, Tom Von Ruden, would occasionally come out to Flagstaff to run tests on the athletes. One of these involved having an athlete run beside a car with Daniels sitting on the hood. A tube was placed over the athlete's mouth and connected to a pipe held by Daniels. The expired air samples were contained in air-collection rubber bags. "Jack was of immense help to each of us in acclimating to altitude and in keeping us healthy," said Ryun.

Debate about the health risks of racing at altitude continued in the sports world leading up to the 1968 Olympics. But Young was reminding himself on a weekly basis that running hard at altitude wasn't a death sentence, even though the odd rep may have felt like it. Ryun also put the burn of running hard at elevation to the test. After contracting mononucleosis in the spring, he was dealing with a lack of energy just as he arrived in Flag. Eventually, Ryun's body adjusted so well to altitude that he ran a solo 880-yard time trial in 1:47 at Lumberjack Stadium.

It was affirming for the city and those who had invested in the track at Lumberjack Stadium to see its new playground used by high-caliber machines like Young and Ryun. But even these impressive workouts weren't enough to convince some that the track was worth the money spent by an athletic department with a tight budget. When rumors began to circulate around town that an international track meet might be held at Lumberjack Stadium two weeks after the U.S. Olympic Track and Field Trials, even the doubters began to realize the new facility's potential.

Jim Ryun (left), Billy O'Neil (center), and George Young take a break from a pre-Olympic workout in Flagstaff in 1968.

The track meet's purpose was to serve as a last opportunity for athletes to get a taste of racing at altitude before Mexico City. Since the opening ceremony would kick off less than two weeks later, competitors could leave directly from Flagstaff on their way to the Olympic village. This made logistical sense and would offer an incredible opportunity to showcase the city ... if local leaders could pull it off.

Young left Flagstaff to compete in the first-ever U.S. Olympic Marathon Trials, due to be contested at 7,500 feet in Alamosa, Colorado, on August 18. The race was open to anyone who wanted to compete—no qualifying time necessary. Young won the trials with a time of 2:30:48 in his debut marathon to earn his spot on the U.S. team for Mexico City. A few weeks later, he won the steeplechase at the U.S. Olympic Track and Field Trials in a time of 8:58.0—six seconds ahead of third-place finisher Nightingale. Ryun went on to win the 1500m in 3:49.0, joining Nightingale as a first-time Olympian.

Three Olympians was an impressive result for the Flagstaff-based training group, although everyone had hoped for four. Ongoing back issues left Mills unable to hit a qualifying mark to get into the trials. The reigning Olympic champion would have to watch the 10,000m in Mexico City from the sidelines.

The group's departure could have been a deflating moment for Flagstaff. Their presence on the trails and at Lumberjack Stadium was proof that this was a place Olympic hopefuls chose to come to prepare for one of the biggest moments of their careers. Thankfully, the rumor of a track meet in Flagstaff soon turned into reality.

What started out as a small idea soon grew into preparations for a world-class meet. Approved by the international AAU (Amateur Athletic Union), the competition more than justified the cost of having laid down a rubberized surface at Lumberjack Stadium. The Flagstaff Chamber of Commerce Olympic Promotion Committee got behind this initiative to bring 131 Olympians from four countries to town.

Holding a meet of this stature required countless hours of preparation behind the scenes. Jim Heihart, chairman of the Flagstaff Olympic Promotion Committee; Jack Raymond, manager of the Chamber of Commerce; and Red, NAU coach and meet director, were the key players. With the help of coaches from throughout the state and NAU officials, the ambitious vision evolved into what the *Arizona Daily Sun* proudly dubbed "a mini-Olympics."

Jack Daniels (center) takes samples of the oxygen expelled by world-record holder Jim Ryun (left) during a training session in summer 1968 outside Flagstaff with the help of his assistant, Tom Von Ruden. The research conducted by Daniels in Flagstaff was among the first to determine the effects on the human body when exerting itself at altitude.

USA
TRACK

On September 29, 1968, the gates to Lumberjack Stadium opened for the much-anticipated event. The expected high was 75 degrees, with strong winds emerging in the early afternoon. Admission was $1.50 for adults, seventy-five cents for under eighteen, and free for under seven. Those who presented a student ID were admitted for a dollar. With twenty-seven events on the schedule and the meet running into the early evening, the six thousand people who showed up to watch certainly got their money's worth.

The day was an international affair thanks to seventy-five West Germans (using Flagstaff as their pre-Olympics training camp to adjust to the altitude and get into the same time zone as Mexico City), five Chileans, eleven Canadians, and fifty Americans. Newspapers reported that the field included twenty-four potential Olympic medalists.

Given the elevation, the middle/distance events weren't expected to produce outstanding times, making way for the field events and sprints to steal the show. At the U.S. Olympic Track and Field Trials only a couple weeks prior, five world records had been broken. The reduced air resistance at 7,300 feet of elevation aided athletes in events requiring less than sixty seconds of exertion. Even the wind threatening some of these performances in Flagstaff didn't stop two world records from falling.

Ralph Boston of the United States almost cleared the pit as he jumped 27 feet 5⅝ inches in the long jump, adding more than an inch to the previous world record. Fellow American Margaret Bailes ran an outstanding 100m in 10.8, taking 0.3 seconds off the previous world record. Some thought the wind would hinder performances on this day; instead, it energized the crowd, even though both performances were later invalidated as wind-aided marks.

The pole vault was another crowd-pleaser. The competition ended in a three-way tie between Americans Bob Seagren and John Pennel and West German Claus Schiprowski.

Among the athletes who competed at the mini-Olympics, ten would go on to medal in Mexico City:

Bob Seagren, United States — gold in the pole vault
Wyomia Tyus, United States — gold in the 100m and 4x400m relay
Ralph Boston, United States — bronze in the long jump

George Woods, United States — silver in the shot put
Randy Matson, United States — gold in the shot put
Madeline Manning, United States — gold in the 800m
Ingrid Becker, West Germany — gold in the pentathlon and long jump
Lieselotte Westermann, West Germany — silver in the discus
Claus Schiprowski, West Germany — silver in the pole vault
Bodo Tümmler, West Germany — bronze in the 1500m

Young and Ryun not competing at the mini-Olympics didn't hurt their medal chances.

Leading the race for Olympic gold as he cleared the final water barrier in Mexico City, Young struggled to call upon his usual kick as Amos Biwott of Kenya went flying by to win the race in 8:51.0, less than a second ahead of fellow countryman Benjamin Kogo. Young was giving everything he had up the home straight, while an excited Nightingale, who hadn't made it out of the first round, shouted encouragement from the sidelines.

Australian Kerry O'Brien was advancing on Young's outside shoulder as they approached the last barrier. This final fifty meters would determine who would go home with the bronze. All the agonizing workouts Young had endured at Lumberjack Stadium and the miles he'd logged on Flagstaff trails would be worth it if his body could handle just a few more steps at elevation.

O'Brien and Young were soon neck and neck with only thirty meters left to run. Using every last ounce of energy to ride on Young's shoulder, O'Brien had nothing left for the last fifteen meters. He leaned forward as Young stayed upright and continued to power toward the line. Without needing to dip, Young finished the race with a hard-earned, third-place effort.

In the 1500m, Ryun wasn't willing to risk an early blistering pace. Hanging toward the back of the pack, he came through the opening 400 meters closer to sixty seconds as the leader clocked 55.9. Ryun had spent enough time at altitude to know how much a lap like that could sting later in the race. If he wanted a chance at winning, he needed to run a tactically smart race and not get caught up in the excitement of an Olympic final.

Kenyan athlete Kip Keino made a move with two laps to go, pressing the pace that had eased off since the opening lap. Coming through the 800-meter mark in

1:55.3, Keino already had a healthy gap on the field and didn't look like he was going to slow down anytime soon.

Ryun's decision to hang back was starting to look like a bad tactic as he came through in fifth place with 400 meters to go—a good twenty-five yards back from Keino, who continued to squeeze down the pace. If Ryun wanted any chance at winning, he would have to unleash an incredible last lap.

Steadily increasing his tempo along the back straight, Ryun began picking off athletes as they paid for the early hot pace. No matter how fit they were, once the altitude exacted its toll, their race was over. Ryun managed to nab second place with less than 200 meters to go, but the gold medal slipped away as Keino held his ground.

Young and Ryun's prediction that it would take around 3:40 to win gold in Mexico City proved quite inaccurate. Ryun finished in second place, running 3:37.8—an incredible time at 7,350 feet. But he was no match for Keino, who won in an astonishing 3:34.9, not far off Ryun's world record time of 3:33.1 set at sea level.

Flagstaff had officially put itself on the running map thanks to the Olympics being awarded to a city at elevation. This paved the way for a high-profile event like the mini-Olympics and for athletes like Young, Ryun, Mills, and Nightingale to consider Flagstaff as a place to train. Performances in Mexico City answered questions in the affirmative about racing at elevation without serious health consequences, and in the case of Keino, proved it was possible to run a nearly world-record performance in the process.

As the Olympians returned home, the future of training in the mountains remained an open question. Experiencing altitude to prepare for competition at altitude was vital. That much seemed clear. But more research was needed to determine the benefits of training high to get ready for races at sea level. Whether future runners would seek out Flagstaff to fulfill their dreams remained to be seen. However, as one lot of extraordinary humans left the city, another continued to train there.

At the cinder fields near Sunset Crater, thirty minutes north of downtown Flagstaff, the National Aeronautics and Space Administration (NASA) and the U.S. Geological Survey, Branch of Astrogeology occupied a closed-off site. Detailed maps of the moon had been drawn with the help of telescopes in Flagstaff to map out an exact replica of where NASA planned to one day land.

Two sections of the cinder fields were manipulated in 1967 using controlled explosives to make craters that matched the maps. Astronauts could then practice driving a rover and testing their equipment on simulated lunar terrain while on Earth. Every astronaut who would one day walk on the moon trained in Flagstaff and northern Arizona at some point.

In more ways than one, Flagstaff was the perfect training environment for pushing the boundaries of what humanity believed possible. And if racing in Mexico City hadn't proved deadly, maybe this 1969 trip to the moon wouldn't be either. △

Chapter 4
Every Tuesday

SIX YEARS AFTER RED HABERLACK TOOK ON THE TRACK AND FIELD program, NAU left the NAIA. The jump to the NCAA occurred on July 1, 1970, when NAU joined the Big Sky Conference—a fitting name evoking the wide-open American West.

Six schools had joined at its founding in 1963: University of Idaho, Idaho State University, University of Montana, Montana State University, Gonzaga University, and Weber State University. The conference expanded in 1970 through the addition of Boise State University and NAU.

Those NAIA years were foundational for NAU, né Arizona State College at Flagstaff. The early rosters were eclectic, populated with athletes from in-state cities big and small, including Steve Cross, Dave Harbster, Joe Lange, Dave Matta, and Joe Valencia from Phoenix, and Leonard Suarez from Bisbee.

They were joined by others from surrounding states, such as Van Johnson, a Native American from Stewart, Nevada; Charlie Appell, Tom Klema, Dan Sauers, and Dan Wood from California; and Rick Jamison, a transfer from NCAA powerhouse University of Kansas. Those squads even had an international flavor with two British runners, Richard Selby and Richard Sliney. In 1969, just three years after the first cross country team was established, the Lumberjacks placed ninth at the NAIA

National Championships. Scorers were Dave Tocheri, seventh; Sliney, eighth; Selby, twenty-first; Sauers, eighty-seventh; and Suarez, 187th.

Red's recruits served as pioneers of a proud program, a gritty and often ragtag bunch that shaped the fabric of the program that remains to this day. They paved the way for the successes later teams would become accustomed to.

NAU tracksters pose with their hosts from the University of Arizona after a meet in Tucson. Richard Sliney is on the far left in the front row beside Ron Mann.

The NAU men's cross country team qualified one runner for the 1970 NCAA Cross Country Championships after an impressive top-ten NAIA team finish the year prior. With temperatures sitting at a modest forty-nine degrees for the start of the race in Williamsburg, Virginia, Sliney grinded his way through the six-mile race to cross the finish line twelfth in 28:44—forty-four seconds back from winner Steve Prefontaine of the University of Oregon.

Sliney's showing was the first step for the NAU program's transition from NAIA to NCAA. Three years later, when the NCAA split into three categories, NAU became a Division I school.

By spring 1971, NAU was already finding success at the national level. The team won their first Big Sky Conference title in outdoor track. A group of athletes celebrated by throwing Red into the steeplechase water pit. Sliney and Tocheri both qualified for the NCAA Outdoor Track and Field Championships, where they finished sixth in the six-mile and seventh in the three-mile, respectively. For Sliney, this rounded out a big year in which he also finished third in the three-mile at the NCAA Indoor Track and Field Championships.

The 1971 cross country season started strong for the Lumberjacks, who won all four of their regular-season meets and were co-champions at their conference meet. NAU could count on two consistent athletes near the front in Sliney and Selby, and runners three through five reliably rounded out the scoring. The result was NAU's first team showing at an NCAA Cross Country Championships.

Richard Sliney (fourth from right) was NAU's first individual to qualify for the NCAA National Cross Country Championships. He finished twelfth in 1970.

Cross country meets are scored by totaling the finishing places of the top five runners across the line for each team, with the lowest combined score winning. Having one or two reliable "low sticks"—a reference to the numbered popsicle sticks handed out to runners as they cross the finish line—such as NAU had with its Brits, is important, but so is enough depth across all five scorers. Teams are allowed to race up to seven people, giving every school the best chance of having

The 1971 cross country team placed ninth in its inaugural visit to the NCAA national meet. Seated from left: Richard Sliney, Wayne Sisson, Richard Selby, Ron Mann, Jeff Rigdon, Dan Sauers, Tsosie Taylor, and Kevin Slotta. Back row, from left: Coach Leo Haberlack, Chris Godsall, Jeff Street, Steve Cross, Gregg Sawyer, Neil Howk, and Eddie Garduno. Not pictured: Dave Tocheri.

five athletes finish. Because of constraints on the team's budget, NAU only sent five athletes, which meant that if any of them had a bad day, it could hurt the team score; or worse, if one of them pulled out of the race, which isn't uncommon, NAU would not be counted as a scoring team.

Sliney used his experience to endure the near-freezing temperatures and lead his teammates, placing sixth out of a field of 285. Prefontaine successfully defended his individual title. Selby and Cross came through the line in thirty-seventh and seventy-ninth, respectively, to give NAU a solid one-two-three punch. Rounding out the top five—and only five—were Sauers in 145th and Tsosie Taylor in 199th. These athletes became the first in school history to score as a team at the NCAA Cross Country Championships, and their 294 points earned them a ninth-place finish.

The program's steady rise came down to a couple of factors. First, Red was able to recruit better athletes and bring over international talents who were already of national caliber when they arrived. Second, a unique team culture was starting to emerge. Ron Mann had observed the positive atmosphere since arriving as a freshman in fall 1968 and embraced it wholeheartedly. He knew he was going to miss being in the thick of it as he began his final semester in spring 1972.

The sun was barely up when Mann's alarm clock started ringing. His reluctant arm reached out from beneath the covers to shut it off and get up. It was a workout day, and there was no time to snooze.

The past four years had flown by, and Mann was doing his best to enjoy his final months as an NAU student-athlete, although that was easier said than done. On February 28, 1972, Mann welcomed his first child into the world. He was born with hyaline membrane disease, the same disease that took the life of President John F. Kennedy's son Patrick. Thanks to the quick decision of doctors to fly the baby down to the hospital in Phoenix six hours after birth, everything was going to be OK.

Visits to see his son down in Phoenix on the weekends, on top of a busy class schedule and a nagging knee injury that hampered his training, meant stress levels were high and sometimes overwhelming during Mann's last semester.

Ron Mann (second from left) and his early 1970s Lumberjack teammates, Dave Harbster (left), Jeff Matthews (second from right), and Richard Selby, were starting to see success at the conference and national levels rather quickly in track and cross country after switching to NCAA competition.

It was just past 6 a.m. and food service was due to begin in half an hour. Exhaustion from Monday's training was still raw in each athlete's body. The first steps out of bed were always the toughest part of the day. Sometimes muscles hurt that didn't hurt the morning before; other times it was the same aches and pains from the cumulative fatigue caused by every pounding mile since the semester began.

The biggest incentive to wake up early was getting to breakfast and catching up with the rest of the NAU track team. On this morning, Mann decided to join the other tired and mildly incoherent students as they made their way over to breakfast. The crisp morning air did the final job of waking everyone up.

Mann had moved out of the dorms and into the married housing at Campus Heights, so he didn't see his teammates as much as he used to. The dorms were split up by gender, and there were strict rules about who could be in which dorm at any given time. Men were forbidden from being in the women's dorms except on Sunday afternoons for two hours. However, this did not mean an "anything goes" situation. Bedroom doors were required to be kept open, and anyone sitting on the bed had to keep at least one foot on the floor. Life in Campus Heights was much less complicated.

Fueling for a big day was the motivator for getting oneself to breakfast, but hanging out with friends was the reason to linger for over an hour. The Central Dining Hall doubled as a social club for the NAU track team. They would catch up on anything and everything that had happened since they saw each other at dinner the night before.

A voice from the end of the table spoke up, "I can't sleep in these dorms. The echo from the football players running around at night is killing me."

"You need to invest in a roll of carpet," suggested Mann. "That's what we had in our room at Tinsley Hall—ten by eight feet—that won't get rid of all the noise, but it deadens it at least."

The floors at Tinsley, concrete with a thin layer of linoleum, amplified the sound of every footstep down the corridors. With a tough workout on the horizon, interrupted sleep was of genuine concern to these guys.

Nervous faces nodded at each other around the table as the men downed their toast and juice. When the nerves register in the body, the stomach shuts off, making every bite feel like a whole meal. They all knew what was ahead: Red prescribed a set of 12x400m reps every Tuesday with the goal of improving on their times week after week.

It wasn't uncommon for training to follow a similar format during this era. When Jack Daniels and many top West German coaches came to Flagstaff for the mini-Olympics, Red had gained insight into current training techniques. Interval training was an integral piece for runners then, while tempo and high-intensity VO_2 workouts became popular later. The best way to get strong in 1972 was to focus on handling the back end of a 400m workout.

With the chatter winding down, the guys left the Central Dining Hall so they wouldn't be late for class. Sharing laughs and commiserating over breakfast was the perfect way to start their day. Running can often feel like an individual sport, especially during track season, so it was important for the team to bond at every opportunity. Somehow, they didn't get sick of one another. The time they spent together forged them into a more cohesive unit.

Mann's morning class, Differential Equations, was taught by Dr. Arthur Adel in the math department. Adel had moved to Flagstaff in 1933 to work at the Lowell Observatory. He became renowned as an astronomer and astrophysicist. In 1948, Adel became a professor at NAU to help fund his research off-campus. Adel had established himself as one of the most brilliant minds in his field and was just four years away from retirement when Mann took his class in 1972. In recognition of Adel's twenty-eight years of contribution to the university, NAU later named a building after him.

Following his math lesson, Mann made his way over to the Activity Center, which was attached to the University Union building next to Central Dining Hall. Students would pass the bowling alley on their left before entering the mini-domed building that multiple NAU sports called home. The indoor track was not in world-class shape, but considering only a few years prior there had been no outdoor or indoor track to speak of, the blue-collar NAU athletes were reserved in their criticism of it—most of the time.

The varsity baseball team used a batting cage on the infield. Much to the track team's dismay, a couple of baseball players had cut a hole in the cage just big enough to hit a ball through. When runners were flying around the tight bends while the baseball team was practicing, this was a disaster waiting to happen. Cross recalled one workout that almost ended horribly.

"I was doing some efforts on the track during the winter, and a baseball came flying through a hole in the cage right down lane one," Cross explained. "After that didn't kill me, one of the baseball players came running after the ball onto the track and we collided 'round the first bend."

Mann shared his teammate's concern. "It's not just the balls flying around, but the dust too. That place turns into a dust storm when you have enough guys running around the infield."

The distance guys could complain all they wanted, but their experiences on the indoor track paled in comparison to what the sprinters had to deal with. The track's rubberized surface didn't extend beyond the outside lane at the end of the home straight. Athletes had to decelerate from top speed before their spikes collided with the concrete. Sparks flew as metal spikes met the concrete at pace. Sprinters frantically tried to slam on the brakes before running through the doors at the end of the track.

Student-athletes joked about the facility's imperfections, but everyone appreciated the fact they had it. Although it wasn't always easy when baseball, track and field, and sometimes even football shared the same space, every sport strove for common goals and respected one another.

The day's training was posted on a bulletin board inside the team's locker room at the Activity Center. Red was never at morning training sessions because of his teaching obligations in the physical education department. Though he was being stretched thin some days, Red always enjoyed time spent working with the track team.

Once the team was dressed and ready to run, they would leave the Activity Center right at 10 a.m. to get in an easy six miles. With a hard workout still to come, nobody wanted to push this training too fast. Their normal loop for this run went west on Route 66, along a trail beside the railroad track, then down San Francisco Street back to where they began. The loop would usually take somewhere between forty-two and forty-five minutes, depending on how the guys were feeling.

After showering, the team dispersed, and Mann headed to his last class before lunch. Already five hours deep into his day, Mann's energy levels and concentration were starting to dip. It didn't matter how brilliant the professor was at this point. Frequent glances at the clock and a growling stomach were commonplace for the second lecture of the day. Mann couldn't wait for class to end so he could replenish his body.

The team reconvened at Central Dining Hall for a quick bite to eat around 1 p.m. There weren't as many jokes at lunch, as most of the guys were discussing President Richard Nixon's run for reelection. Everyone was on some level concerned about the upcoming election and whether the Vietnam War draft would continue.

Ever since 1969, NAU track athletes who were of age to be drafted had been getting together to listen to the lottery over the radio—praying their number would not be drawn. Although they had the safety of being in college, if any of them failed a class or dropped out, they would lose their student deferment and become more vulnerable to being drafted.

This was a tough time for young men in the United States. Being of age to get drafted meant they had friends and classmates from high school who either volunteered or were drafted without any deferment to save them. Having this in the back of their minds added a bit of perspective to the workout awaiting them in a couple of hours. Their pain would be confined to the oval at Lumberjack Stadium and ended once practice was done. That was a privileged position for a young man in 1972.

With the impending workout in mind, the guys were a little more careful about how much food they consumed at lunch. They wanted to eat enough to have energy for the workout but not so much that it would end up on the track. If any workout was going to make these guys throw up, it would be a set of 400m efforts. Between the altitude and the short rest between reps, the stomach was taken through the ringer every week.

Everyone arrived at Lumberjack Stadium right before 3 p.m., ready for their two-mile warm-up. With international recruits Selby, Sliney, Jeff Matthews of New Zealand, and Dave Tocheri of Canada mixed in with U.S. athletes, the workout crew was a fun and dynamic training group that resembled a running brotherhood.

The group's mood was a cocktail of nervousness and excitement. Workout days are a great way to test the body and find out each athlete's fitness level. It's also a time to figure out how much pain can be endured, since that is an inescapable part of the sport. Without pain, or at least serious discomfort, they wouldn't progress as they hoped. They were the ninth-best cross country team in the country, but they wanted to be better. The purpose of Tuesday workouts was to make the body hurt. Sometimes that meant the brain needed to coerce the body into enjoying the ride.

The pace for each 400m rep and the recovery between depended on the weather. On a day with no breeze, the goal was sixty-five to sixty-two seconds per repeat with sixty seconds recovery. However, if it was a typical spring day in Flagstaff, the reps could sometimes be as slow as seventy seconds and the recovery stretched out to a maximum of two minutes. Pushing into a strong headwind up the home straight at 7,000 feet earned vital extra rest.

With only a stopwatch in his hand, Red monitored the splits while his athletes kept track of their own rep times. On earlier repeats, the mood among the group was light, as the workout's toughness hadn't yet set in. There was still enough oxygen in the athletes' lungs to squeeze out a sentence or two during their rest.

"Coach, didn't you have a full head of red hair before you came up to Flag? Did these spring winds blow it all away already?" laughed Mann.

A smile emerged from one side of Red's face as he used the other side to keep his toothpick in place. "It sounds like you're recovering pretty well, Ron. I guess it's time to start the next rep."

By 4:30 p.m. the track work was done. The guys began their two-mile cooldown and finished over at the Activity Center. Tuesdays and Thursdays were weightlifting days for the team. The guys would do a circuit on the center's one Universal gym. The purpose wasn't necessarily to target a specific area of the body, but rather to get the heart rate up. Strength exercises weren't too sport-specific yet, so they were guinea pigs to this new addition to the customary running at practice. Exposed to advanced weight training when the West German team came to Flagstaff in the summer of 1968, Red picked up tips on its importance and incorporated it into the NAU team's weekly schedule.

When the team finished their circuit training, they dashed over to Central Dining Hall to get dinner before service closed at 6 p.m. Nobody would be thrown out if they were still eating beyond closing time, but it would be foolish to expect a fresh plate of food beyond then. The only cooking option allowed in the dorms was a popcorn maker. Students couldn't even have a fridge in their rooms. The only time students could keep a tub of ice cream cold was in the winter by setting it outside their window. The risk was that other students might throw snowballs, trying to hit it off.

The team shared a few more laughs over dinner before heading back to their dorm rooms. With little time free during the day, it was necessary to squeeze studying in at night before heading to bed.

Over at Campus Heights, Mann was starting to crash from his demanding class and training schedule. He looked over at the clock: 9:30 p.m. For the sake of his schoolwork, it would be beneficial to squeeze in another hour of studying before bed. However, if he wanted any hope of getting up at 6 a.m. again the next day, schoolwork would have to wait.

Finally in bed, Mann couldn't help but feel a sense of pride thinking about how far the program had come in his four years as a Lumberjack. Knowing his days as a college athlete were numbered, he tried to savor every moment spent with his teammates. After graduation, his plan was to start teaching, and his years of competing would likely come to an end. Being a part of the NAU program was an honor, one Mann could only dream of continuing after he earned his degree. With that, he drifted off to sleep to get ready for another tough day spent with his friends. △

Chapter 5
A Great Opportunity

AVID RUNNER SCOTT BAXTER WAS TAKEN ABACK BY FLAGSTAFF'S stunningly dark night skies when he arrived in 1966. City leaders had made a purposeful attempt to avoid the effects of light pollution since introducing legal regulations on the use of sweeping searchlights in 1958. Flagstaff and Coconino County adopted comprehensive outdoor lighting codes in 1973. Such efforts would be recognized in 2001, when Flagstaff became the world's first official International Dark Sky Community.

One of the reasons Flagstaff wanted to preserve its dark skies was to allow Lowell Observatory to do effective work. Founded by Percival Lowell in 1894 on a mesa overlooking the original townsite, the observatory was designated a national historic landmark just a year before Baxter came to Flagstaff. In the heady days of the 1960s when the United States planned to reach the moon, the observatory helped astronomers map out sections of the lunar surface.

Decades earlier, in 1930, after a twenty-four-year search for a possible ninth planet, Lowell Observatory was where Clyde Tombaugh first discovered Pluto. Billed at the time as the ninth known planet in the solar system, Pluto was downgraded in classification to a dwarf planet in 2006. Still, Tombaugh's discovery remains a point of pride for the city.

Lowell Observatory would be the impetus for runner Nat White to come to Flagstaff and finish his PhD in 1969. After helping fix some broken equipment there, he was offered a job, and within a year he decided he wanted to stay. Something about the clean air and plentiful trails seemed to attract recreational runners like White and Baxter to the city even though there wasn't yet much of a running community.

As much as Baxter enjoyed looking up at the night sky, the runner in him was drawn to the endless miles of Forest Service roads surrounding the city. Unclimbed rock all over northern Arizona satisfied his love for rock climbing. Flagstaff soon became a magical outdoor palace with everything Baxter could ever need . . . almost.

Baxter, along with fellow runners Ned Frederickson and Jack Welch of Flagstaff, bonded over a common infatuation with the Finnish mystique known as *sisu*. Exemplified by twelve-time Olympic medalist Paavo Nurmi in the 1930s and 1940s and double 1972 Olympic medalist Lasse Virén, sisu describes the spirit of the Finnish people and can be interpreted a few different ways.

The three friends translated it as "pride, determination, and courage," and Baxter silkscreened a few white cotton shirts with "Sisu" on the front and the Finnish flag on the back.They proudly wore their printed shirts during workouts and at races, which soon caught the attention of other runners in the community.

What began as a cool shirt idea evolved into the formation in 1974 of Flagstaff's first running club—the Sisu Striders. The club's first newsletter outlined their motivation:

> The two greatest sources of encouragement for the runner (beyond his/her basic motivation) are competition and companionship. Not just the companionship of having someone to run with but the comradery [*sic*] of sharing the secrets and discoveries of running. There is so much to learn and so much to share that only another runner can understand or relate to.

For an annual fee of $10.00, each person who signed up for the Sisu Striders received a free T-shirt emblazoned with "Sisu Striders," a year's subscription to the club's newsletter, a one-year subscription to *Running—The Journal of the Scientific Study of Distance Running*, and a waiver of entry fees to all local club races. "What's left of the $10, after all these expenses are taken care of, will be used to encourage running in Northern Arizona," read the club's newsletter.

The Sisu Striders set simple goals. "We will first try to educate the public about the physical and emotional benefits of regular running," stated the newsletter. "Secondly, we hope that the enticement of rewards and recognition at local races will stimulate participation."

The Sisu Striders proved an invaluable piece of the emerging running community, laying the foundation for later clubs. It was a complement to the NAU track and field and cross country program, as well as another small group of runners who enjoyed spending time jogging together.

In the same spirit, NAU professors Chuck Eaton, George Kyte, Bob Packard, and John Zark ran together in the Activity Center during their lunch breaks, often joined by White. Kyte had supported NAU track and field and cross country since the team's inception, and White would occasionally join the NAU team for workouts at Lumberjack Stadium. In the first decade after the formation of the college program, the university campus became a hub for the synergetic connection among student-athletes, professors, and the larger Flagstaff running community that continues to this day.

Entering his eleventh year at the helm of NAU track and field and cross country, Red Haberlack had cemented himself as one of the best coaches in the Big Sky Conference. So it came as a surprise to Athletic Director Hank Anderson when Red walked into his office to talk about taking a one-year sabbatical during the 1976–1977 school year.

It wasn't uncommon for teachers to take a sabbatical to further their own education, but most teachers weren't also heading up a successful track and field program. Leaving for a year meant someone else would have to take charge, potentially halting the program's progress if the interim leader were unprepared for the role. To make the sabbatical option work for his athletes, Red would need to find someone who could make the team feel like he'd never left.

"I know just the man," a confident Red told Anderson.

Down the mountain at Sunnyslope High School in north Phoenix, Ron Mann had begun his own coaching journey at his alma mater. The father of two was happy to be back in the district where he had grown up. Putting his NAU education to use, Mann taught woodworking and mathematics and coached the distance runners at Sunnyslope. During his nearly four years coaching the program, the Vikings had fielded multiple regional champions and established themselves as a force within the state. Coaching and teaching gave Mann a sense of purpose as he exercised his love for people and sport to mentor young athletes. He knew coaching was what he wanted to do; he didn't yet realize it was his destiny.

Red had kept in regular contact with Mann after he graduated in spring 1972. The two often discussed the NAU program, and Mann eagerly followed the team's progress. Red had expressed interest in furthering his own education at some point during those conversations, but Mann was still surprised that once Red finally committed to doing so, he wanted to leave the program in Mann's young hands.

"Whaddya say, Ron, you think you could handle looking after the team while I'm gone?" Red asked Mann over the phone.

Although Mann was content with his job and coaching responsibilities at Sunnyslope, the opportunity to lead a collegiate program was exciting. Mann could also further his own education and obtain a master's degree during his year in Flagstaff.

"I have big shoes to fill, Coach, but I am up for the challenge," Mann replied.

Anderson breathed a sigh of relief when he learned of Mann's willingness to take over the program for the school year. "I'm delighted that Red has the opportunity to work on an advanced degree," the athletic director said. "By having one of Red's former athletes, Ron, come for a year, we can keep the continuity of the program going."

With his athletes enjoying the summer break, Red and Shirley packed up and drove north to Utah. Red was enrolled in a health education PhD program at the University of Utah. Typically, a PhD takes several years to complete. Red was going to attempt it in a year. It was an ambitious goal, but Red's proven work ethic and ability to juggle teaching, coaching, and family made it seem possible.

Mann arrived in Flagstaff in late-July 1976 to give himself a few weeks to adjust before the school year kicked off. Lying in bed at Campus Heights was a flashback moment for the twenty-six-year-old. Not long had passed since he slept in this same complex as an exhausted athlete just trying to make it through each day. Soon he would be an exhausted coach trying to do the same thing. But that didn't deter him. Being a part of the NAU program, whatever his role, was still a privilege.

Mann took a trip down memory lane walking the NAU campus before school officially started. Not a lot had changed on the part of campus where he had spent most of his time as a student, but as he ventured farther south, he could see the university starting to expand.

On the corner of South San Francisco Street and East Pine Knoll Drive, a structure was being built on a twenty-six-acre land parcel the Arizona Lumber and Timber Company had donated in 1975. The massive building would house a multi-purpose sports stadium for the Lumberjacks. The $8.1 million domed stadium was expected to be finished by fall 1977.

Construction of the ensphere in the mid-1970s transformed NAU's emerging south campus.

The construction site utilized a natural amphitheater of excavated stone, saving money on a costly supporting wall. Architectural firm Rossman and Partners oversaw the design, and Mardian Construction Company of Phoenix did the heavy lifting to erect the 97,000 square-foot dome.

The idea for a domed stadium originated in the early 1970s, after the success of the Minidome at Idaho State University in Pocatello—a rival school within the Big Sky Conference. Turning the "ensphere" into reality required a substantial financial outlay, and the money had to come from multiple sources. Legislative funding covered $1.5 million, while $4.6 million of the final cost came from voluntary student fee increases, approved by a vote of the student body. The remaining funds came from vending machines around campus. Since the 1950s, this money had accumulated interest in a fund that had amassed $2 million by the time of the dome project. One reporter highlighted the grassroots effort, noting that "the nickels and dimes of NAU students and staff helped pay for the dome."

The ensphere represented a significant investment, not only in NAU and the athletic department, but also the community of Flagstaff. Its artificial turf would be the new home of NAU football. With 15,300 seats (not including expandable end-zone seating), NAU could pull in more money through ticket sales than had been possible at Lumberjack Stadium. The world-class facility could help attract top football talent in the state and beyond.

Under the turf, a 352-yard track would be put to use during the indoor season while snow blanketed the city. This would be the new home of the NAU track and field team over the winter. Looking up 142 feet and taking in the massive 500-foot roof span overhead was an incredible sight. Athletes and fans could be proud of their impressive facility. It wasn't until 2002 that the original rubberized granular track was converted to the Mondo surface used at most Olympic sites and reconfigured to 300 meters to comply with new NCAA rules governing indoor qualifying marks.

Red's track and field program wouldn't have exclusive access to the space during the indoor season. A basketball court was installed on the infield against the back straight, an ice-skating rink fit into the bend coming into the home straight, and a softball field sat inside the first curve. This made for a cluttered infield from a track runner's perspective, but it was still a significant improvement to the old Activity Center, which would eventually cease to exist as an athletic venue.

Athletes had continued flocking to Flagstaff as a training base in the years following the 1968 Olympic Games in Mexico City. With Lumberjack Stadium and the new dome providing versatile training opportunities, the decision to include a 352-yard track proved a wise one. At five laps to the mile, NAU's dome boasted one of the largest indoor tracks in the country, distinguishing Flagstaff as a premier year-round altitude training site. The ensphere may have been seen primarily as a drawing card for NAU football, but it became an even bigger one for some of the world's best runners.

As a young coach taking the reins of an NCAA Division I program, Mann faced his own daunting climb. Trying to gain the respect of his athletes was tough at first, as some resisted the forced transition from temporarily losing their veteran coach.

Mann's years of coaching at the high school level and experience as a collegiate athlete gave him the tools for a successful year. He just needed the team's buy-in.

The biggest roadblock to Mann's success was his workload. His typical day consisted of teaching, coaching in the afternoons, taking classes at night, and trying to squeeze in time for his family.

"I realized three or four weeks into the position that I had taken on too much," said Mann.

By that time, it was too late. He had already committed to his teaching, studying, and coaching roles. Red wasn't coming back for a year, so Mann had to figure out how to juggle his schedule without getting burned out.

On top of it all, subsisting on a graduate student stipend left the young coach scrambling to cover his family's expenses. Red was getting two-thirds of his normal salary while he was away in Utah, which left Mann with the remaining one-third. A tuition waiver helped with the cost of the master's program, but overall, the situation was physically, emotionally, and financially draining.

With a wife and two kids to provide for, it became apparent that this coaching position was more of a gamble than a definitively great opportunity. On some occasions, Mann's parents and mother-in-law would come up to Flagstaff from Phoenix and bring new clothes for their grandkids and sometimes a meal or two. The support from Mann's extended family was crucial.

Somehow amid the stress, Mann realized college coaching was his calling. This was what he believed he was put on this planet to do. It took a couple months to get used to the schedule, but eventually Mann began to derive satisfaction from being busy. "I found the challenge a motivation rather than a detriment," he said.

With the coaching assistance of recent NAU graduate Freddie Espinoza, NAU placed second at the Big Sky Cross Country Championships, and Jim Trapp and Ruben Reyes qualified for the 1976 NCAA national meet. When it came to track season, where Mann and Espinoza had to manage multiple event groups (something that was common at mid-major programs), their fall success didn't carry over. "I didn't do a good job of coaching the technical events," admitted Mann. The team finished fifth at the Big Sky Outdoor Track and Field Championships, putting a damper on Mann's year in charge of the program.

As the 1977 track season ended, so too did Mann's stint as a coach at NAU. Mann had secretly hoped that Red's PhD might lead to an administrative position, opening the door for Mann to continue coaching at NAU. But that dream remained far-fetched. Not a single job offer came in from another college, leading Mann to question his newly developed passion for coaching at that level.

"I made tons of mistakes during this year," said Mann. Early missteps are commonplace and entirely expected in novice coaches, but that didn't help his immediate situation. "I walked away from the year and didn't have a job offer. I didn't even get an assistant job offer. This led me to think, 'Am I really cut out for this college coaching thing?'"

"Maybe I was meant to be a high school coach," Mann reflected as he and his family headed down the hill to Phoenix.

The domed stadium, now known as the NAU Skydome, was completed a couple of months after Red's return. Its roof was visible from planes flying over the city, and it became a landmark for identifying the NAU campus from atop nearby peaks.

The first football game hosted in the Skydome was held on September 17, 1977, and the Lumberjacks won by one point. An average of 13,029 people attended the five regular-season home games, an impressive 60.4 percent increase in attendance over the 1976 season.

Once the football season wrapped, Red's track team finally got their turn in the Skydome. The air may have been thin and dry in there, and the five laps to a mile may have felt never-ending, but this facility made the team feel validated. That was a special feeling for a group of guys running in borrowed sweats and worn-out shoes.

The NAU Skydome was renamed in 1979, becoming the J. Lawrence Walkup Skydome in honor of the longtime university president. Or, as students would come to shorten it, simply the Dome. That same year, the twenty-five-foot-tall Muffler Man statues that stood outside the Lumberjack Cafe on Sitgreaves Street were relocated to the Dome when the business was sold and the new owner donated them to NAU. One of the statues went inside, while the other proudly stood watch by the main entrance. △

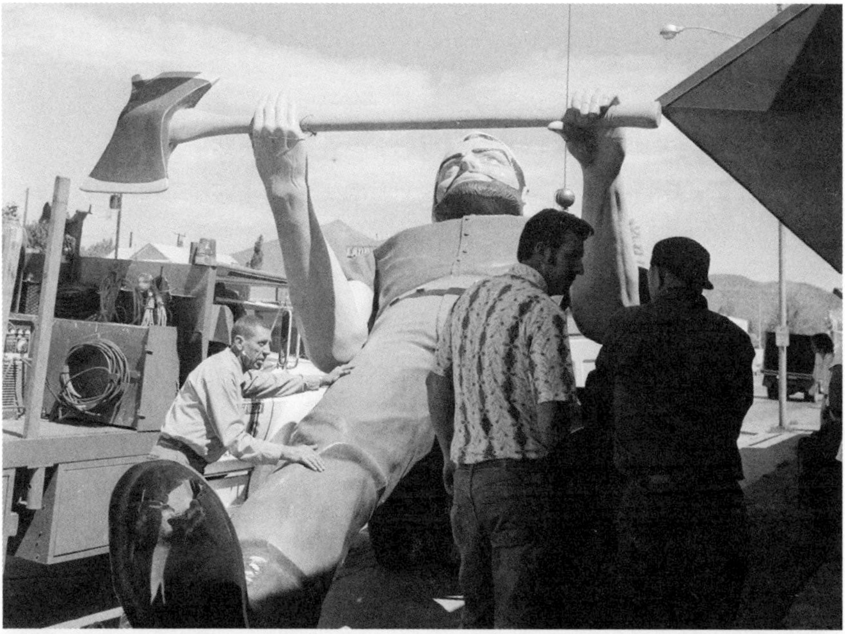

The Lumberjack that once stood outside a local restaurant was relocated to campus in 1979 (top). Ever since, he has watched over fans as they enter the Skydome (bottom).

Chapter 6
Welcoming a Women's Program

IN AN EMPTY CLASSROOM AT PARADISE VALLEY HIGH SCHOOL IN Phoenix, Ron Mann sat at his desk looking out at chairs that would soon be filled with eager students. Mann appreciated his role as an educator for vocational construction and didn't have a problem connecting with his students—being a teacher suited him. A natural people-person and an experienced athlete and coach, Mann knew what it took to get the best out of others. Applying those skills to the classroom came naturally to him.

When Mann wasn't teaching at Paradise Valley, he coached the track and field team at Glendale Community College, a fifteen-minute commute from the high school. The part-time gig let Mann keep his hands in the college coaching scene. With the added advantage of living close to where he had grown up, Mann had found a comfortable place in life. But comfort wasn't really the dream he'd been chasing.

The lesson Mann had planned for the day fogged in his brain as he glanced out the window to the north. Visions of another place began to dominate his thoughts. His body may have been in the classroom, but his mind had taken a trip up the mountain. Mann could almost feel cool air entering his lungs as they worked harder to pull in oxygen with every breath. He remembered the familiar burn in his legs as he closed out a sixteen-mile run at Schultz Pass. He reveled in the satisfaction of watching his athletes crush a workout at Lumberjack Stadium.

The year Mann had spent as head of the NAU track and field and cross country program was firmly etched into his consciousness. It had been the most rewarding experience of his coaching career thus far, and it would be a lie to suggest he wasn't longing to return to it.

Mann had hoped his accomplishments over that season with the NAU team would set him up for a varsity coaching position. Instead, he'd spent the next three years back down in the Valley of the Sun as a part-time coach at local community colleges. The work felt rewarding, but far removed from his ambition of heading up an NCAA track program.

The daydreaming had become more frequent since Red Haberlack had contacted Mann to inform him that a new head coaching position was about to open at NAU. The athletic department was adding a women's track and field and cross country program to its list of varsity sports. Red encouraged Mann to apply for the position.

The NAU men's program was well established by 1980. They had been a top-ten team over cross country and notched standout performances on the track. This meant the NAU athletic department wasn't looking for just anyone to fill the role of women's head coach. The successful candidate would need to show their ability to bring the new program up to the level of the men's achievements.

Mann fancied his chances when he applied for the position. Beyond his experience as a coach, Mann possessed a keen insider's knowledge of Flagstaff and NAU. He reasoned that would help him stand out among other candidates. "I knew the university so well," he said. "I knew what majors were available, the athletic environment, and the challenges of running at high altitude."

What Mann lacked on his résumé was experience working with female athletes and more than a year of coaching at the NCAA level. If other candidates were considerably stronger in these areas, Mann's background with the program and city likely wouldn't be enough to convince the selection committee he was the right person for the position.

His thoughts rushed back down the mountain as his students flooded into the classroom. Daydreaming would have to wait. One day Mann may be the head coach of an NCAA program, but for now, he was a teacher ready to do his best for the kids who sat in front of him.

NAU's decision to add a women's track and field and cross country program in 1980 came about because of changes to discrimination laws in the United States going back more than fifteen years. In the summer of 1964, around the same time that Red was preparing to make his first trip to Flagstaff, Congress passed the Civil Rights Act and President Lyndon B. Johnson signed it into law. Labeled one of the most significant legislative achievements in American history, the law prohibited discrimination based on race, color, religion, sex, or national origin.

The Civil Rights Act of 1964 was a step in the right direction for the country; however, in many ways it still didn't go far enough to protect every population from overt discrimination. Title VI of the Act prohibited discrimination based on race, color, or national origin in educational programs or activities receiving federal financial assistance. Since sex was not on the list of protected classes, women continued to be excluded from educational and sporting opportunities after the law took effect.

It wasn't until the Education Amendments of 1972 were signed into law that the issue was finally addressed. Title IX of these Amendments established that: "No person in the United States shall, on the basis of sex, be excluded from participation in, be denied the benefits of, or be subjected to discrimination under any education program or activity receiving Federal financial assistance."

The roadblocks that had prevented women from studying certain college subjects or competing in sports at all educational levels shifted. This was a great starting point, yet it was hard to ignore the damage already done. When Title IX passed in 1972, only 30,000 women were competing in college sports, compared to 170,000 men. It would take an enormous effort to even out those numbers and provide women with the opportunities they'd been denied for so long.

College athletic departments around the country scrambled to bring their sports programs into compliance with Title IX requirements. For the Big Sky Conference, it was expected that every competing college would have at least six teams for men and women. If a college couldn't reach this number by a certain date, they would be ineligible to compete within the conference.

NAU President Dr. Eugene Hughes was happy about the push for more women's programs. Aside from the obvious desire to maintain the flow of federal funding to the school, Hughes could see how fast the university was growing and that the availability of women's sports would attract athletes who might be unsure about coming to Flagstaff. For NAU to fulfill its potential as the state's third major university, alongside Arizona State University and the University of Arizona, Hughes knew there would be value in a well-rounded athletic department.

With the success of the men's track and field and cross country program under Red's guidance, adding a women's track and field and cross country program was an obvious choice. This would also be an easy and cheap way to add a lot of athletes at once. Lumping indoors, outdoors, and cross country all into one program under one head coach made sense for an athletic department on a tight budget. Red was on board with having a women's program join what he had built. However, he wasn't willing to take on the extra load of coaching twice the athletes.

Arriving back at his family's home in Phoenix following a much-deserved holiday in Hawai'i, Mann was greeted by smiling faces the moment he walked in the door. Most of the smiles were from his kids, but the curious looking smile on his dad's face from across the room caught his attention.

"I have good news and bad news," Mann's dad told him. "The bad news is you've got to be in Flagstaff on Monday morning. The good news is you're interviewing for the women's head coaching position."

Mann couldn't hide the excitement he felt. Being asked to come for an interview meant that he was one of the top candidates for the position. Although he had only just arrived home, Mann couldn't wait to take one more trip before the school year started. Monday couldn't come soon enough.

Mann arrived in Flagstaff Monday at 9:00 a.m. ready for a full day of interviews. Since the head coaching job also required the successful candidate to teach at NAU, Mann's first interview was with the head of the physical education department. Having a master's degree in exercise science meant he was a perfect fit for that department's criteria.

Mann then met with President Hughes, followed by Hank Anderson, the school's athletic director. Every meeting was important, but the toughest awaiting Mann was the five-member selection committee.

It was clear from the beginning that about half the panel favored a female coach to lead the new program. Mann knew that some of the other candidates were women and at least two had extensive résumés of success coaching female track and field and cross country teams.

The swing vote, in Mann's opinion, was Marge Cibik. During the panel interview, she looked directly at Mann and asked the all-important question: "For a male who has never coached women's athletics before, what makes you capable of coaching and being a role model for young women?"

Mann took a sip of water before answering in the most 1980s way possible. "It is my experience that young women take quality direction from a male role model. They look up to a father figure, and that is exactly what I plan to be to these young women."

Although Mann is the first to admit such an answer wouldn't win anyone over in the decades that followed, on this day, Cibik resonated with the response, as her daughter had that exact experience as a high school volleyball player in Flagstaff. This was what Cibik wanted to hear.

Mann continued: "No matter who you're coaching, coaching is coaching. You don't coach events; you coach people."

Mann's passion for coaching and working with track and field athletes, regardless of their gender, was obvious to everyone on the panel. He wanted to lead the soon-to-exist women's varsity program up the same mountain the men had started to climb in 1965.

In the end, Mann persuaded the panel he was the right candidate. He explained to Anderson how he would run a program from a logistical standpoint. He assured the head of the physical education department he could be a great teacher at NAU. He convinced Hughes he would be a positive addition to his staff. The only person already on board was Red. He knew the kind of person Mann was and considered him the ideal candidate for the job; he just needed everyone else to see it too.

When choosing what college to attend, the decision for Jennifer Martin was an easy one. The Flagstaff local who would be graduating from Coconino High School in spring 1978 was determined to stay in-state due to the excessive cost of out-of-state tuition. That narrowed her choices down to Tucson, Tempe, or Flagstaff. Since

Martin didn't see the appeal of living in a low desert, NAU was the only option that remained. The final selling point for NAU was the scholarship it offered Martin. Attendance would only cost $125 a semester plus the cost of books.

Martin wouldn't have the option to compete in college sports at NAU until fall 1980. She learned through her brother, who had run for the men's track and cross country teams, that a women's team was forming. Having competed on the first girls' cross country team at Coconino High School, Martin felt it was fitting that she help make history once more as a member of the first women's cross country squad at NAU.

Women's sports were seeing a nationwide surge in participation, thanks to Title IX. By the time Martin graduated from high school, six times as many high school girls were participating in sports as there had been in 1970.

The sign-up day for this new program drew more attention than Mann or Martin had imagined. Although Martin was excited about the new program, she did have doubts about how many women would be interested. "The only people I ever saw out running were the Coconino High School boys when I was in school," she said. A part of her own motivation to join the NAU team was to add numbers. "I didn't want this to be created and no one go for it."

The women who turned up included students from the physical education department, those interested in competing in a college sport, and athletes from a running group started by Red with the help of assistant coach Jim Trapp in anticipation of a women's program. With women's sports only just starting to grow, there was no telling who out of this group would develop into a strong runner. More than likely, most of these women hadn't had access to good coaching, adequate facilities, or generally positive direction for their running up to this point.

Mann couldn't afford to be picky. "I tried to recruit anybody I could," he said. "I was just trying to assemble numbers."

That didn't mean Mann wasn't trying to recruit women who were good runners. Eighty percent of his time was spent looking for "tier two" runners who would contribute to the numbers, and the other twenty percent was focused on finding top-level athletes. His connections to community colleges in the state helped him get the attention of athletes finishing up their two-year degrees.

It was tough for Mann to put a lot of time and energy into recruiting, considering he had a whole program to operate on his own. In the late 1970s, Red had added Trapp to his staff since he was instrumental in recruiting efforts in Arizona, nationally, and internationally. Trapp was well-known as a Canadian star runner. Mann was a one-man show, much like Red had been in the beginning.

With teaching commitments thrown into the mix, this made for a very demanding first year as head coach. Building a women's program on par with the men would take time, determination, and a lot of patience. Mann had all of these in spades.

The year 1980 initiated a new era at NAU with the first women's varsity cross country team. Here at the AIAW District Championships are, left to right, Lori Oliver, Sandra Lazo, Diana Herera, Leslie Carroll, Tina Lick, Shawnee Bolden, Connie Blackwater, and Coach Ron Mann.

The Mann family packed up their car and set out on the five-hour drive to Durango, Colorado, for a vacation. Late July to early August in 1982 was a beautiful time on Colorado's Western Slope. With three kids and camping equipment crammed into the car, the appeal of Durango was its proximity to Flagstaff. Mann wanted to get out of the state but didn't want to travel so far that the trip with restless kids wasn't worth the eventual destination.

Durango had become popular with tourists and outdoor enthusiasts. Mann's three sons, Steve, Ryun, and Brandon, looked forward to fishing in the stream near the Lightner Creek Campground. If they didn't have any luck along the Animas, they could go back to the trout farm next to the campground and cast on a separate pond where kids paid a small fee to fish.

Looking to catch some trout of his own, Red had also decided to take time away from Flagstaff and his demanding head-coaching role. Red headed southwest of Page, Arizona, to his favorite spot at Lees Ferry. Located on the Colorado River, where many boats put in to run the Grand Canyon, this was the perfect place to escape and enjoy the feeling of being dwarfed by 1,000-foot canyon walls while hauling in a twenty-inch wild rainbow.

With the school year due to kick off in only a few weeks, Red and Mann wanted to make the most of their last bit of freedom before the grind of coaching resumed. They liked their jobs, but between the recruiting trips, practice, travel for meets, and teaching, it was easy to get burned out if they didn't take time to relax throughout the year. These holidays weren't just for fun; they were necessary.

Back in Flagstaff, Dean of the College of Education Charlie Faucet and Athletic Director Anderson came by the Haberlack home looking for Red. They needed him back in Flagstaff immediately. There was no easy way to get ahold of Red at remote Lees Ferry. Shirley told Faucet and Anderson their news would have to wait until Red's return the next day.

The day after Red arrived back in Flagstaff, Mann used the pay phone at Lightner Creek Campground to see if he had any voice messages from NAU. He hadn't anticipated anyone would need to reach him in his few days away, but there was a message from Anderson that would change his life:

> "Hi Ron, I do apologize about bothering you while you are away with your family, but an urgent matter has come up.
>
> "Dr. Helen Oswald, who was the head of Physical Education, has passed away suddenly. Since the school year will begin soon, they needed to find a replacement quickly. The department feels strongly that Red is the best person to fill that role.
>
> "He accepted the job, Ron.
>
> "We need you back in Flagstaff to determine the future of the track program. Give me a call back when you get this message." △

Part 2 – The Climb
(1982 – 2009)

Chapter 7
Raising Expectations

RON MANN SAT NERVOUSLY OUTSIDE ATHLETIC DIRECTOR HANK Anderson's office. The biggest meeting of his life was waiting beyond Anderson's door. There were several plausible scenarios for how this meeting may play out, but Mann knew exactly how he wanted it to end.

The five-hour car ride back to Flagstaff from Durango had given Mann time to discuss the impending meeting with his wife. Fortunately, his family understood having their holiday cut short. There would be other chances to catch fish at the trout farm, but there would likely never be another opportunity where Mann could choose between coaching positions within a college program. Anderson was preparing to hand Mann the coaching equivalent of a blank check.

Red Haberlack accepting the job as chair of the Department of Health, Physical Education and Recreation was not a surprise to Mann. The unfortunate circumstances in which the position had become available—the unexpected death of department chair Helen Oswald—was. Oswald had seemed settled, so if Red were looking for an administration job, he would have likely needed to move to get it.

Suddenly, that reality had changed. Mann had long expected Red to move into administration, ever since Red went on sabbatical to Utah during the 1976–1977 season to gain his PhD in health education. But Mann also had anticipated more time to prepare for an orderly transition of power within the track team's coaching staff.

Anderson knew all too well about the draw to administration over coaching. After starting out as a college basketball coach, he'd changed occupations when the athletic director job at NAU opened. Anderson understood Red's decision on a personal level, but that conflicted with his desire to retain a leader of Red's talent working closely with the athletes. "I consider Red to be the finest track coach in the Big Sky," he said. Anderson's priority was to make sure Red's departure didn't leave a gaping void in his department.

Red ticked all the right boxes for the department chair. He was a great coach and a positive face within the community, and he cared deeply about student success on and off the track. In a conversation with one of his athletes, Red explained, "Not too many track and cross country athletes are making a living running," an observation that has stood the test of time. He continued, "You had better work on getting an education, young man."

Getting an education was a baseline expectation to Red. During his coaching career, around ninety percent of his athletes graduated with either their bachelor's or master's degree. While working hard in the classroom, they also produced stellar performances outside of it. Red's teams won seven Big Sky Conference titles—four in outdoor track, one in indoor track, and two in cross country (one of these being a tie). He coached seven NAIA All-Americans and eight NCAA All-Americans. Although his college coaching tenure ended suddenly, he left the program as one of the most respected coaches on campus.

Red did not regret moving on from his role as coach of the team he had started. "It was my time," he said. "I had been on the road so much; I was ready to hand the job to someone else." Red had originally seen Flagstaff as a temporary position, not one where he would be stationed for eighteen years. "When I came here, I sure didn't think I'd stay that long. Probably a few years, then move on. But I love it here."

Anderson opened the office door and welcomed Mann inside. As the two sat across from each other, tense silence filled the room until Anderson spoke.

"Well, what do we do?"

Before Mann had the opportunity to answer with the elaborate plan he had in mind, Anderson continued.

"Do you want to take the men's program, or do you want to stay with the women's program?"

The current setup of separate men's and women's coaches had been working, so there was no reason for Anderson to come up with an alternative. But Mann had a different vision in mind.

"It isn't common for the head men's and women's coaches to get along like Red and I did," Mann said.

Sharing the same space and equipment can cause issues, but that never happened when Mann and Red were working together. If NAU was to hire another head coach to take over whichever team Mann decided not to work with, that could upset the current environment within the two teams. The way forward in Mann's mind was a more innovative approach for the time.

"What if we combine the men's and women's programs and you let me hire an assistant coach?" proposed Mann.

The idea of combining programs was progressive for 1982. Mann had seen the success Tom Tellez, head coach at the University of Houston, was having after combining their two programs. If they could make it work, there was no reason NAU couldn't. This practice became normalized in later years, but its practicality wasn't obvious when women's programs were first added at the NCAA level.

Anderson was very receptive to Mann's idea and appreciated his persuasive argument that it would benefit the whole track program. With only a few weeks before the school year began, there wasn't time for the two to go back and forth. The decision needed to be made wisely and expeditiously, and that time crunch worked in Mann's favor.

After just two years as a coach at the NCAA level, Mann heard the words he had dreamed about since his coaching journey began.

"You are now the head coach of the combined men's and women's track and field and cross country program here at NAU," Anderson said.

Some people work their whole lives for an opportunity like this one and never get it. Mann knew how fortunate he was to be in this position at just thirty-two years of age.

Eleven years. That's how long it had been since NAU had sent a full team to the NCAA Cross Country Championships, back in 1971.

In 1978, the Lumberjacks came close to qualifying with a strong team consisting of Randy Espinoza, Benito Lazo, Mark Lomeland, Larry Martinez, Nick Martin, Art Menchaca, Ruben Reyes, and Rob Stanley. They won the Big Sky Cross Country Championships but were unable to advance beyond the juggernaut that was NCAA District 7. The University of Texas at El Paso, the University of Colorado, Colorado State University, and the University of Wyoming all finished ahead of NAU, blocking the Lumberjacks from qualifying for nationals. Nine days later, those same teams finished first, fifth, ninth, and thirteenth at the 1978 NCAA Cross Country Championships in Madison, Wisconsin.

The NAU cross country program had everything it needed to become successful, and Mann knew the team's potential to finally reach the next level to become a national powerhouse. Watching the University of Arizona men's and women's cross country teams finish seventh and eighth, respectively, at the 1981 NCAA Cross Country Championships, as well as Big Sky Conference rival Idaho State's men finishing twenty-third, Mann's competitive nature heightened.

"My mind was always set on the one thing—winning a national championship at Northern Arizona," said Mann.

This wasn't something Mann wrote on the walls in the locker room or reminded his athletes of every day at practice. It was a goal he expressed through the high standards he set for them.

Seventeen years of competitive experience had shaped the program into a conference powerhouse. The natural progression was to take the team one step farther up the mountain.

The biggest problem Mann faced when taking over the entire program was the persistent mentality of some athletes who couldn't see past the fact that the team hadn't made nationals for over a decade.

"I don't think we really knew yet that we belonged there," said sophomore Mark Souza.

Overcoming the barriers some of his athletes had built for themselves wasn't going to be easy. Mann knew that strengthening an athlete's belief in what they were capable of began at practice, through cultivating an environment where athletes felt comfortable expressing their big goals.

"You had boatloads of energy, a contagious enthusiasm, and were a nonstop fountain of optimism," Souza later said of his new coach.

Some of that energy came from Mann's ability to let someone else take over the field events. After accepting the position as head coach of the combined program, Mann called his friend—field events specialist Greg Hull—to see if he wanted to come on as assistant coach.

"Can I think about it overnight?" Hull asked.

"Of course you can."

The next morning, when Mann went outside to grab the newspaper, he found Hull asleep in a sleeping bag on his front porch.

"I guess that's a yes," laughed Mann.

Having Hull on staff helped free up Mann's time, which he reinvested into the rest of the program.

Coaching legends. From left, Ron Mann (turned sideways), Olympian and long-time Central Arizona College coach George Young, Leo Haberlack (in hat), Greg Hull (back turned), and veteran University of Arizona coach Dave Murray mingle at Fort Tuthill in Flagstaff.

The men ran 85–100 miles a week during the season, and Mann occasionally joined them on an easy run. This allowed Mann to engage with his athletes in a relaxed and informal setting, except when they purposefully tested his fitness. Some of the guys used to bombard Mann with questions as they ran up hills, hoping to tire him out before they reached the top. Eventually, Mann caught on, and after struggling for air at the top of one particularly difficult hill, he abandoned the men's tempo and joined the women's more tolerable and courteous pace for the remainder of the run.

When Mann wasn't putting in miles with the team or following them on country road workouts in his yellow Honda, he was working hard at recruiting domestic and international talent. NAU had a history of successfully recruiting overseas athletes.

For the two-year-old women's team, recruiting internationals was a little more difficult. A tight recruiting budget meant these athletes would not take official visits. They had to rely on information from coaches. Mann could say Flagstaff was one of the best places in the country to train, but results mattered. The women's team had little performance history to tout, and certainly none at the national level. That gap cut against Mann's description of a scenic long run on A-1 Mountain Road, no matter how accurate he was.

Luck was on Mann's side, however, as he recruited a Canadian who had been dealing with injuries during her final year of high school. Angela Chalmers had been on track to secure herself a scholarship at a big U.S. university after a stellar junior year and a spot on the Canadian national junior track team. When colleges looked for recent results and her name didn't come up, it was the little school in Flagstaff that saw an opportunity. Chalmers came highly recommended by one of Mann's Canadian contacts. He knew that if NAU's medical staff could keep her healthy, she had the potential to excel.

When Chalmers arrived on campus in fall 1982, expectations of the women's team started to shift. Her presence set an example of excellence the women's team needed to become conference and national contenders. Everyone could see that Chalmers was someone who could compete with the best.

Chalmers benefited from the combined programs. A level above her teammates, she would join the men for weekend long runs and the occasional fartlek interval session. Although she had a hard time keeping up with their faster efforts, Chalmers would catch back up on the easy efforts in time for the next rep to begin.

"Watching her train and especially watching her race with ferocity was educational and helped establish a work ethic and mindset that NAU was a team that should be mentioned as contenders," said Souza.

In her first track season as a Lumberjack, Chalmers placed third at the 1983 NCAA Indoor Track and Field Championships in the mile. The following year, she took second at the 1984 NCAA Indoor Championships in the 1500m and fifth at the 1984 NCAA Outdoor Championships in the same event.

Watching Chalmers succeed at the highest levels under Mann's training gave her teammates a much-needed confidence boost. Even as she redshirted the 1984 cross country season, the men's team returned to the national meet and placed seventeenth at Penn State University. It wasn't quite the ninth-place finish the team had in 1971, but it was a big step in the right direction.

The next year, Chalmers placed second in the 3000m at the 1985 NCAA Outdoor Track and Field Championships before getting third in the 3000m at the World University Games known as the Universiade in Kobe, Japan, and eighth at the 1985 NCAA Cross Country Championships. Everything was lining up for her to have a big track season and a shot at winning an individual title.

On the outside, Chalmers seemed unstoppable, but on the inside, she was struggling. After the death of her dad, enduring grief started to catch up with her. In spring 1986, Chalmers stopped going to class. The bright student's grades dropped to the point that she was going to fail the semester. The NAU athletic department stepped in and deemed Chalmers ineligible to compete at the 1986 NCAA Outdoor Track and Field Championships. All the work she had put in was slipping away.

Losing her eligibility for the spring was only the first of many consequences for Chalmers if her grades didn't improve. "It seemed impossible for her to become eligible for the fall," said Mann. "She had to pass twelve credits in the summer [up to four classes]."

The most successful athlete NAU had ever recruited was suddenly on the verge of ending her storied college career in disappointment. If she couldn't regain her eligibility, losing an entire year of competition would likely stall the progress of this rising star.

Mann, who had developed a strong coach-athlete relationship with Chalmers, called her into his office for what was bound to be a difficult and heartfelt conversation. She was at a crossroads, and Mann presented the task ahead as a challenge—just like she approached racing. Her coach knew Chalmers's inner drive to succeed was high, so he spoke about the importance of continuing her education and her last chance to win a coveted national title. Finally, they spoke about her love for her teammates with whom she would be able to travel that next fall, and the pride she would feel wearing the NAU jersey one more season.

Chalmers, known for her ability to kick and overtake competition late in races, gave Mann the same look he had often seen before she toed the starting line. The look exuded confidence, the self-assuredness that she knew what it took to succeed in all aspects of her life and this setback was not going to define her. Mann knew as Chalmers left the room what the result would be . . . another come-from-behind victory.

After talking with Mann, Chalmers decided to spend summer 1986 in Flagstaff and work toward becoming eligible for the fall. The willpower to make this decision was a testament to Chalmers's character. It was going to be an incredibly difficult workload to take on; there would be no break, and her days would consist of studying and running.

As everyone else went home for the summer, Chalmers put her head down and got to work, determined to keep her running story alive.

Staying in Flagstaff proved a blessing in disguise for Chalmers. Not only did she become eligible again, but she also built a strong base from training at altitude that she wouldn't have gotten at her parents' home in Brandon, Manitoba.

Chalmers had dealt with minor injuries in her buildup that led to Mann being more conservative with her racing schedule. After not competing at NAU's only home meet, the George Kyte Classic, Chalmers opened her season at the Aztec Invitational in San Diego, where she placed thirty-second. The instruction she received from Mann heading into this race was to run with her teammates. If she could feel good doing that, she would get the green light to have a more honest effort for her next race.

At the Lobo Invitational in New Mexico, Chalmers looked like herself again and came through for the individual win, while the team placed third. Two weeks later at the NCAA District 7 meet, Chalmers notched another convincing win that put her in the conversation for an individual title at nationals in eleven days.

"If one had to choose the hottest runner coming into the meet, Chalmers would definitely have to be considered," stated the race preview in the official program for the 1986 NCAA Cross Country Championships.

This positive endorsement didn't mean Chalmers was the overwhelming favorite. That title was reserved for Stephanie Herbst from the University of Wisconsin, who won the 5000m and 10,000m at the 1986 NCAA Outdoor Track and Field Championships. Polly Plumer from the University of California, Los Angeles, was lining up as the top returner from the 1985 NCAA Cross Country Championships. Also in consideration was Suzy Favor, the University of Wisconsin freshman and U.S. junior record holder in the 1500m.

Angela Chalmers answers questions after becoming NAU's first individual cross country national champion.

The women's 5k race over the golf course at the Canada Hills Country Club in Tucson, Arizona, was going to be a must-watch up front. After getting out to an aggressive start, Chalmers stayed glued to the front pack as they navigated the grass, dirt, sand roads, and hills of this tough course. Also navigating the course was Mann, from the sidelines. He made sure to reach as many spots as possible before heading toward the finish line to see the last half-mile of the race.

Appearing from behind a hill with 800 meters left to run was Chalmers, who had broken from the pack. After a whirlwind year, Chalmers had fought every step of the way to open her lead on the best female collegiate distance runners in the country.

Mann couldn't contain his excitement as he watched Chalmers power through the finish line to win NAU its first NCAA individual national title in any sport. Mann knew the fortitude Chalmers possessed to make this achievement a reality. She had lifted herself out of a deep canyon that had nearly prevented her from reaching this crowning moment.

"It was very emotional having her win," said Mann. "It was in our home state, and NAU was considered the third-best school in the state."

Chalmers's face was plastered all over the front page of the *Arizona Daily Sun*, unprecedented coverage for the NAU cross country program.

Chalmers had blazed the trail. She had demonstrated how to convert ambition into action for her teammates to see. Her story was a reminder that accountability is the rope that prevents anyone from falling into an abyss. The tracks she left would be there to guide her teammates and future Lumberjacks. △

Chapter 8
A New Horizon

WALKING OUT OF PHOENIX SKY HARBOR INTERNATIONAL AIRPORT, Chris Bray was surprised by scenery that didn't match his expectations of what Flagstaff would look like. Not even close. *There is no way I am going to school here,* he thought.

Little did he know that a two-hour drive stood between him and the NAU campus. The farther Bray got up the mountain, the more he appreciated the changing landscape and the more it reminded the Nevada Union High School runner of Northern California where he was from. "It felt like home," said Bray, recalling the transformation from cacti to red rock to pine trees along Interstate 17.

After getting over the initial shock of touching down in the middle of a Roadrunner and Wile E. Coyote cartoon desert, Bray was blown away by Flagstaff's cool serenity. The city lived up to the high praise his former high school teammate, current NAU athlete Cameron Mitchell, had given it in advance of Bray's official recruiting visit.

Touring Flagstaff, the NAU campus, and nearby trails with Mitchell as his guide convinced Bray this was where he wanted to go to school.

In summer 1987, Bray came to Flagstaff for the second time, now as an incoming freshman at NAU. Driving across state lines with his dad at the wheel, the two reached Sechrist Hall—the dorm that would serve as Bray's home for the next few years.

After a long day of driving and unpacking, Bray sat exhausted in his dorm room with his dad when there was a knock at the door. It was the NAU men's cross country team.

Bray opened the door to a group of sheepish-looking guys who were not expecting to see a parent in the room. While most of the team tried to hide behind the door, Chris Curry emerged from the crowd. The guys had knocked on Bray's door to continue an important team tradition, and that wasn't going to stop just because Mr. Bray was in the room.

With absolute confidence, Curry boldly asked, "Hey Mr. Bray, you want a beer?"

Mortified, the younger Bray thought to himself, "I'm screwed. This is the end of my college career." Then to Bray's surprise, his dad replied, "Yeah, I would love a beer."

Bray left his dad alone to enjoy that cold beverage in the dorms while he headed out with the team to enjoy drinks of their own. College was getting off to an unexpected, yet exciting, start for the freshman.

Taking Bray out on his first night in town was a way of quickly introducing a new athlete to the team while getting to know the new runner better. It also served the purpose of showing Bray that the team had fun when the time called for it.

"The feeling was that we have fun, but when it's time to work, it's time to work," said Bray.

This piece of NAU team culture had evolved over the years. As the program saw more success, it was easier to instill the expectation of working hard. If the team wanted to scale new heights, they would have to do things that hadn't yet been done. But it was important that achievement didn't come at the sacrifice of enjoying the process.

The men of NAU were halfway into their warm-up when Kim White shouted, "One-ten."

Everyone stopped in their tracks. Those who needed to pee made their way over to the barely hidden bushes while the rest of the team waited nearby. Calling "one-ten" was a simple signal to wait patiently while a teammate took care of business.

With one of the most imposing workouts before him, Bray felt a tight knot in his stomach as he stood at the base of Snowbowl Road, looking up at the imposing mountain. Taking several deep breaths, he looked around at his teammates who were squeezing in last-minute strides before the workout began.

"How hard is this going to be?" Bray asked Mitchell.

Mitchell laughed while shaking his head. "You don't want to know," he replied.

Snowbowl Road is six-and-a-half miles of pavement with a consistent six percent gradient. By the time the NAU team reached the top, they would have climbed over 2,000 feet to reach an altitude of 9,200 feet. Like Mitchell said, it was probably better that Bray didn't know what lay ahead.

The climb would take the NAU athletes up to one of the oldest ski areas in the country. First opened in 1938, Arizona Snowbowl has served the Flagstaff community and visitors for decades. Snowbowl was where this NAU workout would finish, but if they ever wanted to go higher, there was the option of continuing on to tougher terrain to reach Arizona's highest point. At 12,633 feet, Humphreys Peak is host to Flagstaff's best views. Visible from the top are the red rocks of Sedona, the cinder cones of the San Francisco Volcanic Field, and the rim of the Grand Canyon.

A similar climb for the team was a run to the summit of Mount Elden. What Elden lacks in distance, it makes up for with steeper sections, sharp corners, and dirt mixed with loose rock for more difficult footing. Athletes who reach the radio towers at the top of Elden get an incredible view of east Flagstaff from 2,000 feet above the city.

Easy access to roads that lead up to 9,000 feet is one of many factors that makes Flagstaff a world-class altitude training site. It's a twenty-minute drive to the base of Snowbowl Road from downtown and a fifteen-minute drive to the base of Mount Elden. Testing the body at these higher elevations makes running at 7,000 feet feel just a little closer to sea level than it did before.

Ron Mann called his athletes up to the imaginary starting line, men and women. They glanced at the long, straight road ahead. The start of Snowbowl Road is generous, but beyond that first bend waited a world of hurt, a kind of pain every runner hoped they were ready for.

"Is this dog one?" Bray asked the team.

Mitchell laughed, "It sure is."

"Dog one" had become code for the hardest rep within a workout, and since running up Snowbowl Road was six-and-a-half miles of hard effort, it fulfilled that criterion.

With the men and women ready to go, Mann started the workout with the two words that had started every workout since Red Haberlack was in charge: "Ready … Ho!"

The journey of self-discovery had begun. No matter how fit or tough an athlete may think they are, this road will break even the strongest mind if they underestimate it.

After a short time as a full team, by the end of the straightaway the group would break into two—one of men and one of women.

In their single-file lines, the men and women of NAU each resembled cycling pelotons more than they did a running team as they navigated their way up the road. To avoid letting the head of the pack burn out from dictating the effort for too long, the person in front would frequently pull to the side and let the team train go by before latching onto the back. This gave temporary relief so the previous leader could then just focus on the body in front of them.

If the constant grind up the mountain wasn't bad enough, Mann had a plan to make the team's legs feel like they were being dipped in a pot of acid. Standing at the one-mile-to-go mark, Mann waited for the team to get close before he made his announcement.

Once the heavy breathing reached him, Mann shouted, "Take it to the top!"

Without hesitation, Bray later recalled, the guys all took off. Somehow, among all the physical and psychological pain they were in, they found another gear and started grinding even harder for the remainder of their mountain climb.

The body is capable of incredible feats, and this effort by the NAU team proved that. The runners may have looked composed when dealing with pain on the way up, but when they finally reached the top, they were exhausted.

The tourists who had come up the mountain for sightseeing were mortified by the scene in the parking lot. There were bodies laid out on the ground, people hunched over the side of the mountain dry-heaving, and others with their hands on their knees, desperately trying to take in the little oxygen that existed in the thin air at 9,200 feet.

Bray looked around at his teammates. They didn't just run up this mountain for the sake of doing so. They did it because, as a collective, they wanted to do something special as a team this season and continue creating a legacy for all the seasons to come. Every athlete that gave their all had done so to better themselves for the sake of the team. It was a selfless task to get to the top.

The specifics have changed somewhat, but snaking up Snowbowl Road remains a staple of the training program. As Bray and many other Lumberjacks have discovered, the challenge of pushing yourself beyond your limits and doing so as a *team* is the fabric of what NAU was, and remains so today.

"It was exciting to see how strong these guys were," said Bray. Having only been at altitude for a few months, he could label this as the hardest workout he had ever done.

"It was really hard, but it was awesome," laughed Bray.

While the NAU team was running up mountains, the Flagstaff Urban Trails System (FUTS) Ad Hoc Committee was discussing the establishment of a trail system that could one day connect all the community's favorite recreational areas. The project was the brainchild of Flagstaff Community Development Director John Silva.

Since the summer of 1987, the committee had been meeting at different sites around the city to figure out where the trail system could run. Plots of private land that were unlikely ever to be developed would provide the perfect setting for a trail.

After spending the fall and winter figuring out all the logistics, the FUTS Ad Hoc Committee presented their final report on March 17, 1988. The committee stated that, "The most critical and opportune time to create an Urban Trails System is now, before any more obstructions and impediments develop along the proposed routes."

The estimated cost for the proposed trail system was $36,510, with an annual maintenance fee of $1,805. Considering the potential benefits of such a trail system to the city, this would be worth every penny.

The city council approved the plan, and the first link of the FUTS was built from Thorpe Road to Meade Lane. "The Thorpe link was already a social trail, which supported the rationale of starting there," said committee member Nat White. "One part of the strategy for future developments was: if it is being used now, formalize it and incorporate it into the system where logical and practical." Improving upon Flagstaff's recreational opportunities was important, but so was preserving the spaces that already existed.

After Buffalo Park was forced to close in 1969, it was repurposed as a municipal park for recreational purposes in 1973. Then in 1985, the Flagstaff City Council, aiming to relieve the traffic snarls in the downtown corridors during the busy summer tourism season, voted to put a road through Buffalo Park as a shortcut to the Grand Canyon.

A group of local runners and other community members partnered to stop this proposed project. Buffalo Park was becoming a popular recreational site, and putting a highway through it could have an irreversible impact. The referendum gained momentum from people who opposed the road and supported the protection of Buffalo Park from future forms of development—it ended up getting twice as many signatures as needed and passed by a two-to-one margin.

Ever since Buffalo Park had become an open, empty space for community use, people had been trying to figure out how to make it better. Building a mini-Stonehenge as a tourist attraction was one idea, while building baseball fields was another. All these plans were attempts to develop the space in some way. Ultimately, Flagstaff leaders deemed less to be more. The space remained mostly unfettered and still is today. In time, it would become one of the city's most popular recreational areas, especially among runners of all capabilities for easy miles or a structured workout without any added glamour—just a two-mile dirt loop and a stunning backdrop of Mount Elden and the San Francisco Peaks.

Although she had used up her eligibility, the Chalmers effect was still embedded in NAU as the team headed into the 1988 fall season. The men's cross country team had finally passed the Haberlack-era ninth-place finish by placing eighth at the 1987 NCAA Cross Country Championships. Meanwhile, the women were coming off an eleventh-place finish in their first appearance there as a team. The level of excellence Mann expected, and then was embodied by Chalmers, was driving the program to new heights.

Chalmers finished her college career as a six-time All-American, the holder of four school records, and the winner of NAU's first individual national title. She went on to place seventeenth in her 1500m heat and fourteenth in the 3000m final at the 1988 Olympic Games in Seoul, Korea, a year after graduating.

At the 1990 Commonwealth Games, Chalmers won both the 1500m and the 3000m before getting bronze at the 1992 Olympic Games in Barcelona, Spain. The standout NAU athlete had carved out a storied athletic career, and her performance while a Lumberjack would set a high bar in steering the program to enduring success.

Having watched their old teammate compete at the Olympics early in their season, the NAU men's cross country team went into the 1988 NCAA Cross Country Championships at Jester Park in Granger, Iowa, with more determination to succeed than ever before.

The guys knew they had a shot at the podium. With a strong front end and enough dependable depth to not bleed too much at the back, anything was possible if everyone could just log a solid day.

NAU's first NCAA team trophy came in 1988. Front row, from left: Vince Firlotte, Darren Stonerock, Milfred Tewawina, Scott Pestka. Back row: Coach Warren Mandrell, Cameron Mitchell, Eric Grubbs, Chris Bray, Bo Reed, Coach Ron Mann.

Bo Reed and Milfred Tewawina had an incredible day at the front of the race, finishing third and eighth, respectively. All they needed was for their teammates to hold their own and a podium spot was within reach.

Next across the line were Mitchell in forty-second, Daren Stonerock in fifty-first, and finally Scott Pestka in 110th, to round out the top five scorers.

It wasn't the perfect race across the board for NAU, but it was enough to secure their spot in the history books. Unable to top the dominant 100-point performance of the University of Wisconsin, NAU finished in second place with 156 to earn their school its first NCAA Division I team trophy.

"I sort of saw it coming," said Mann. "This was building; it didn't just happen."

Red's teams used to celebrate a victory by throwing him into the steeplechase pit, but Mann enjoyed much warmer water for his celebrations.

After arriving back in Flagstaff, Mann met up with NAU throws coach Pete Corkery at his apartment's hot tub to discuss the race. With a cigar in one hand and a beer in the other, the two talked and bathed in the excitement of all the good to come.

"This type of celebration carried on for a few years until I realized it wasn't a good health idea," laughed Mann.

Coach Mann chomping on one of many victory cigars.

The media exaggerated the tradition for comedic effect. "Ron Mann likes to smoke a fat cigar after one of his track or cross-country teams wins a championship," wrote Neil Hayes of the *Arizona Republic* on January 26, 1991. "That ritual puts Mann on the American Cancer Society's most wanted list. After 10 years as the coordinator of track and field at Northern Arizona, Mann has smoked more cigars than Archie Bunker."

While the NAU team experienced fluctuations in success, Mann emphasized what was important outside of running. The goal was to win a national title, but even if that didn't happen, there was no reason a road trip couldn't be enjoyable.

Endorphins permeated the team members throughout the men's stellar 1988 season. The next year, the women had a solid thirteenth-place finish at the NCAA Cross Country Championships and the men didn't qualify. Then at the 1990 championships in Knoxville, Tennessee, the women placed fourteenth and the men nineteenth.

Whether getting within breathing distance of a national team title, finishing outside the top ten, or missing the meet entirely, some disappointment was natural. But Mann didn't let his runners feel down for long.

After their Knoxville race, Mann told his athletes they would be going out for dinner at a restaurant in Gatlinburg. The teams were fine with this decision until they learned it was an hour away.

"Can't we just go somewhere closer?" said Bray from the back of the van.

Mann was quick with his response. "When will you ever get the chance to be in Knoxville, Tennessee, and when will you ever get the chance to go to Gatlinburg the rest of your life?"

That was the first time this clicked for Bray. "Going places wasn't all about the run; it was also about the experiences in these places."

Just because nationals didn't go their way didn't mean they couldn't enjoy the time spent away together. Bray thought back on his first night in Flagstaff. When it's time to work, it's time to work, but after the work is done, no matter how it went, it's important to have fun with friends.

There was something about being back in Tucson, Arizona, for the 1991 NCAA Cross Country Championships that gave Mann a good feeling. It was hard to forget the incredible emotions of that day, five years prior, when Chalmers won there. This time around, the women did not have an obvious individual title contender, but they were capable of a strong team performance.

Coming off their fifth-straight Big Sky Conference title, the NAU women won the NCAA District 7 Championships in the week leading up to nationals. The Lumberjacks were rewarded for their stellar season by heading to Tucson as the sixth-ranked team in the country.

For a team that had only existed for eleven years, to be ranked sixth seemed like a steep progression. It took the men's program twice that time to achieve a similar ranking. The women's team had learned to perform at a high level thanks to Chalmers and the example of the men's successful 1988 performance. NAU junior and team leader Larah Treadwell aptly summarized the women's perspective, "If the men can do it, then we can train and do it too."

The team's mentality had shifted, filling the women with confidence heading into nationals. Finishing fourteenth the year before, they were the underdogs seeking an ambitious top-five finish. If they came up short, they would still outperform anything they had ever accomplished as a team; and if they exceeded expectations, NAU could be proud.

For a fun team event before driving south to Tucson, the women decorated white cotton T-shirts with different inspirational quotes and entertaining designs. One of the shirts stood out to Treadwell. Her teammate had written a quote that

The 1991 NAU women's team placed third at nationals, the highest finish in the program's eleven-year history. The men placed nineteenth. Front row, from left: Kim White, Rick Jarman, Donald Guess, Nate Hammer, Greg Lopez, Bret Bonnenberger, Chris Bray. Back row: Coach Warren Mandrell, Kristi Klinnert, Tracy Jarman, Larah Treadwell, Grace White, Calley Nelson, Mary Fein, Christy Michaels, Coach Ron Mann.

came directly from the unofficial NAU cross country rule book. The shirt read: "If you're gonna die, die from the front."

Cross country is a sport in which an athlete must endure inevitable pain to be successful. How a team chooses to embrace that pain as a collective will determine whether they'll meet their goals. For the women to discuss and embrace this pain in a healthy way was an indication of what was to come in Tucson.

The Lumberjacks pushed a strong top three across the line at nationals, with Tracy Jarman getting twenty-first and Kristi Klinnert in twenty-sixth to earn All-American honors. Next through was Treadwell in thirty-seventh, Calley Nelson in sixty-second, and Christy Michaels in 109th. The result was a significant improvement upon the team's four previous appearances at nationals. Mann knew they had just done something special.

"We got third or fourth," Mann said to his team as he tried to do the quick math in his head.

No one wanted to get too excited about their podium possibility until official results were read.

"In fourth place with 189 points is Cornell University," said a voice over the loudspeaker. The women looked at one another, their hearts racing. The announcement continued, "In third place with 168 points is Northern Arizona University."

Anyone there would have thought these women had won. Pure elation poured from the NAU team camp as they realized what the women had pulled off. The celebrations were loud enough that supporters four hours away, back up the mountain in Flagstaff, could have heard.

"This is just absolutely great. This is the best. Even I'm surprised by this," Mann said.

Jarman shared Mann's surprise with the result when she talked with the *Arizona Daily Sun*. "We came in ranked sixth and our goal was to get into the top five. Our little school got third. With all these huge schools here, we take third—how great is that?" △

Chapter 9
End of an Era

"I WANT TO EMPHASIZE THAT I'M NOT UNHAPPY AT NAU," RON MANN told the *Arizona Daily Sun* reporter who asked him about the University of Colorado coaching position for which he was a finalist.

Mann was in hot demand by the time the 1995 fall season came around. After his thirteen years as head coach of the NAU program, thirty-four Big Sky Conference Championship team titles, three NCAA Cross Country Championship podium finishes, and one individual NCAA champion, Mann's résumé made him attractive to other programs when coaching positions came available.

Mann loved working at NAU, but the constraints of its tight budget made the thought of serving a more financially robust institution appealing. Two years prior, the NAU athletic department was forced to cut its dependence on state funding by $500,000 over a three-year period. By 1995, Mann was still finding ways to tighten his already-impoverished budget. Sacrificing opportunities for his athletes because the university was unable to afford travel costs had become a sobering reality of Mann's job.

The recommendation to apply for the Colorado position came from previous NAU throws coach Pete Corkery. Corkery had accepted the same position at Colorado a few years prior, and when the head coaching job came available, he knew Mann would be the perfect fit.

Located at 5,318 feet above sea level, the University of Colorado ranked as one of the best training sites in the country. The city of Boulder had hosted world-class runners like 1972 Olympic Games gold medalist Frank Shorter. The Colorado program already had a standout collegiate athlete in Adam Goucher, who came in second as a freshman at the 1994 NCAA Cross Country Championships. To simply dismiss the prospect of coaching there would have been a regrettable decision for Mann.

Mann flew out to Colorado to conduct his interview in the middle of the 1995 cross country season. He returned home with a heavy decision to make.

There was no certainty he was the Buffaloes' first choice. The three finalists were Mann, UC Irvine's Vince O'Boyle, and Colorado's current assistant track coach, Mark Wetmore.

As the decision was being made back in Colorado, Mann felt conflicted about the tough situation that awaited him if he were to be the successful candidate. It looked unlikely that his entire family could make the move to Boulder, meaning he would have to commute back and forth to spend time with them.

"On a personal level, it was too much of a price to pay," said Mann, who withdrew his name from consideration before the final decision was made. The budget and salary challenges Mann had faced at NAU before he applied for the vacant position would continue. The University of Colorado hired Wetmore as their new head coach.

With the possibility of losing their coach behind them, the NAU cross country teams shifted focus back to their seasons. The men were coming off a strong fourth-place podium finish at the 1994 NCAA Cross Country Championships, while the women missed qualifying for the national meet for a third straight year.

The final kilometer of the 1995 NCAA Cross Country Championships in Ames, Iowa, was a bittersweet moment for Mann, who was convinced his men were going to take the team title. He shouted down the walkie-talkie to assistant coach Ed Beathea on the other end, "We're gonna win this thing!"

Then Mann watched as the University of Arkansas team surged over the last kilometer and up the finish straight. Once again, NAU had to settle for second place, while Arkansas took home the gold with a forty-two-point lead over the Lumberjacks.

NAU's top five athletes on that day were Jama Bile in twentieth, Tim Martin in thirtieth, Theodore Martin in thirty-second, John Howell in thirty-third, and

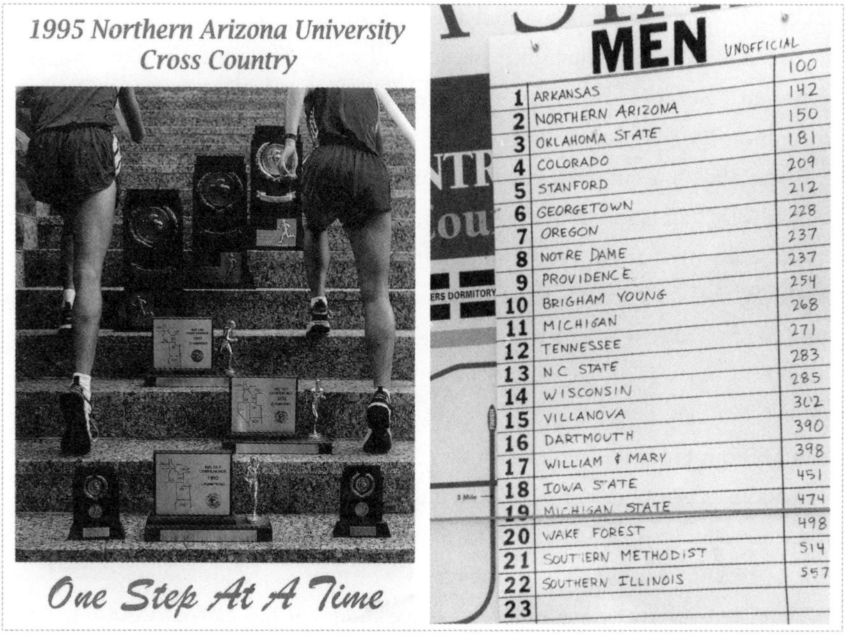

The 1995 cross country yearbook showed off the school's growing collection of hardware. By season's end, NAU's second national runner-up finish in eight seasons was impressive, but the Lumberjacks had not yet crested the mountain.

The 1995 national men's runner-up Lumberjacks, from left to right: Coach Ron Mann, Ryan Ferguson, Jama Bile, John Howell, Matt Smith, Tim Martin, Jim Cera, and Theo Martin.

Jim Cera in eighty-second. Although they'd lacked a top-ten individual finisher and the depth to back him, the tightly packed and strong NAU team could leave Iowa with their heads held high, knowing their efforts helped bring another national trophy home to Flagstaff.

It was almost a fairy-tale moment for Mann, who, when put to the test, had decided Flagstaff was the place for him. Although the coaching position at the country's trendy running mecca in Colorado didn't fit, with the way word was spreading about Flagstaff's desirability as a training site, Mann wouldn't have to wait long for the new mecca to come to him.

Sean Anthony graduated with a business administration degree from the University of Wisconsin before landing a job in the corporate world. The problem was, the business world wasn't meant for him. Anthony loved the outdoors, and working a nine-to-five office job didn't suit the lifestyle he envisioned for himself.

In 1993, Anthony took a leave of absence and made his way out west to Sedona. There, his passion for mountain biking took off as he explored the city's endless trails. As an outdoor enthusiast, Anthony had found a near-perfect place to *play*, but it wasn't until a friend invited him on a trip up to Flagstaff that Anthony found the perfect place to *live*.

There, Anthony would discover another world. The drastic change in scenery, from red rocks to towering pine trees, beckoned him as he gained some 3,000 feet in altitude in less than an hour's drive. What Arizonans affectionately call going up the mountain from the state's lower elevations into Flagstaff is, in truth, scaling the Mogollon Rim. It's the steepest stretch for motorists to reach the southern edge of the monolithic Colorado Plateau that, within the states that meet to make up the Four Corners, contains some of the country's most stunning scenery. Anthony had never been to Flagstaff before this biking trip, but everything about the city and its trail system meant he wouldn't consider living anywhere else.

Two years later, Anthony moved to Flagstaff with no plans and no job. "I just wanted to live here," he said.

Anthony had been in Flagstaff for only a few weeks when Jim Garretson, part-owner of Flagstaff Athletic Club (FAC), hired him. First opening in 1979, FAC had been serving the athletic community in Flagstaff for sixteen years. Anthony had done strength and conditioning work in college, which gave him enough background to be a health and fitness pro at FAC's west location. With his increasing interest in the exercise profession, the FAC job gave Anthony valuable experience within a community where he saw himself living for the indefinite future.

After his first year working at FAC, one of Anthony's clients talked with him about her internship in Flagstaff. The Finnish athlete had been working for the recently established High Altitude Sports Training Complex (HASTC) located on NAU's campus. The HASTC provided a hub to support the growing population of international and domestic athletes converging on Flagstaff for altitude training. Its purpose was to accommodate their needs, including access to campus facilities, finding lodging, and pointing them toward services such as sports massage and physical therapy.

Anthony liked how the HASTC operated and its contribution to making Flagstaff an even more desirable training location. The Finnish athlete gave Anthony her boss's number to discuss possible job openings.

Rick Smith, director of the HASTC, invited Anthony to interview for the position of assistant director. Although Smith was pleasant to talk to, the interview didn't go the way Anthony thought it would. Smith was more interested in Anthony's previous summer spent living in a Zen Buddhist monastery than his experience in business and his work in the fitness sector. Believing Anthony was an enlightened person, Smith hired him on the spot. "My hiring had nothing to do with my professional qualifications," laughed Anthony.

The idea for the HASTC in Flagstaff was conceived in 1994 from conversations between Flagstaff Mayor Chris Bavasi and former football coach Smith. It began as a joint economic development partnership between NAU, the City of Flagstaff, and the State of Arizona, with the invaluable support of NAU President Dr. Clara Lovett and Senator John Wettaw. The future website for the HASTC described it as "a center for excellence in the areas of sports performance, education, sports science and altitude sports training."

Once Anthony began his role as assistant director, he soon learned that there were problems with how the HASTC was set up. The pricing structure for athletes was unsustainable, the center had to pay NAU to use its facilities, all the money the center relied on to survive was controlled by others, and it didn't provide any services from its headquarters at Lumberjack Stadium.

"I don't think anyone had any idea what they were getting into," said Anthony. "In all fairness to Rick and Chris, they just didn't know this."

Two benefits of the HASTC's existence were its altitude training symposiums and distance coaching clinics.

In addition to the symposiums and clinics, USA Track & Field (USATF) funded an elite athlete information and training camp in Flagstaff in 1997. These camps provided U.S. athletes with information about how to incorporate altitude training into their yearly periodization schedules by experiencing it firsthand. Among the athlete attendees were three-time American record holder Bob Kennedy and two-time Olympic marathoner and former Brigham Young University standout Ed Eyestone.

Dr. Dave Martin, a pioneer in exercise science research, was a lead presenter at these camps and USATF event chair for the marathon. Dr. Robert Chapman was an advisor to the group and presenter. Legendary University of Minnesota coach Roy Griak was event chair for 10,000m, Kelly Sullivan was men's distance chair of USATF Development, and Mann was event chair for 5000m. They were responsible for keeping track of developing athletes in their event areas and recommending who to select for the camps and symposiums.

In 1998, the HASTC hosted its first International Symposium on Altitude Training. The early symposiums included renowned experts in altitude science and training, such as Dr. Ben Levin, Dr. Hans Gunderson, Chapman, Dr. Randy Wilber, and Norway's Dr. Orjan Madsen. The goal of the symposium was to bridge the gap between research and coaching applications on a topic of increasing interest in the sports world. For three packed days, participants devoured the latest information.

The HASTC's symposiums would emerge as one of the largest and most prestigious annual gatherings on the planet for discussions on altitude training. The symposium's exploding popularity indicated just how prevalent the subject had become in the athletics world. While incorporating altitude training was clearly becoming of paramount importance, misconceptions lingered on how to use it to your benefit as a coach or athlete. Though training high held great promise, it also could be perilous to the uninitiated.

High altitude, despite its clear benefits, is not a panacea.

Coaches can unwittingly destroy their athletes, and not all runners respond equally. Mann, Haberlack, and their colleagues from around the world had been figuring out how to use the tool of altitude training effectively. These symposiums, also held at Olympic Training Centers in San Diego and Colorado Springs, were meant to marry the science and practice for optimal results.

"The symposiums helped with getting to know people at the U.S. Olympic Committee," said Anthony. "We talked to them about how we could be more involved."

Even with its structural shortcomings, the HASTC was establishing its value within the Flagstaff community and the sports training world. It was also on its way to drawing more attention to the city as an altitude destination. In 1968, Flagstaff served as an unofficial Olympic training site for George Young, Billy Mills, Jim Ryun, and Conrad Nightingale. Now, three decades later, that designation would become more official.

The head distance coach at Indiana University and guest speaker from the altitude training symposiums—Chapman—walked up to his volunteer assistant and asked him one simple question, "Have you ever heard of Northern Arizona University?" After taking a moment to think, Eric Heins replied, "No, I haven't."

Heins quickly jumped to his own defense. "I grew up in Ohio," he told Chapman. "I've never been west of the Mississippi." It was 2001, and without the easy accessibility of information through outlets such as MileSplit or FloTrack, one of the country's best distance programs had managed to fly under his radar.

Chapman, on the other hand, knew NAU well. As an esteemed scientist in the area of altitude training, he had met with Mann on several occasions in Flagstaff. "The reason I ask is because there's a graduate assistant position opening at NAU beginning in the fall," Chapman told Heins. "I think you should apply for it."

The thought of moving to the Southwest wasn't appealing to Heins. He had grown up in the small city of Zanesville, Ohio, and was content in this part of the country. This was where he had spent his whole life.

After high school, Heins stayed in-state to study aerospace engineering as a student-athlete for the University of Cincinnati. It wasn't until he got a D in calculus his first semester, an F in calculus his second semester, and a D in physics, that Heins realized his dream of being an aerospace engineer was looking unlikely.

This led to Heins asking his college coach about the possibility of pursuing a career in coaching. His coach advised him that a change in degree would be a good start. Heins switched his focus to studying exercise science before getting accepted into the master of kinesiology program at nearby IU.

Chapman became Heins's advisor for the coaching portion of his master's program and gave him a group of six athletes to write training plans for. "This was my first true experience writing programs," said Heins. "I learned about how to communicate with college athletes and figure out what they needed."

NAU was a nationally recognized program, and there were no guarantees that a volunteer assistant from Indiana would be the ideal candidate. But Heins knew that the best way to continue gaining experience as a coach was to find a graduate assistantship in a reputable program. On Chapman's recommendation, Mann offered Heins the position of graduate assistant for the 2001–2003 school years.

Moving out to Arizona to assist Mann in coaching one of the best distance programs in the country would prove to be a life-changing experience for Heins. He joined an energetic staff at NAU that included sprint coach and previous NAU student-athlete J.W. Hardy.

Hardy was recruited by Mann in 1989 as a 400m runner after a successful home visit. Originally wanting to attend the University of Southern California, Hardy appreciated Mann's persistence. "I am a pretty loyal person," said Hardy. "The fact Ron took the time to come to my house really did it for me."

After graduating from NAU, Hardy got a job working at an elementary school in Phoenix, where he also coached track and football at Alhambra High School. Then, in 1997, Mann called Hardy, asking if he would be interested in a sprints position.

Returning to work under the coach who had guided Hardy's successful NAU athletic career excited him. "My wife, Amy, was from Flag," said Hardy. "It felt right that God had put this into play."

Mann complemented the stellar staff he had assembled with some outstanding student-athletes. He hit a gold mine in recruiting Swedish steeplechaser Ida Nilsson after she reached out to him, hoping to transfer from the University of Arkansas at Little Rock. The transfer went smoothly, and Nilsson arrived in Flagstaff ready for the 2001 fall season.

She made an immediate impact on the program. In her first outdoor season as a Lumberjack, she placed second at the NCAA Outdoor Track and Field

Championships in the steeplechase. Nilsson kept alive a tradition of Swedish athletes coming through the program, a lineage that stretched back to 1987 with shot-putter Kent Larsson. From there, Mann and assistant coach Anders Axlid, a Swedish national and NAU alum, recruited several other throwers, and eventually jumpers and distance runners from Axlid's home country.

Having Nilsson join the program was significant for the distance group; equally as significant was her help in bringing another Swedish runner into the program.

NAU has benefitted from a long-running international pipeline. At the 2002 Great American Cross Country Festival in Charlotte, North Carolina, Swede Henrik Ahnström (786) takes first place (left), while Somalia-born Nurani Sheikh (789) passes Georgetown's Mike Smith for runner-up (right).

"I have a younger sister who has more speed than me," Nilsson told Mann.

An accomplished steeplechaser herself, Ida wasn't just being humble. Johanna Nilsson was fast, especially at the shorter distances. And she joined her sister on the NAU team in fall 2002. At the 2003 Indoor Track and Field Championships, Johanna won the mile in her freshman year. This was the first national title for an NAU track and field athlete since Anna Soderberg won the discus at the 1996 NCAA Outdoor Track and Field Championships.

A few months later, Ida earned another second-place finish in the steeplechase at the 2003 NCAA Outdoor Track and Field Championships. The Nilsson sisters were proving to be a dominant force, and they were far from done.

With his graduate assistant position coming to an end, Heins looked back fondly at the past three years. Any doubts he had about applying to coach at this remote outpost had long ago dissipated. His time in Flagstaff had transformed into an invaluable experience. "I had a blast," he said. "The time there was one of my best memories as a college coach."

Mann made sure Heins enjoyed his stay at NAU, whether having Heins write a winter training plan for a group of athletes, traveling to the occasional workout in Mann's Porsche, or even teaching him about how to work with athletes coming from different parts of the country and the world.

"You can't treat some of these kids from California the way you would a kid from Michigan," Mann told Heins. "They're not used to it. They're a little more laid back, so you have to be laid back while working with them."

Heins was impressed at how Mann could be red in the face, upset about a facility scheduling issue or myriad administration dramas, then show up to the track for practice with the athletes having no idea he had been so angry just a short while ago. It was important to keep practice a fun environment and, for Mann, it was also an enjoyable break from the behind-the-scenes challenges that came with being a college coach.

Heins had hoped his experience as a volunteer assistant at IU, combined with his work as a graduate assistant at NAU, would open a coaching door in Flagstaff or elsewhere; unfortunately, that wasn't the case. It was a situation Mann could empathize with. Heins's college coaching future was looking uncertain until Matt Sparks, from Southern Illinois University, told him of an opening at Southeast Missouri State University.

The position was part-time, paying just $12,000 a year. Heins would have to mow lawns in the summer and work evenings at a fitness center to make ends meet. Though far from glorious, the coaching job gave Heins the opportunity to continue working at the Division I level and lead a group of athletes.

Southeast Missouri State would be a step back from working with what was becoming a perennial top-ten contender at nationals, but Heins didn't have much of a choice about leaving the part of the country he had come to love. "I didn't leave NAU because I wanted to; I left because the position was done," he said.

It was a beautiful sixty-degree day at Buffalo Park for the 2003 George Kyte Classic. NAU's traditional season-opener and only home cross country meet gave the Lumberjacks a welcome chance to put on a show for the local community, who rarely got to see them compete in-person.

The meet was named after Dr. George Kyte, who had developed an interest in the newly started track and field and cross country program when he first moved to Flagstaff. The program had only existed for two years when Kyte identified a problem. The NAU football team held a banquet dinner at the end of their season, but cross country never got the same treatment. That didn't sit right with Kyte.

At the conclusion of the 1967 cross country season, Kyte invited the NAU team to the Elks Lodge for dinner . . . and he paid the bill! The runners ate free steak, and—as George Young could testify—nothing tastes quite as good as that.

Coach Mann and avid NAU cross country supporter George Kyte enjoy the 1988 annual team dinner, compliments of Kyte.

Thus began an annual tradition, and Kyte would always pay out-of-pocket to support the athletes he loved. In 1980, as NAU made the decision to add a women's cross country program to the athletic department, Mann asked Kyte a very important question: "Would Elinor [Kyte's wife] be interested in sponsoring the women's team so they could join the men at the Elks Lodge each season?"

Kyte chuckled, "Well, Elinor won't go to the Elks Lodge, but I will sponsor them."

From that moment on, both the men's and women's cross country programs were treated to a season-ending banquet.

The year before Red Haberlack accepted the administrator position, he and Mann made a decision to commemorate Kyte's generous patronage. "The home meet was named the George Kyte Classic," Mann said. "He was very honored when we told him."

The first George Kyte Classic began in 1981 with Kyte himself firing the gun to start the race.

Always held in early September, the George Kyte Classic serves as a true rust-buster for the NAU team. Most of the athletes are coming off a big summer training block and are still readjusting to altitude after a few months at home. Some runners will thrive at Buffalo Park while others will barely survive—neither scenario necessarily offers a true indicator for how the season ahead will look.

The NAU cross country team had two major advantages over their competitors for the 2003 meet. They would be the only school that lived and trained at 7,000 feet, and they knew Buffalo Park like the back of their hands.

The Lumberjacks knew the first kilometer doesn't look uphill but feels like it; the next 400 meters is a healthy downhill; the second mile is fast until the hill; and the hill, once crested, will take about 600 meters to fully recover. Trying to run Buffalo Park like any other race will certainly come back to bite you. The deceiving toughness of the course, mixed with the altitude, early afternoon sun, dry air, and gravel underfoot, combine to make the George Kyte Classic one of the country's toughest opening cross country meets.

Mann was confident his athletes were prepared for these conditions. He even had a workout that mimicked possible race-day moves by visiting teams.

The notorious workout—Secret Surges—consisted of Mann giving all his athletes a piece of paper with a different number written on each one. This number corresponded to the length of a surge that the runners would have to enforce in the workout. Everybody kept their numbers a secret from the others, including their coach. Mann rode beside the group on his bike as they did laps around Buffalo Park. At a moment of his choosing, Mann said an athlete's name and they had to surge for the length of time scrawled on their bit of paper. Workouts like this were designed to be both tough and fun, with the athletes getting to decide how hard they made their surge.

Seth Watkins (174) and Andy Weilacher (175) during the 2003 national meet.

With countless hours of experience navigating the Buffalo Park loop, it wasn't surprising that both teams kicked off their 2003 season by perfect-scoring the meet with the top five finishers across the line in each race. This was a great start to the season, while at the same time it set the tone for an emotional end. Ten days after the team's victory, Kyte, the cross country program's number-one supporter virtually from the beginning, passed away at age eighty-five.

As the season progressed, the men's cross country team looked likely to perform well at the 2003 NCAA Cross Country Championships. They were coming off seventh-, fourth-, and seventh-place showings the previous three years. On the women's side, the runners were struggling to get back to the team that had placed third at nationals. But they were consistently making the national meet, and with Ida and Johanna making waves on the track, it was only a matter of time before they would shine on the grass too.

Mann's nerves heading into nationals were different from years past. He still had that enduring sense of excitement about the possibility of a podium finish, but as the team showed more success, getting on the podium was transforming into a deep internal expectation for Mann. It felt like he carried more pressure and stress on his shoulders now.

When the men placed third at the 2003 NCAA Cross Country Championships, Mann was excited for his athletes, but Mann's wife, who was traveling with the team, knew something was off.

The 2003 NCAA third-place team. Front row, from left: Travis Laird, Henrik Ahnström, Tyler Williams, Seth Watkins. Back row: Coach Brice Allen, Coach Ron Mann, Taylor Beckley, Mint Henk, Shiloh Mielke, Andy Weilacher.

"What's wrong?" she asked her husband.

"I am more relieved than I am excited," Mann replied.

That comment was the clue that something had to change. Mann loved working at NAU, and Flagstaff was home. That didn't change the way he felt, however. The pressure of leading a program that was expected to succeed while constantly working within a tight budget finally became too much to handle.

After a podium finish in 2003, Mann announced it was time for him to move on from NAU.

While the team enjoyed themselves at the infamous athlete-hosted annual cross country party (a tradition that still continues), Mann was planning a full squad meeting for the Monday after Thanksgiving.

As the entire NAU track and field and cross country teams filed into the north end of the Dome and took seats near Mann's office, everyone sensed that something was up. Mann struggled to hold back tears once he began to address them.

"The 2004 spring season will be my last here at NAU," Mann told his athletes.

His twenty-four years of coaching, on top of four years as a student-athlete for the NAU program, were coming to a sudden and unexpected end. △

Chapter 10
"Start of the Downfall of NAU?"

AN EAGER CROWD FILLED NAU'S BABBITT ADMINISTRATIVE CENTER on May 12, 2004, to hear an announcement from Jim Page, U.S. Olympic Committee Managing Director of Sports Performance. The HASTC was being designated as an official U.S. Olympic Training Site! It would also become an official site for the Community Olympic Development Program for distance running. As part of this new branding, the HASTC would be renamed the Center for High Altitude Training.

"Endurance athletes have to train at altitude," Page told the crowd. "You can't succeed anymore without good altitude training."

This announcement was not only exciting for the center and NAU but also for Flagstaff. Mayor Joe Donaldson gave Page a key to the city in appreciation of what the designation meant for the community.

The center had lived up to its motto, "Where the world comes to train," during its ten years of operations, a reputation that NAU president, Dr. John Haeger, was very proud of.

Natalie Harlan had the evidence to support this claim. Harlan, the director of the Center for High Altitude Training, told those in attendance that more than 4,500 athletes and coaches from thirty-nine countries had utilized the center. Of those athletes, 106 had won Olympic medals since the 1996 Atlanta Games.

Sitting next to Harlan on stage was Ron Mann. With less than two months left as head coach at NAU, Mann had accepted an offer to coach the elite distance running program and the Olympic Development Program at the center.

Hiring a proven running coach was one of the requirements for the center to attain these lofty new designations. Mann's retirement announcement in the fall, just before the search for such a coach began, was convenient timing. Mann could continue living in Flagstaff by working at the new position and selling real estate with his son, Ryun.

This plan seemed solid until Mann got a call from University of Louisville Athletic Director Tom Jurich. Jurich had been athletic director at NAU from 1988–1994 and accepted the position at Louisville in 1997 after a stint at Colorado State University. With the program set to join the Big East Conference, Jurich was looking for a coach who could bring the distance program to the level of, and eventually beyond, the other schools in his conference.

Having built a relationship with Mann during his time at NAU and knowing how well he worked within a tight budget, Jurich knew Mann could build a successful program with the more significant resources the University of Louisville could provide.

Mann interviewed in the middle of June 2004 and learned he was the candidate of choice later that same week. He was to begin the new contract and be announced as the new director of cross country and track and field at the University of Louisville on July 2, 2004.

Mann called Sean Anthony to tell him the news. "I want you to hear it from me first," Mann said. "I'm taking an offer I can't refuse." Instead of beginning his job at the Center for High Altitude Training on July 2, Mann would be making the move to Louisville to continue coaching at the collegiate level.

Mann provided further justification to Anthony for why he felt he wasn't the right fit for the center. "I saw myself working with high-performance athletes, and the focus at the beginning was for the center's coach to be working with community athletes," said Mann. "I also felt like I would be a fundraiser and a PR person when I worked there, and my desire was to always just be a coach."

After their conversation ended, Anthony and Harlan walked into what was supposed to be Mann's office at Lumberjack Stadium and stared blankly at his new business cards on the desk. Anthony turned to Harlan, "What are we gonna do?"

The center had to have a high-performance distance coach, so the only thing they could do was begin a new search. Anthony had a pile of applications sitting on the left side of his desk from everyone interested in the position. Only one application sat on its own on the right side of his desk.

"What choice do we have?" Anthony told Harlan while looking at the lone application. "No one can compare in terms of his experience."

Looking for a final opinion on the decision, Anthony reached out to esteemed coach Joe Vigil, who summarized perfectly what Anthony would be getting himself into if he hired Dr. Jack Daniels: "Coaches and athletes love him. And administrators hate him."

As an administrator, Anthony had to decide what to do with that last sentence. He knew Daniels was the best person for the job, and ultimately he and Harlan decided the Center for High Altitude Training would be fortunate to have his expertise.

Mann left an immense legacy at NAU. The athletic department threw a big party wishing Mann well on his new journey. The cake was iced by Ida Nilsson's win in the 2004 NCAA Outdoor Track and Field Championships steeplechase—a final flourish on the end of the Mann era.

Of the countless memories Mann had during his twenty-four years as a coach at NAU, one stood out. On a flight home from an NCAA team trophy–winning weekend, a coaching friend approached him. "Can I hold the trophy for a minute?" his friend asked. "I am going to retire, and I've never had one of these."

Mann felt blessed to have experienced such lofty achievements so early in his career. Only a select few ever get to coach a team that will win an NCAA trophy for a top-four team finish. That was all well and good—until the desire to win became more of an addiction. Then, big races carried more stress and pressure for Mann, who eventually decided the healthiest way for the NAU program to grow was for him to step aside for the next leader.

It was important for Mann that he leave the program in a better place than it was when he took over from Red Haberlack. He unquestionably did that. During his tenure, Mann was the most accomplished coach in NAU history. The statistics speak for themselves.

Mann won fifty-six Big Sky Coach of the Year awards, while his teams brought home fifty-eight Big Sky Conference titles and six podium finishes at nationals.

His athletes tallied five individual national titles, had sixteen top-ten NCAA finishes, and 103 All-American honors. Mann was inducted into the NAU Hall of Fame as both an athlete and a coach.

The most decorated coach in NAU history left with a smile on his face, knowing he had done everything he could to elevate the program.

The year before Mann decided to retire, his assistant coach, J.W. Hardy, was considering a move to full-time ministry work. Hardy loved coaching, but he felt a pull toward his other calling. Not long after Hardy decided that coaching, not ministry, was his destiny, Mann announced his retirement. Hardy would be selected as one of three finalists for the position.

"God has a sense of humor," laughed Hardy.

The other finalists for the director of track and field and cross country position gave Hardy pause about his chance for promotion. Joe Franklin of Butler University was a distance specialist who could build upon NAU's area of dominance. So, too, could Robert Chapman, an expert in the science of altitude training.

"I thought Robert Chapman would be the new head coach," said Hardy. If NAU wanted to continue with a distance coach at the helm—one who knew exactly how to take advantage of Flagstaff's high elevation—Chapman was the obvious pick.

It came as a surprise to Hardy when Chapman withdrew his name from consideration. In Hardy's mind, this put him in a good place to get the job. He believed his strengths were his combined NAU experience as a former student-athlete and coach and having worked with multiple event groups, which could make NAU a more well-rounded program.

Newly appointed Interim Athletic Director Dave Brown called Hardy into his office. Brown liked Hardy's vision for the program and knew he would be a safe bet for the job, but the committee didn't share his sentiment. They were looking for someone different, presumably someone with more of a distance background, based on the program's success under Red and Mann.

Brown went to President Haeger's office following the meeting to push his case for Hardy's hire. After the meeting with Haeger, Brown named Hardy as Mann's successor.

"When I accepted the position, it was a humbling and scary moment," said Hardy.

Hardy envisioned building on Mann's success, much like Mann had done when taking over from Red. The difference was that Mann's twenty-four years as head coach had lifted the program to a point on the mountain where the only way up was to win a national team title.

"I remember the devastation of thinking I don't know if that can be done," said Hardy, considering the caliber of coach Mann was and even he came up just short.

This didn't mean Hardy wasn't going to try. He was intent on finding the best distance coach he could for that dream to become a reality.

While that search began, some in the broader running community were casting doubt on the future of the NAU program with Hardy at the helm. Hardy had made the questionable choice of visiting the online running forum LetsRun.com to see what people were saying about his job announcement. The first headline made his stomach drop. It was titled: "The start of the downfall of NAU."

J.W. Hardy took over as NAU's track coach in 2004.

This was a brutal and sobering reminder that some within the distance ranks saw him as a sprint coach taking over one of the best distance programs in the country. That could have easily rattled Hardy; instead, it lit a fire inside. To prove his critics wrong and continue the NAU legacy, he knew he needed to hire a highly successful distance coach to complement his staff.

Bringing on Daniels as the new coach of the elite distance running program and the Olympic Development Program at the Center for High Altitude Training in spring 2005 was an exciting development for the running community in Flagstaff.

Daniels held a doctorate in exercise physiology and had published *Daniels' Running Formula*, one of the sport's most successful training books. When he coached at State University of New York at Cortland, his athletes won eight NCAA team crowns, thirty-one individual titles, and 130 All-American designations. In the mid-90s, *Runner's World* magazine went so far as to declare him the "World's Best Coach."

Aside from the obvious benefits of having someone of this caliber working at the center, it was special for the city of Flagstaff to have Daniels back. "The world's best coach" had played an instrumental role in helping the quartet of Americans that trained in town before the 1968 Mexico City Games.

Daniels told other staff at the center, "In all my years of altitude research and training distance runners, I can't imagine a better place for this type of program. The weather and environment are ideal, facilities are outstanding, and there is a group of individuals involved who are very experienced and successful in working with elite and emerging athletes."

Anthony was glad to have Daniels on board, but he quickly learned why Vigil said what he did about Daniels being tough for administrators. "Jack always did what he wanted to do," said Anthony, adding that he never doubted Daniels's intentions of helping his athletes in any way he could.

The stories and knowledge Daniels loved to share were a constant reminder to Anthony of why he was the right person for the job. Often, Anthony would go into Daniels's office to ask him a question and walk out an hour later in a complete daze from all the information he just absorbed. "Then you realize that he never answered your question," laughed Anthony.

While the Center for High Altitude Training was making waves with its emerging distance program, Greg McMillan started the first professional running group in Flagstaff in spring 2006. The newly formed adidas McMillan Elite was created to help American distance runners compete with East African athletes. The group covered kit and travel costs while also giving members a housing stipend.

Mike Smith was one of the athletes who came to Flagstaff to train under McMillan, and he managed to qualify for the 2008 U.S. Olympic Marathon Trials. For Smith, who grew up in Washington, D.C., the move to Flagstaff was a pleasant change of pace. The community resonated with him.

"The way that some people who are not from the Southwest are really attracted to the Southwest is special," said Smith. The openness of the forest provided a welcoming environment compared to the populated metro area where he grew up, and it was serendipitous that it also happened to be a fantastic place to train.

Smith had put his English degree to good use after graduating from Georgetown by teaching at an elementary school for two years before coming to Flagstaff. "I knew I wanted to work with people, and I really liked working with young people," said Smith. "It was gratifying work, but teaching was the hardest thing I did in my life. I wanted to do something like that, but not actual teaching. Coaching became that thing."

Smith began working with Daniels for two hours a week at a middle school after-hours program run by the Center for High Altitude Training. As this position evolved, Smith picked up more hours each week, then moved into a coaching office at Lumberjack Stadium. There, he spent hours picking Daniels's brain and developed a real passion for coaching.

"Jack is a true scientist," said Smith, pointing out the contrast between their respective approaches. Without a background in exercise physiology, Smith was curious about how Daniels formulated his training plans and the way he worked back from race day to discover what stressors (workouts) were needed for an athlete to be ready to perform. Smith thrived on this problem-solving aspect of coaching.

Intent on learning all he could from the coaches around him, Smith volunteered for the NAU track and field and cross country team during the 2006–2007 season. "I was involved on a very minimal level," said Smith. "I ended up only doing it for one year because I had to pay the bills."

The Community Olympic Development Program eventually extended beyond middle school kids to adults. "We had kids running, but we saw an opportunity to have a weekly workout program," said Smith. "In December 2006, we started advertising a running club that would be coached by Jack. We got maybe ten people to sign up for it. We had to choose a name, and we chose Altius because it means *higher*."

Team Altius helped keep the running club scene alive in Flagstaff. The Sisu Striders that had started in 1974 faded out later in the decade when Ned Frederick and Jack Welch moved away from Flagstaff and Scott Baxter became more involved in climbing. "Since we were the core of the Sisu Striders, the club just kind of evaporated," said Baxter.

Next in line to take the place of the Sisu Striders was the Flagstaff Road and Track Club. "The Arizona Road Racers was a prominent group in Phoenix, and we felt that Flagstaff needed an organized group," said Mann. Some of the original members who helped get this club off the ground and sustain its existence were Nat White, Jack Boehle (Coconino High School cross country coach), Dusty Sullivan (Flagstaff High School cross country coach), Molly Carter, Cynthia and Wayne Sjoberg, Bob Packard, and Mann. Other running enthusiasts were also fundamental in the club's early years.

The FRTC helped prevent the overlap of local races. At times there would be four races on the same Saturday. Race directors in the area got together and created a summer circuit with the FRTC putting on a couple of their own races that incorporated different terrain.

Neil Weintraub, a Kaibab National Forest archaeologist who came to town in the 1980s, saw the work that the FRTC was doing. When the club began to drift away in the early '90s, he knew there was still a demand for racing in the area. In 2001, the Northern Arizona Trail Runners Association (NATRA) was formed with a mission to promote trail running in northern Arizona to folks of all abilities. Cofounder Weintraub devoted lots of volunteer energy to achieving that mission in the decades to come, not just through NATRA's Saturday morning runs but also as the town's running Everyman, the mouthpiece on social media for whatever upcoming races and newsworthy happenings needed promoting and whatever local history needed telling.

He also helped build up a summer running series that became a popular gathering place for the entirety of the local running community through races such as Gaspin' in the Aspen, Run for the Mountain, the Sacred Mountain Prayer Run, and his beloved Big Brothers Big Sisters Half Marathon (the second-oldest half in the state—45 years as of 2022).

Whether directing races while also taking and posting hundreds of photos for participants, being an aid-station fixture at regional races such as the Sedona Marathon and the Flagstaff to Grand Canyon Stagecoach 100-Miler, or keeping the infamous War Dog and the Soulstice Mountain Trail Run and its season-closing post-race party churning along, Weintraub was influential in expanding the local running presence in the early 21st century.

The running community in Flagstaff was flourishing at all levels with the work being done at the Center for High Altitude Training, NAU's ascension onto the national stage, and emerging community and recreational opportunities. It seemed like nothing could derail the city's momentum as it barreled toward becoming the country's premier running destination.

Hardy felt John Hayes was the right fit to serve under him as head men's and women's cross country and assistant track and field coach for multiple reasons. Hayes was motivated, a fierce recruiter, and had an appreciation for middle and distance running. Hardy had picked up the middle-distance group while working for Mann but would offload them to Hayes to free himself up for the administrative and other tasks his job required.

The 2005 NAU women's cross country squad, including coach John Hayes (back row, second from left, in sunglasses) and national individual champion Johanna Nilsson (front row, far left).

With Hayes at the wheel, NAU went on a streak of winning individual national titles nearly every season. Ida Nilsson won the 2005 NCAA Indoor Track and Field Championships in the 5000m to round out her collegiate career as an eleven-time All-American with three school records, three top-ten NCAA Cross Country Championship finishes, and two individual national titles.

Johanna Nilsson kept this momentum rolling into the 2005 fall season, where she became the second NAU athlete to earn an NCAA Cross Country Championship individual title before grabbing an electric double gold at the 2006 NCAA Indoor Track and Field Championships in the mile and 3000m. She finished her collegiate career with four school records and four individual national titles.

The Nilsson sisters, recruited by Mann, rewrote NAU's record books. But soon Hayes could lay claim to bringing in one of the most recognizable athletes in the history of the school. Lopez Lomong was recruited to NAU in 2005. The Sudanese athlete came from unimaginably tough beginnings that he would later detail in his autobiography *Running for my Life: One Lost Boy's Journey from the Killing Fields of Sudan to the Olympic Games.*

Lomong's career took off at NAU. In 2007, he won the Indoor Track and Field Championships 3000m before going on to win the NCAA Outdoor Track and Field Championships 1500m. For good measure, he also gained U.S. citizenship and a year later he made the 2008 U.S. Olympic team. The entire U.S. delegation—not just the track and field squad—voted Lomong to be flagbearer at the Opening Ceremony of the Beijing Games.

In spring 2007, Hayes announced he would be accepting a head coaching position at the U.S. Air Force Academy at the end of the track season. Hardy was once again in a position of filling this pivotal coaching role. Hayes had only been with the program a short time, but he left an enormous legacy behind.

When Hayes's position came available at NAU, it was a no-brainer for Eric Heins to apply. He was working at Texas Christian University after having spent three years coaching at Southeast Missouri State.

While in Missouri, Heins met his wife, Kaci. They moved to Fort Worth, Texas, for the TCU job and she began teaching. The two were settled, but Heins was constantly searching for a better coaching opportunity elsewhere.

Having been a graduate assistant at NAU for two years and knowing Hardy from their time working together, Heins was able to secure an interview for the position that would begin in fall 2007.

Kaci was happy to accompany Heins on this trip to Flagstaff. The two rented a car in Phoenix and made a nighttime drive up the mountain. When they arrived in Flagstaff, Kaci got out of the car, smelled the pine trees, looked up at the stars and said, "Eric, you have to get this job."

Johanna Nilsson's national championship in 2005 earned her the Cross Country Female Athlete of the Year trophy.

Having Kaci's approval meant the world to Heins. They began to imagine how their lives could look while living in this inviting mountain town. It was a tough reality check when Hardy called Heins to inform him the job was being offered to someone else.

"It was hard to see how upset Kaci was about it," Heins said. Their dream of living in Flagstaff was shattered.

The next day, Heins was out at lunch when Hardy called again. "Hey, are we good?" Hardy asked.

Although he was disappointed, Heins understood this was part of the business. His only criticism regarded the bluntness with which he had been told.

"You're one of my mentors," Heins replied. "I would have just liked more feedback from you about what I could work on as opposed to just getting called and told I didn't get the job."

Hardy paused before responding, "Well, do you still want the job?"

Although he was a little confused by the question, Heins replied, "Heck yeah!"

"The other guy turned it down," Hardy said. "He went home, talked to his wife, and they didn't want to move out here."

Heins could confidently tell Hardy that wouldn't be the case for him. He called Kaci to tell her the good news.

"We're moving to Flagstaff!" ∆

Chapter 11
Running Takes a Hit

"WHERE IS SEAN?" ASKED NANCY DANIELS AS SHE SEARCHED EACH OFFICE at the Center for High Altitude Training. Nancy was understandably upset. Sean Anthony had just handed in his resignation as assistant director of the Center for High Altitude Training. Nancy and her husband, Jack Daniels, had shifted their lives to Flagstaff with the intention of staying until Daniels retired. Daniels was already in his seventies, so it was a big commitment to come out to Flagstaff in the first place. Anthony had been keeping the center operating despite countless challenges; now his departure threatened the positions of everyone else who worked there.

Anthony could empathize with Nancy's concerns, but his resignation occurred because of a litany of frustrations of his own. In spring 2008, the director of the Center for High Altitude Training, Natalie Harlan, announced she would be accepting a job with the Flagstaff Medical Center. This shouldn't have placed leadership of the center in jeopardy because Anthony, who was second in charge, was twelve years into his time there. He was the natural choice to take over from Harlan. Unfortunately, NAU didn't see it that way.

"The university put us under the NAU Foundation because we operated partially on soft money," said Anthony. "The person in charge of that at the time structured things so the director position required fundraising experience, which rendered me ineligible to even apply for it. After all the years I'd spent helping to build the program into what it was, I wasn't exactly happy about that, especially as I had ideas about a more sustainable way to do things."

Anthony was worn down by bureaucracy. The center was operating under the auspices of the university, but catering to the needs of elite athletes was just not a priority during a time of budget cuts. The center was allowed to do increasingly less for athletes over the years, and by August 2008, Anthony didn't have any fight left in him.

After Harlan gave notice, "I announced that I would be resigning as well," Anthony said.

Sean Anthony (left) talking with Canadian coach Wynn Gmitroski (right) and his former athlete Heather Hennigar, who was transitioning into coaching during this visit to Flagstaff. Gmitroski has frequently used Flagstaff for altitude-based training.

The NAU Foundation began a desperate search to fill the vacant positions, but this process proved problematic once they realized how few people were interested. The first-choice candidate would have had to take a fifty percent pay cut to accept the offer. The second candidate said they'd only take the position if Anthony returned. "Nobody was willing to do what Natalie and I were doing for what the university was willing to pay them," said Anthony.

After submitting his resignation in August, Anthony officially left his position with the center in October. NAU scrambled to fill the vacant positions, but still with no luck. The decision to let Anthony leave instead of allowing him to be eligible for the director job was the first nail in the coffin for Flagstaff's future as a U.S. Olympic Training Site.

While the Center for High Altitude Training was sorting through issues with leadership, so too was the NAU track and field and cross country program. "I feel like next year will be my last year," J.W. Hardy told his head cross country and assistant track coach, Eric Heins, in spring 2008. If the NAU athletic department's financial situation didn't improve—and a looming global financial crisis made that highly unlikely—then Hardy knew it would be difficult to stay in his current role as program director.

The budget woes for Hardy began in 2006 when his salary was cut by five percent. This led Hardy to interview for a coaching position at Ohio State University the same year.

During his interview, when someone suggested that Ohio State was a level above NAU, Hardy bristled, "Make no mistake, the teams we have at Northern Arizona will light you up."

NAU may have had a small athletic budget and only a forty-year program history, but Hardy knew something about Lumberjack pride: the gritty blue-and-gold from a humble mountain town will punch above its weight every single time. What NAU had accomplished with little far outweighed what many big programs had achieved with a lot.

The Ohio State job may not have worked out for Hardy, but he continued to entertain the possibility of other opportunities outside of Flagstaff, especially after the financial crisis sent ripples around the globe in 2008.

Without a distance coach as director of the entire track and field and cross country program, the cap on how much they could get paid meant the university would lose great distance assistant coaches to bigger programs once they started having success. "You need a distance coach in the director position. The only way you prevent the cross country coaches being stolen is to have them as the head coach," conceded Hardy.

Hardy loved the NAU program and Flagstaff but recognized that it was time for new leadership. Though his specialty was not distance, he had the foresight to hire both Hayes and Heins, who maintained the national caliber of the distance program. Hardy knew that the next director needed to have that expertise. It was a critical piece in order to continue the legacy already emerging.

With remarkable humility, Hardy told Heins, "I don't know if my being here will allow us to get to the next level."

As the time came to find the right position for himself elsewhere, Hardy was not going to pack up and leave without helping ensure an orderly transition of power.

When he offered assistant coaches Mo Saatara and Heins an opportunity to show their interest in learning what it took to be the director, Heins stepped up. He knew this was an opportunity too good to let pass. If Hardy's job was going to open, Heins would apply for the position.

The news broke on January 20, 2009, through a statement posted by the NAU Public Affairs Office that the Center for High Altitude Training would be closing the next day. The rationale given was statewide budget cuts as a result of the ongoing financial crisis, which by then had been officially declared a recession.

Closing the Center for High Altitude Training would save NAU $230,000 annually at a time when the university, at the direction of the Arizona Legislature, had to cut $31.2 million from its 2009 financial plan. Expenditures deemed less essential to the educational success and experience of NAU students were most vulnerable. The center's nearly fifteen-year-long contribution to sport in Flagstaff had come to a sudden end.

NAU President John Haeger said that beyond the immediate need to save money, NAU could not meet the conditions of a multi-year, $3 million contract with the U.S. Olympic Committee.

The staff that had kept the center going during a turbulent few months lost their jobs without being consulted. With the top two positions remaining vacant there was no one to advocate for the center.

Daniels was openly disappointed by the closing, but remained optimistic about the future of running in Flagstaff. He told the *Arizona Daily Sun*, "There is no question in my mind that Flagstaff is the best place in the world to train for distance running. I really don't know if doing away with the center will do away with elite, high-altitude runners who come here. I think the elite runners will continue to come here, and I'd love to continue to work with them."

Staying in Flagstaff and continuing to work with elite athletes may have been Daniels's immediate goal, but without institutional support, he decided to continue his work elsewhere.

"One of the biggest losses for the Center for High Altitude Training was that they lost Jack Daniels. And it felt like they didn't know what they were losing," said Mike Smith.

Along with Daniels, Flagstaff lost its designation as a U.S. Olympic Training Site. Since the 1968 Mexico City Olympic Games, athletes had sought out Flagstaff to get in an altitude stint before major racing blocks. In recent years, the trickle that began with four Olympians had become a steady stream of hopefuls and stars. The community had worked hard for the Olympic rings, and many felt they were emblematic of what this running hotbed deserved. Then, in one swift blow, the rings were gone.

The center's closure may have seemed like a micro event to those who had little to do with sport in the city, but that indifference was precisely where Smith believed the biggest issue lay.

"It was always an uphill battle making it easier for people to train here," said Smith. "I thought, 'Why is it so hard?' We are missing this opportunity over and over again to celebrate who we are as a destination for training. If only the people outside of our sport knew it was the best place in the world to train. Flagstaff needs to embrace its identity."

The tough realization for people like Smith and Daniels was that not only had they lost their jobs, but all the hard work they had put into the Flagstaff running community was now in jeopardy. The one ounce of hope that remained was university officials stating it was possible the center could open in the future with the aid of corporate sponsors or financial support from the City of Flagstaff.

Smith bought into the idea that this might not be the end of a high-performance training center in town. In a 2009 interview with *Runner's World* magazine, Smith said, "There's been a huge outcry of support, and I think something will pop up and maybe three years from now, there might be a center that is doing more than what we're doing now."

The person who was least surprised about the closure of the Center for High Altitude Training was Anthony. "I could see the center needing to close from a mile away," he said.

From Anthony's perspective, that closure would be a disservice to Flagstaff only if something better didn't take its place. That's why, after he officially left his position there in October 2008, he began to develop a new and improved business plan that could be implemented once the inevitable happened.

Internal discussions years prior had identified why the Center for High Altitude Training didn't work well funded by NAU. Anthony had seen an opportunity to turn the functioning pieces into a private entity and improve upon them to create a self-supporting business.

As with any good entrepreneurial venture, this one needed a name that would help it stand out. Anthony used the term *hypobaric hypoxia*—which refers to the reduced oxygen content in the air at altitude—to come up with a five-character word, a subtle nod to the five Olympic rings, that would resonate with athletes who came to Flagstaff to train. Anthony's business name would highlight the physiological state of training at high elevation. Rising from the ashes of the Center for High Altitude Training would be a new approach, appropriately named HYPO2.

"When I left in October, I came up with the name, filed for the LLC, and waited to see what would happen with the Center for High Altitude Training," said Anthony. "When they announced the closure, I swooped in and said 'We can do this as a private entity' to all those who had just been fired."

HYPO2's goal was to pick up where the university left off. Even though the Olympic Training Site designation was gone, Anthony's entrepreneurial turn offered services that continued to attract elite athletes who wanted to train at 7,000 feet. Anthony was able to offer roles at HYPO2 to those who had recently been let go. One of the people taking him up on that offer was Smith. "I felt very fortunate that someone like Mike wanted to come and work for me," said Anthony.

Smith's work with Team Altius would continue while at HYPO2, although the U.S. Olympic Committee made him change the name because of its association with the Olympic motto, "Citius, Altius, Fortius" (Swifter, Higher, Stronger). In 2009, Team Altius rebranded itself Team Run Flagstaff (TRF), continuing to provide opportunities for community runners to stay connected and do track workouts together.

Smith believed it was important to keep the community running program alive despite the challenges of doing so. Nat White, an original member of the board for TRF, gave Smith a great perspective on how to keep a club operating as inevitable leadership changes were made. White told Smith that previous clubs in

Flagstaff—like the Flagstaff Road and Track Club that stopped operations in the mid-1990s—couldn't sustain themselves once people moved out of town or got older and lost interest in running. This advice was helpful for Smith, who was determined to not let that happen with TRF.

Since Anthony was the face of the Center for High Altitude Training when international athletes came into town to use NAU facilities, it was easy for him to shift the existing clientele over to HYPO2 because they trusted him. The same spring that the Center for High Altitude Training closed, HYPO2 hit the ground running, ready to work with athletes excited to train in Flagstaff.

As HYPO2 grew, it marketed itself as a one-stop shop. Anthony's venture would provide essential training services such as VO_2 max testing, blood work, chiropractic, and massage. It would even facilitate lodging, transportation, and booking a lane at the pool or a time slot for the track, if necessary. There would be nothing elite athletes needed that HYPO2 could not accommodate.

HYPO2's offerings stood in stark contrast to those provided through the Center for High Altitude Training. "At the end of my tenure, we weren't allowed to offer massage because the university was so risk-averse," said Anthony. An issue with a massage therapist with whom the Center for High Altitude Training subcontracted had caused NAU to feel there was too much liability in offering massages. No longer allowed to recommend any massage therapists to athletes who came through the center, Anthony effectively gave them the yellow pages to figure it out themselves. To avoid similar legal concerns, HYPO2 would instead offer its own, properly vetted, massage therapists on site.

Anthony's passion for going above and beyond for the athletes who utilized HYPO2 was partly motivated by famous restaurateur Danny Meyer.

"He has a notion of something called enlightened hospitality," explained Anthony. "You don't want to just meet people's needs so they're satisfied, you want to meet their needs in creative and gracious ways, so they are happy—so they feel like you actually care about their happiness. I wanted us to go above and beyond to create that kind of training experience for all the athletes and coaches that we work with."

Not everyone bought into this positive take on working with people. A business mentor to Anthony once told him, "If I ever see you picking an athlete up from the airport, I'll throw a rock at you." Anthony laughed as he recalled the humorous comment, but he firmly believed that kind of service demonstrated why HYPO2 was on a successful path.

"You can form a relationship in a ten-minute car ride, through showing that you care about somebody, that will last a lifetime."

The closing of the Center for High Altitude Training was a low point for the Flagstaff running community, but HYPO2's opening provided hope that what it represented and the value it brought to town would not be lost for good. The new business venture showed there were people who cared deeply about preserving the city as the ultimate training destination for athletes from all over the world.

That same spring, the coaching job at Boise State University came available. Hardy knew he had to give it a shot. Boise State had always been on his top-ten list. Oddly enough, after he applied, Hardy was initially reluctant to take the interview because at that point, after so much uncertainty, he was happy living in Flagstaff. He decided to proceed out of respect for Gene Bleymaier, the school's athletic director and a passionate track and field supporter.

After a positive trip to Boise State and what Hardy felt was a successful interview, he arrived back home in Flagstaff. As he walked up the steps to his front door, a call came through from Bleymaier. He offered Hardy the head coaching position with an attractive salary.

Less than an hour later, NAU Athletic Director Jim Fallis called Hardy asking how the interview went. "It went well," Hardy told Fallis. "They offered me the job."

Fallis tried to convince Hardy to stay. "We will match whatever they are offering, resurface the track, install new locker rooms, and get you that assistant coach you've been asking for."

This counteroffer was too good to pass up, and Hardy told Fallis it looked like he would be staying in Flagstaff. After hanging up the phone, Hardy called a jumps coach he knew and told him that he was about to have an assistant coaching position to fill.

The decision to turn down the Boise State job was tough for Hardy, but with all his needs being met at NAU, there was suddenly no reason to leave.

When Hardy went to bed that night, dread that he might have made the wrong decision began eating away at him.

"I woke up in the night," said Hardy. "By the morning, I'm crying." Hardy turned to his wife, Amy, and said, "We're supposed to go to Boise."

Hardy was a guest preacher at his local church in Flagstaff, and the week prior he had delivered a sermon on the book of Joshua, about the Israelites crossing over the Jordan River with the Ark of the Covenant into the promised land. "Be strong and courageous," he had told his congregation.

Now it was time for Hardy to embrace those words and go where his heart was taking him.

Hardy believed he was meant to be at Boise State, so he told Fallis his time at NAU would conclude at the end of the 2009 spring semester.

The NAU track and field and cross country program was the heartbeat of the mountain town's running culture. The university needed to find the right replacement for Hardy, someone who understood the great possibilities of leading the Lumberjacks. Fallis believed that person was throws coach Saatara, because he had been working at NAU the longest.

Hardy disagreed.

"It would be foolish not to hire Eric," he told Fallis. As he had previously emphasized, NAU needed a distance coach in the director's position.

Fallis trusted Hardy enough to promote Heins, but he held off on making Heins the official program director. For the 2009–2010 season, Heins would be interim director of NAU track and field and cross country. If he passed that test, he would have "interim" removed from his title.

"It was a little scary being put in charge because of NAU being such a big program," said Heins. "It was exciting, but you still don't want anything to go wrong under your watch."

Heins was in the right place at the right time to land the assistant coaching position at NAU, but the second act of his coaching career would not be due to chance. He was going to make sure of that. △

Part 3 – The Summit (2009–2019)

Chapter 12
Consistency Starts to Pay Off

DAVID MCNEILL HAD BEEN RECRUITED BY JOHN HAYES IN SPRING 2007, only to be told a few weeks before he was due to arrive in Flagstaff that Hayes had left. Although McNeill was assured by Hayes he would be in good hands with the incoming coach, that didn't alleviate the stress of traveling halfway across the world to a city he'd never seen to run for a school without a confirmed distance coach.

The stress of a big move momentarily subsided for McNeill when his rickety plane touched down at Flagstaff Pulliam Airport. Stepping out onto the tarmac, McNeill was "pummeled" by the smell of ponderosa pine trees. "I had never smelt anything like it," he said. This aroma, carried by late-summer monsoon rains, became synonymous with those first steps in northern Arizona for McNeill.

Adjusting to life in a new country proved more difficult than the twenty-year-old had imagined. McNeill arrived with fellow Australian athlete Ben Ashkettle as part of the 2007 recruiting class. Having his countryman on the team was helpful, but McNeill still had to navigate the pressures of living off campus, managing finances, and being submerged into a new culture.

"If Ben wasn't there, I probably wouldn't have lasted very long," McNeill admitted. "There were some tearful conversations in Heins's and [J.W.] Hardy's offices."

The culture shock continued when McNeill and Ashkettle walked into the NAU locker room. The team revered its storied history embedded with traditions that the upperclassmen were familiar with and invested in. McNeill and Ashkettle were initially cynical about their teammates' obsession with the program.

Aussie David McNeill overcame initial doubts about NAU to continue the Lumberjacks' powerful international legacy.

Being part of the NAU program wasn't just about running workouts together and traveling to races; it required complete buy-in to what the team was trying to achieve. The Lumberjacks wanted to be the best program in the country, and protecting the team's culture was fundamental to achieving that goal. It may seem silly to do chants after workouts or to stop on a run when someone shouts "one-ten," but those were as much a part of being a Lumberjack as putting on a racing singlet. Such traditions were the direct ties to the program's past.

As the months went by, McNeill and Ashkettle acclimated to their new environment. NAU's history of multinational teams meant the presence of Australians didn't feel foreign to anyone. "The Americans loved having the random internationals," McNeill said. "It was a nice cross-cultural melting pot."

The 2007 fall season concluded with a fourth-place podium finish for the NAU men's cross country team at the NCAA Cross Country Championships and an individual tenth-place finish for McNeill, while the women finished seventh with their second-highest place in program history. Seeing how the team performed and how close the guys were, and how team culture played into all of that, McNeill's eyes opened and his skepticism melted. "This was when the team culture started to infiltrate us," McNeill said. "Ben and I fell in love with Flagstaff and NAU running."

While his investment in the team was growing, McNeill experienced significant progress in his performances. At the 2009 NCAA Outdoor Track and Field Championships, he placed second behind the University of Oregon's Galen Rupp in the 5000m before earning another second-place finish at the 2009 NCAA Cross Country Championships, this time behind Liberty University's Sam Chelanga. These back-to-back second-place finishes, mixed with the lessons he learned training in Europe with the Melbourne Track Club in the lead-up to the 2009 World Athletics Championships over the summer, provided McNeill with the motivation and tools to chase a national title.

A brutal winter in Flagstaff, which included fifty-four inches of snow in five days during January, had McNeill struggling in the first months of the 2010 indoor season. Even so, he managed to gain momentum and confidence in time for the 2010 NCAA Indoor Track and Field Championships. Determined to break his string of second-place finishes, McNeill won the 5000m ahead of Chelanga to earn his first individual national title. He backed up this performance by winning the 5000m at the 2010 NCAA Outdoor Track and Field Championships at historic Hayward Field in Eugene, Oregon, with his parents flying in from Australia to watch.

For an athlete to leave their mark on the record books before they graduate is a significant achievement; so too is the ability to leave a positive mark on the team's identity. Despite his initial skepticism of how the bonds of team tradition and performance intertwined, McNeill had grown to not only embrace the team's culture, but to also make his own unique contribution.

At the start of each cross country season, the men's team would take an informal camping trip in the Arizona wilderness, typically consisting of cliff jumping into Clear Creek near Winslow, telling stories, and talking about the upcoming season.

As the sky turned to dusk, McNeill brought out the "Australian Lumberjack Cake" he had baked for the occasion. The dessert was a dense mix of apples and dates with a shredded coconut top layer, an interesting combination of ingredients that worked well together, much like the team that stood in front of McNeill as he explained how special it was to share this cake with his friends. Future generations of NAU athletes have enjoyed the taste of a Lumberjack Cake at the start of each cross country season since, baked by a senior athlete as he kicks off the discussion of goals for the upcoming season.

Midway through his third season as director of the NAU program —the "interim" designation had long since fallen off his title—Heins spent spring 2012 watching hordes of professional athletes and international teams train on the track outside his office window. Flagstaff wasn't a secret anymore. On any given day during the buildup to the 2012 London Olympic Games, the track at Lumberjack Stadium would be reminiscent of the mini-Olympics in 1968. Altitude training was no longer an intriguing unknown; it was a well-researched necessity.

No matter how many Olympians came and went outside Heins's window, his memories of the London Games would always focus on the three athletes who graced a photo framed on the wall that split the windows overlooking the track. They were athletes who called Flagstaff their home, not just their training camp.

Lopez Lomong, who last ran in an NAU singlet in 2007, had qualified for his second U.S. Olympic team in the 5000m. He was joined over the same distance by 2010 graduate McNeill, who had qualified for the Australian team, and NAU junior Diego Estrada, who was running for Mexico in the 10,000m after a phenomenal 27:32.90 spring showing at Stanford's Payton Jordan Invitational in Palo Alto, California.

Though his time couldn't count as a school record because Estrada ran it in a redshirt season, his 13:15.33 in the 5000m the next spring did. Estrada's 2013 clocking made him the second-fastest 5000m runner in collegiate history, a performance anyone could appreciate. His 4:04.36 raw time for the mile record in the Dome was one that those who understood the physiological challenges at altitude could get excited about.

These three Olympians spanning just over the past half decade represented the level of international recruits NAU was able to attract. It was one factor moving the needle for the program, and Heins was brimming with confidence about the future. When Nike Cross Nationals champion and Foot Locker runner-up Futsum Zienasellassie, an Eritrean who moved to Indianapolis, Indiana, with his family when he was fourteen, arrived on campus in fall 2012, Heins told him the NAU men would win a national team title before he graduated. This was music to Zienasellassie's ears and something he felt the team was positioned to achieve by fall 2013.

NAU Assistant Track and Field Coach Leah Rosenfeld pulled the old and well-worn team van into the parking lot at Foxglenn Park. Affectionately named Big Blue, this van had faithfully served the NAU program for more than two decades. In fact, it was older than some of the athletes sitting inside. Big Blue had seen three head-coaching changes and had been around since the first version of the workout the team was about to do.

NAU's Big Blue has carried runners through the Mann, Hardy, Hayes, Heins, and Smith eras and remains in use today. How many workouts has it seen? How many miles has it traveled to transport countless All-Americans and student-athletes to get their miles in?

In the late 1980s, Ron Mann came up with a workout called "The Signature." The athletes would do sets of 4x400m, two-mile tempo, 4x400m, two-mile tempo, and finish with a final set of 4x400m. The tempo sections were run on a road loop around campus, while the 400s were on the track. Eventually, the workout would move to Cardinal Field next to the Dome to get a feel for grass during the fall.

When Hayes took over as head men's and women's cross country and assistant track and field coach at NAU, he rechristened the workout "The Lumberjack." The name stuck when Heins took over as director, although he did change the tempo portions to ten minutes and the location to Foxglenn.

Diego Estrada (383) leads early at the 2011 national cross country meet, where he placed fourth.

Foxglenn is the best public space in Flagstaff to mimic the feel of a cross country race. With the city being situated in a dry, high-elevation forest, there isn't an abundance of open grass area to use for cross country-specific workouts. The team relies on the L-shaped, 600m-perimeter field at Foxglenn and the 400m perimeter at Cardinal Field for that.

Ahead of the 2013 Nuttycombe Wisconsin Invitational, Heins prescribed the Lumberjack workout to test the men's fitness. With FloTrack in attendance, athlete Matt McElroy was asked about what this workout meant to him. "It means hard work," he responded.

At Foxglenn, the coaches marked a 400m, U-shaped course stretching across multiple soccer fields before the athletes arrived. Each rep would consist of a slight

incline for the first straight, two tight bends, and a slight decline to the finish. There was enough variation and unevenness under foot to keep athletes from settling into a comfortable rhythm. Every rep would be a grind—exactly what Heins wanted.

The Lumberjack's first set of 400s is designed to be a slight shock to the system yet still meant to be run at a controlled pace that doesn't cause too much fatigue. The fastest athletes had no problem running sixty-seven, sixty-eight, sixty-five, and sixty-six for these 400s. Each rep started two-and-a-half minutes after the previous one began, so the faster an athlete ran, the more recovery he would get. However, going too fast to get an extra couple seconds of rest was hardly worth it.

At the end of the first set, the team was given two minutes to prepare for the ten-minute tempo. Everyone would start together and head out along a dirt trail before flipping at five minutes and coming back. If anyone was faster on the way back, they would keep running past the start until the time was up. Although the tempo wasn't a measured two miles, the front end ran five-minute pace, exactly what Mann used to have his athletes do.

After the tempo, the team took another two-minute breather before starting their second set of 400s. With the guys thoroughly warmed up, there was no excuse not to lean into the pace a bit more. This time they started out with the fastest rep from their previous set—sixty-five, sixty-five, sixty-three, sixty-three.

With their legs starting to burn, the team lined up to start the final tempo segment. Trying to flush out the heaviness in their muscles while maintaining a decent pace was the aim of this rep. The upcoming Nuttycombe Wisconsin Invitational would see significant pace changes throughout the race, and the team had to be prepared for that feeling while trusting they would still have gas for a final kick.

Some athletes had been switching between spikes and flats for each set, but with just one final set of 400s left, everyone on the line was wearing spikes. This part of the workout mattered most. All the prior work had been in preparation for these four reps. Each athlete had their own version of fatigue written across their face—some more visceral than others. No matter how they felt, when Heins shouted, "Ready . . . Ho!" every runner took off without a second thought to how they'd feel sixty seconds later.

The front group came through their first rep in a sixty-four. This wasn't as fast as they'd hoped, but considering they were coming off tempo pace, it was an acceptable start. From there, they cut it down. The next two reps were a sixty-two and sixty-one. Their legs were on fire heading into the workout's final and fastest rep. Everyone wanted to run sub-sixty for this effort, but the unforgiving nature of this Foxglenn course meant few would be capable of it.

Zienasellassie led the charge, rounding out the workout in a fifty-nine-second final 400m, with Brian Shrader on his shoulder and McElroy a couple of steps behind.

The team's confidence radiated from their exhausted faces as FloTrack weaved in and out of the finish-line carnage. "Watch out for Wisconsin," Zienasellassie told the cameraman. "We're coming for it."

Although the Nuttycombe Wisconsin Invitational was their immediate focus, the team had their sights set on November. After finishing fourth at the 2012 NCAA Cross Country Championships, the team knew they had a shot at dethroning the

Futsum Zienasellassie (246), Matt McElroy (241), and Brian Shrader, shown here in a dominating 2012 Big Sky Championships performance at their home course at Buffalo Park, helped put NAU on the cusp of a national championship.

defending champions, Oklahoma State University. This belief was supported by what Heins witnessed as the best "Lumberjack" workout ever.

"The mood is fantastic," Heins told FloTrack. "It's gonna be a challenge for sure [to win nationals], but I believe in our guys. I believe we have a very talented team. I believe they show up when it matters most. And I believe that if all the stars align, we have a shot."

Standing by the kilometer-to-go mark, Heins took a deep breath as he waited for his athletes to race past. The Lumberjacks had been leading the 2013 NCAA Cross Country Championships in Terre Haute since the five-kilometer halfway mark. At eight kilometers, the NAU men's cross country team, which had secured the number-one ranking the week before nationals, was still holding off the University of Colorado by twenty points. Heins was doing quick math as he watched each NAU and Colorado singlet fly by.

It was a historic race for the University of Oregon at the front, with freshman Edward Cheserek taking the individual title in dominant fashion. Twenty-four seconds back, NAU sophomore Zienasellassie crossed the line fourth. The first NAU athlete home wasted no time in turning back to the finishing straight to eagerly receive his teammates.

Left: Flagstaff native Brian Shrader finishes strong at 2012 nationals. Right: Matt McElroy at the 2014 NCAA national meet in a singlet showcasing the new NAU logo.

McElroy couldn't contain his excitement when he came through in twenty-fifth and was met by an excited Zienasellassie, who pulled him in for a hug. The joy among the Lumberjacks was heightened when Shrader joined the embrace, having finished just a second behind McElroy in twenty-eighth. The three athletes stood arm in arm in the finish chute waiting for their fourth and fifth runners to come through the line.

The emotions shifted from elation to concern as Josh Hardin (seventy-fifth), Nathan Weitz (seventy-sixth), Caleb Hoover (141st) and Andy Trouard (202nd) came through the chute. Uncertainty began to rise. Colorado had been right on their tails, and if NAU had slipped back too much over the last portion of the race, their national title hopes would be dashed.

If Heins had had a walkie-talkie in hand while standing at the kilometer-to-go mark with his assistant coach on the other end, he would have likely shouted, "We're gonna win this thing," as Mann had done in 1995 on the same course, from the same spot—with the same result.

"When the final results came in and I saw we lost to Colorado, my heart broke," said McElroy.

The Lumberjacks had hoped this would be their year, but once again the team's lack of depth denied them a golden moment. They needed to close the spread from their first to seventh man to have any chance at topping a team like Colorado. They would have to wait another year to find out if they were capable of it.

Car after car slowly pulled off to the side of Lake Mary Road. For those looking for soft-surface miles, this unofficial parking area was perfectly located at the head of a run called "Mailboxes"—officially Crimson Road—a dirt stretch that is frequently plowed in the winter months, making it an ideal escape from the pounding of road, indoor track, or treadmill when snow covers the ground.

For those athletes arriving for a road workout, this parking area was referred to as the four-mile mark. It lies six miles up from where Lake Mary Road starts in Flagstaff at the corner of South Beulah Boulevard and West University Heights Drive, but four miles from where the measured and desirable workout portion of the pavement begins heading southeast out of town. The entirety of Lake Mary Road has become a popular spot for runners, bikers, and other outdoor enthusiasts who enjoy the three lakes and many camping areas along its fifty-three-mile stretch.

While the NAU team didn't use Lake Mary Road much, runners training for marathons and other road races ran it often. The wide shoulders, unnoticeable camber, gradually rolling hills, and mild traffic made this a perfect location to get in long tempo efforts. Its lowest elevation sits at 6,730 feet, its highest, 7,500. This lack of extreme variation means athletes can get into a nice rhythm without interruption.

Newly formed professional group Northern Arizona Elite frequently used Lake Mary Road. Founded in January 2014 with a combination of athletes from the dissolved adidas McMillan Elite group and others who were excited to work with Coach Ben Rosario, NAZ Elite was quickly becoming the local team to root for. However, they weren't the only professional group that popped up at this time.

Vince Sherry—owner of the popular local store Run Flagstaff—started his own professional team, Team Run Flagstaff Pro. This elite squad was a great addition to the community running program, Team Run Flagstaff.

Starting a professional running team in Flagstaff wasn't always Rosario's plan. After graduating from Truman State University in 2003, he joined Hansons-Brooks Distance Project, where he ran for two years in Michigan. Rosario then moved back home to St. Louis, Missouri, and co-founded the Big River Running Company.

The opportunity to visit Flagstaff for his first time came in fall 2007, after Rosario started being coached by Greg McMillan. Rosario spent three weeks training with the adidas McMillan Elite team—which included Mike Smith—for the buildup to the 2008 U.S. Olympic Marathon Trials. Within these three weeks Rosario squeezed in a twenty-four-mile run on Waterline Road, a long run at Bellemont Road, and a workout at 3,100 feet at Camp Verde, a forty-five-minute drive south of Flagstaff.

It was a fun time to be training in Flagstaff, but Rosario learned the importance of adequate recovery when he arrived at the Olympic Trials completely fried. He ended up finishing 100th in 2:36:09—modestly better than Smith's DNF performance but no match for Heins's 2:25:01 for sixty-eighth.

Five years after his first trip to Flagstaff, Rosario and his family made the move from Missouri to Arizona. Just a few months later, Smith left to become head women's cross country and assistant women's track and field coach at Georgetown University.

This was an emotional move for Smith and his beloved running community in Flagstaff. Erin Strout, a senior editor at *Running Times* magazine and an active member of the local running scene, wrote in the *Arizona Daily Sun*, "Laughter is one of hundreds of gifts Smith, founder and director of Team Run Flagstaff, has given us over the past six years as a coach talented beyond his years, a phenomenal runner, a thoughtful neighbor and a best friend."

It was unlikely that Flagstaff would find anyone else like Smith, but that was OK, as Strout highlighted, "Without him [Smith] we wouldn't be where we are, but because of him, we've all assumed a responsibility to sustain a thriving running community simply through our continued dedication and participation." Losing Smith just a few years after Jack Daniels's departure was a tough blow to Flagstaff, but his years of committed effort had successfully established a running community that could continue to thrive without him.

Rosario knew that starting and sustaining a professional group, even in the best training site in the country, wouldn't be easy. He invested $40,000 of his own money into NAZ Elite during the first year before the team signed a deal with HOKA in 2015. This investment was necessary to secure high-caliber talent. Athletes like

Steph Bruce, Ben Bruce, Scott Smith, Kellyn Taylor, Matt Llano, Amy Van Alstine, Jordan Chipangama, David Rooney, and Eric Fernandez legitimized the team's elite credentials. "If we started with lower-level athletes, we would have been pegged as a developmental group," explained Rosario.

Zambia-born Jordan Chipangama, shown here at the 2009 NCAA national meet, was one of a number of elite Lumberjacks who stayed in Flagstaff after an outstanding NAU career to run professionally.

Flagstaff's evolving professional scene was a positive addition to the community and collegiate running environments that were already thriving. For these world-class athletes, the city was becoming a place worth staying for longer than just a month or two out of the year. On top of the incredible facilities Flagstaff offered, these coaches were also developing relationships with local tracks at nearby lower-elevation towns such as Sedona and Cottonwood. These opportunities were an extension of the years when Mann would shuttle his NAU team in Big Blue down the hill to Camp Verde High School's dirt track for speed development or Montezuma Well Road for downhill training. At under 3,500-foot elevation and less than an hour away, the Verde Valley increased athletes' access to the proven benefits of living high and training low.

Locals couldn't drive to work or the grocery store or stroll through Buffalo Park without glimpsing a runner flying by. The sport became increasingly visible, meshing perfectly with the city's adventurous and outdoorsy vibe. Most people who lived in Flagstaff had no idea if the runner they passed on their way to work was a professional, a college athlete, or even an Olympian. That ability to hide in plain sight was an attractive part of training in Flag.

Since taking charge in 2007, Heins had turned a solid cross country program into a model of consistency with six podiums in eight seasons, including another fourth-place finish in fall 2014.

The 2015 season was shaping up very differently, however, with some big decisions at hand that would carry short- and long-term consequences. Zienasellassie walked into Heins's office and declared he wanted to redshirt the upcoming cross country campaign. Redshirting would mean Zienasellassie would be ineligible to race in the fall. Instead, his final year of eligibility would extend to 2016.

Heins was hesitant to redshirt the junior athlete, a move that might interrupt the momentum of his fourth and third place individual finishes at the two previous national championships. He also preferred to be the one to approach an athlete with the idea, not the other way around. However, Heins agreed a redshirt was the right decision.

With Zienasellassie out, dashing NAU's national title hopes for 2015, Heins continued to move his chess pieces. The coach decided to hold out Geordie Beamish, Andy Trouard, and Nathan Weitz as well. With four of the top seven sidelined, not only were NAU's chances of getting on the podium in jeopardy, now the Lumberjacks might not even make the national meet.

The two key players during a trying 2015 campaign that concluded at the NCAA Mountain Regional Championship were freshman Tyler Day and University of Michigan transfer Cory Glines. Heins knew it was going to be a tough season when the guys finished thirtieth at the mid-season Nuttycombe Wisconsin Invitational. After the race, Heins told his athletes with clear frustration in his voice that they "got beat by guys in basketball shorts and Jordans."

Although things were looking bad for the Lumberjacks from an outsider's perspective, Heins remained quietly confident about what the 2015 decisions would mean for the 2016 season. With all the key players racing, and with the addition of a twenty-one-year-old transfer from New Zealand who'd arrive in the spring, Heins felt he had done his part to align the stars this time. △

Chapter 13
The Overlapping Season

"DO YOU HAVE A MINUTE?" ERIC HEINS ASKED ATHLETIC DIRECTOR LISA Campos in spring 2016.

"Sure, Eric, come in and take a seat," Campos replied. "What's on your mind?"

"Well, I don't really know how to put this, but my wife, Kaci, applied for her dream job at the Space Center in Houston, and they've just offered her the position. She'll start work there in the fall," Heins said.

Campos took a deep breath. She knew exactly what was coming next.

"Kaci has supported my dream as a college coach for over a decade, and now it's time for me to support her dream." Heins paused before verbalizing the last and most difficult sentence: "After much discussion with my family, I have decided to resign from my coaching position at NAU."

There was an uncomfortable silence as Campos digested the situation. Heins was the most accomplished coach on her staff. He'd done an admirable job of continuing to elevate the premier athletic program on campus.

"I'm guessing nothing I can say will change your mind," Campos said.

Heins looked her in the eyes with certainty. "No, there isn't."

With Kaci planning to leave Flagstaff that summer, Campos assumed Heins would finish up the 2016 spring semester so he, Kaci, and their son could all move to Houston at the same time. But Heins had a different idea.

"I really want to coach this next year," Heins told Campos. "But I respect any decision you make, since I'm the one telling you that I'm leaving."

Having Heins stay for the 2016–2017 school year would give the athletic department ample time to find a replacement, and it would give Heins time to slowly transition out of the role. This unconventional, yet courteous, request could play in everyone's best interest.

Campos decided to meet Heins in the middle. He would stay for the 2016 fall season, but after that, he would be done. Heins respected her decision and appreciated the opportunity to have one last season with his team.

Since taking over the program as director in 2009, Heins had kept the dream alive of one day bringing home a gold NCAA team trophy to Flagstaff. Having gotten fourth twice and second once in the past four years, he held more than an ounce of hope the team could win in his final season—provided the veterans and newcomers could rebound from the 2015 results.

The stage was set for the NAU team to send Heins out on a high note for the cross country program's fiftieth anniversary. This motivated and determined group was truly within striking distance of the summit after all these years. Then Campos threw a curveball Heins's way.

"We are going to start your replacement in the fall," Campos told Heins. "They'll shadow you all season and take over the program after nationals."

This plan made sense logistically; it is better not to bring in a new coach halfway through the school year. But there is a reason schools never do this. The potential for the two coaches to clash and cause unnecessary drama that impacts the athletes presents a risk usually not worth taking. Campos was confident the arrangement could work, and Heins, even if he were inclined, wasn't in a position to change her mind. All he could do was hope they found the right fit, not only for the sake of the fall season but for the future of the program.

The team's success during this unorthodox passing of the torch would depend on the willingness of both coaches to set ego aside. Heins's fairy-tale ending hung in the balance.

Mike Smith logged onto his Instagram account and saw a message from a friend at the Run Flagstaff store. It was a screenshot of Kaci's announcement that she was accepting a job in Houston. "Surely she wouldn't be moving out there by herself," Smith mused.

NAU was at the top of Smith's dream job list. If the opportunity ever arose to return to Flagstaff and coach for NAU, he would move heaven and Earth to get that job. Prior to Kaci's announcement, he was realistic in believing the job wasn't coming available any time soon. "Heins wasn't even close to retiring," said Smith. "This thing will open up in twenty years, and that's when I'll have my résumé ready."

With that assumption at the back of his mind, Smith began coaching at Georgetown University and didn't think about the NAU job again. Flagstaff never left his mind though. Smith spent summers in Flag to escape Washington, D.C., and reconnect with friends in the community he'd come to love.

When the NAU position opened, Smith found himself in a difficult spot. "I had just signed a five-year contract the month before to be the new director at Georgetown. I was settled in and really liked the kids I was working with."

Regardless of his current situation, Smith knew he had an obligation to himself to apply. "What are the chances of this job coming up again?" he reasoned.

Heins was quick to give Smith a heads-up. Although he was a very qualified candidate, he would be one of over a hundred coaches chasing after the plumb position. "Don't get your hopes up," Heins warned.

Once the athletic department narrowed down their candidates to three, they invited Ron Mann to help with the final selection process. He was asked to call the three candidates and determine who he thought was best suited for the position. Mann was happy to be an advisor but refused to be any kind of decision maker. "You're not going to ask me who I would choose, because I am not going to be that person," Mann told Campos.

Smith fondly recalled that the first time he ever spoke to Mann was during one of these phone conversations. The two talked about the history of the NAU program and how Mann had seen Flagstaff change over the years. Unsure as to what role Mann was playing in the decision process, Smith did what he could during the call to show his suitability for the position.

"I didn't know if you were running the show in the background," laughed Smith.

Mann was quick to reply, "I was not."

While the decision was being hashed out back in Flagstaff, Smith was on a trip with friends in Vail, Colorado. Near the end of the vacation, Campos finally reached out to deliver the good news.

"I'll never forget the call saying they are going to extend the offer to me," said Smith. "It was a life-changing moment."

Heins could breathe a sigh of relief. "If I didn't know who it was, I would have been a little apprehensive. Knowing it was Mike made me feel a whole lot better about the situation."

To avoid any confusion, Smith wanted to be clear Heins was in charge. "Coach Heins is fully coaching every day of the season," he reminded himself. "For the first time in four years, I'm not the head coach. I'm in the background."

As it turned out, Heins and Smith were an ideal pairing for NAU's quest for victory at the 2016 NCAA Cross Country Championships in Terre Haute.

Tyler Day hesitantly walked into the dimly lit men's locker room and slid into a chair. As the camera was still being adjusted to the right height, Day started some friendly conversation with his interviewer to break the ice.

The locker room had been Day's second home for the past year. He'd spent countless hours there, preparing for workouts and enjoying the company of teammates. He was used to feeling nervous in the locker room, but he wasn't used to the nerves that came with the weight of being asked difficult questions.

"Let's get started," the interviewer told Day. "Tell me about how you felt when Coach Heins told the team this was his last season with NAU."

The usually talkative sophomore took a few seconds to find the right words. "I initially was scared," Day admitted. "I actually had thoughts of probably transferring. Like, oh man, this is probably not going to work out."

After Day was finished in the chair, Peter Lomong, brother of NAU legend Lopez Lomong, took his place. He was asked the same question. "I didn't know what to do," Lomong told the interviewer. "I just started crying."

Next was Cory Glines, who said, "It sucked," while NAU's number one runner Futsum Zienasellassie described the situation as "sad."

One after the other, the guys told FloTrack—who had come to film their 2016 cross country season for a documentary called *The Program: Northern Arizona*—about the devastation of finding out Heins was leaving. Although they were told their new coach would be a great fit, it was safe to say that most were skeptical of any replacement measuring up to their current coach.

"When I first saw Coach Smith at the outdoor track before Heins introduced him to the team, I was angry," said New Zealand transfer Matt Baxter who had only been on the team for a semester. "I thought, 'This is the guy who might make me regret my decision to come to NAU.'"

Smith was attuned to the reality awaiting him. It wasn't just that he would be coaching another guy's recruits—something all new hires must deal with—it was that his beloved predecessor would be right there with the team all season. "Coaching changes are hard," Smith said. "I had to recognize that these people didn't want to lose their coach."

Heins might have been convinced Smith was the right person to take his place, but there was a lot more convincing to do before the athletes would come on board.

Smith had been watching the men's cross country team train for a few weeks when he had to ask Heins, "Do you think the guys are a little too loose with how they act at practice?"

Heins couldn't help but laugh as he recalled asking Mann the exact same question when he worked with the team.

"Being loose is how they perform, and it's how NAU teams have always been," Heins replied.

Smith had not yet seen them compete in a big meet setting. He was still a little puzzled at how this excessively relaxed and joking atmosphere at practice would translate at race time, when they really had to focus. There were times when Smith thought to himself, "Do they understand how hard this is?"

When it came time to toe the line, the team's demeanor shifted markedly. Sometimes they would be laughing right up until they stepped into the starting box; then they looked like "killers" (as Smith would describe them). Their ability to flip the switch from relaxed to laser-focused was a unique quality that proved effective as the fall season got underway.

The men annihilated the competition at the thirty-sixth annual George Kyte Classic by putting five runners in the top six. They took a small breather after crossing the finish line before logging a ten-mile cooldown for a total of eighteen miles on the day. The cooldown was miserable in the afternoon heat, with guys hacking from having just raced at 7,000 feet.

A week later, the men's team traveled to Terre Haute for the Sycamore Invitational, run over the same loop where nationals would be held in a little over two months. The team had to rely on their depth to pull off the win, with Day sitting out because of a hip injury and Heins not ready to race Zienasellassie just yet.

Baxter finally got his first chance to race on the grass since arriving at NAU in the spring. He took the individual win with Glines not far behind. The team showed they could survive this first test of the season without two of their top runners, winning the meet with a mere eighteen points.

These early races, although not significantly impressive, showed that NAU had the depth to be a contender when it really mattered later in the season. The U.S. Track & Field and Cross Country Coaches Association took note, ranking the men's team number one in the country in the third week of the polls.

Heading into the Nuttycombe Wisconsin Invitational on October 14, the top-ranked team was confident they were ready to take care of business. The Lumberjacks were coming off a solid month of training without any interruptions. With 207 athletes lining up in Madison, this was the first real opportunity of the season to measure themselves against some of the best teams in the country.

Smith was complimentary of the "killers" as he watched them tear up the Wisconsin course. "I liked their poise, patience—they played the game," he said. They'd been ranked number one for the two weeks leading into this race, so Smith was curious to see how they handled having a target on their backs. "Champions respond to pressure. They like pressure," Smith said. "With the men you always ask, can they do that for two more kilometers? And I think that is their strong point. Two thousand more meters is going to be their comfort zone."

Heins was beaming as he talked to FloTrack after the race. "This has been a year in the making," he said. "We want to have a good chance to win [at nationals]. We're not hiding from that."

Seeing how loose the team was and then watching them execute when it mattered was a promising realization for Smith. He'd been told that keeping the mood light at practice was beneficial; he was only starting to see how well that methodology applied to race day.

While Smith was impressed with how the team enjoyed themselves, Heins was taking note of how Smith interacted with the athletes. "His post-race evaluations were great," said Heins. Smith always gave the athletes immediate feedback once they finished a race. He treated it as an invaluable opportunity to find out how things went, before time eroded those raw emotions. This was something Heins intended to implement with any athletes he worked with in the future.

It was an eight-mile tempo at Buffalo Park that got Heins pumped for his team's prospects later in the season. Eight guys stayed together for the fastest combined effort their coach had ever seen. After the workout, Heins addressed the team, almost in tears as he shared his excitement over what he had just witnessed.

Although the team was ranked number one, they still viewed themselves as underdogs every time they raced. That was one of the reasons they could go into meets looking and feeling as relaxed as they did. They believed they had nothing to lose and everything to gain.

The team felt this way even as they finished with a perfect score of fifteen points at their conference meet, with all seven athletes finishing in the top nine. The men then watched the women's team take the win to top off a golden career for Heins as a Big Sky Conference coach.

It was a quick turnaround of two weeks before the Lumberjacks would line up for their first 10k race of the season at the NCAA Mountain Regional Championship in Logan, Utah. The Mountain Region is perennially the strongest in the country, and with three top-ranked teams in attendance (NAU in first, University of Colorado in second, and BYU in fourth), it would provide a preview for the national meet. However, with nationals just eight days later, teams often hold out some top runners and replace them with alternates if they have the depth to pull off such a strategy.

NAU had no intention of holding anyone out, but on race day Geordie Beamish got on the bus looking pale and desperately asking for something to eat. He'd been unable to hold down food all morning, and that finally caught up to him as the team departed their hotel for the course.

As warm-ups began, Heins pulled the team aside to deliver the bad news. "No Beamish today. He's sick. So we're only going to have six guys on the line. Every one of you needs to go out there and do your job."

Heading into the homestretch of an emotional and highly anticipated season, the Lumberjacks had cruised through every obstacle along the way. Now, with a man down and no alternate ready to race, the guys didn't have much room for error.

Thankfully, Zienasellassie saved the day up front by taking home the individual title, with Glines finishing sixth and Day seventh. Baxter had his roughest outing of the season, coming in twenty-second, with Nathan Weitz twenty-fourth and Andy Trouard thirty-sixth.

"This was our worst meet of the year," Heins admitted after the Lumberjack men still somehow managed to win as a team. Even on their worst day, they could dig deep enough to get the job done. However, they couldn't count on that happening again at nationals.

Heins took the team away from all the hype at the finish line and gave them an important piece of advice for how to move forward from this disappointing performance. "Forget about the race," he said. "We have bigger things to accomplish."

Back in Flagstaff, the team found a surprise from adidas in their locker room. Every athlete had a blue box with a gift inside. The team had never received anything like this from their sponsor before, so there was a Christmas morning–like excitement about the moment.

Pulling open the box, Glines saw a square yellow sign that read, "Ready . . . Ho!" Beneath it was a pair of casual adidas shoes, black with a gold heel. There was no better way to arrive in Terre Haute than wearing shoes whose heels displayed the color of the trophy they hoped to win.

The last gift in the box was a blue jacket with a gold NAU logo on the chest. Somehow adidas hadn't gotten the memo that the school's logo had changed a few years prior. Day was quick to point this out to his teammates. "Dude! It has the old logo on it."

When the athletic department found out, the team was advised not to wear the jackets while they traveled and instead wear the accurately logoed apparel they already had. Since the logo was a fun throwback to Heins's beginnings as an assistant coach at NAU, and with the jackets now being the nicest piece of adidas apparel each athlete owned, the guys respectfully disregarded that request.

It was undeniable: Heins had accumulated the deepest NAU men's team in program history for the 2016 season. In the past, the Lumberjacks were typically strong through four runners, but the lack of a dependable fifth or sixth man always seemed to stand in the way of their reaching the top of the podium.

For this season, the team had a proven low stick in Zienasellassie. His performances at the NCAA Cross Country Championships since 2012 were thirty-first place as a freshman, fourth as a sophomore, and third as a junior. During his last outdoor season for NAU, Zienasellassie broke the 10,000m school record with a 27:52.70 at the Payton Jordan Invitational on his way to placing second at the 2016 NCAA Outdoor Track and Field Championships. In the hunt for a team title, Zienasellassie would surely contribute by fighting up front for the individual title.

Eric Heins assembled a powerhouse men's team for his final season at the helm in 2016.

The remainder of the top four would be filled out by some combination of Glines, Baxter, and Day. Glines had clocked standout performances at the George Kyte Classic and NCAA Mountain Regional Championship, while Baxter was solid through conference but had a sub-par day at regionals. For his part, Day was steadily returning to competitive form after the hip injury that had hampered his early season.

The biggest question mark surrounded the team's fifth man. Weitz was fast and strong on the grass but struggled when two kilometers were added at late-season meets. Beamish was finally healthy and running confidently, until getting ill at regionals put his preparations in doubt. If he could get to the line feeling good, he was NAU's best shot at having enough depth through the top five.

Trouard faced the longest odds. He'd performed well at the conference meet but had an off day at regionals. If one of these three had a good day in Terre Haute, then NAU might just make school history.

As if the pressure to perform wasn't high enough by the last week of the season, the final moments of FloTrack's documentary dialed up a little extra motivation for each athlete. Released just four days before nationals, the storyline was abundantly clear: the team's expressed desire to take home a historic victory for their school and a fitting send-off for the man who brought them all together.

"To win the team title with this being Coach Heins's last year is what we have been thinking about . . . we're all driven, and we want to make that happen," said Zienasellassie.

Glines echoed his teammate's thoughts, adding, "I don't think we really need these out-of-this-world performances. I think if we have the guys that show up and do what they're capable of, then I don't see why we couldn't bring it home."

The comments made on camera echoed those made on training runs during the season. Everyone wanted to pull off this win for Heins, and no one was hiding from that. For the athletes, the tough part of watching this documentary so close to nationals was hearing how their coaches felt about the upcoming race.

"I'm still losing sleep over whether we're gonna win this national title or not," Heins said, before Smith concluded, "How many chances does anyone ever get at that?" △

Chapter 14
History on the Line

THE NAU MEN'S CROSS COUNTRY TEAM STOPPED IN THEIR TRACKS TO look up at the flock of vultures circling overhead. It seemed like a bad omen to be followed like prey on a local Terre Haute trail just two days out from nationals. But by this point in the season, the team was used to having eyes on them.

Undeterred, the Lumberjacks continued to navigate their first run in Terre Haute. The mixture of hidden single-track trails in dense brush and dirt roads with open space made it likely someone would get lost. A small gap formed between the team's front and back halves, and a wrong turn from the back half split the group in two. They ran separately until the two groups popped out at opposite ends of a dirt road.

Tyler Day started toward the other group, snapping his fingers. The rest of his group followed his lead until the sound of synchronized finger-clicking reached the ears of their teammates.

Snapping fingers echoed through the trees as the two groups approached each other in true *West Side Story* fashion. At the center of the trail, the runners collided with laughter and hugs, greeting one another as if their miles spent apart were the length of summer break.

Goofy, loose, funny, maybe even a little weird—these adjectives perfectly described the NAU men's cross country team. The men gave the appearance of taking nothing too seriously. That was their greatest strength. And it was on display during the entire season.

The guys looked sharp as they attended the pre-competition banquet rocking flannel shirts—paying homage to their lumberjack roots. While some teams wore three-piece suits, the NAU team dressed like their outfits were sewn from their personalities.

Once the dinner concluded, all teams in attendance made their way to an auditorium up the street for the awards presentation. Two incredible careers at NAU were honored that evening, with Eric Heins being named Mountain Region Cross Country Coach of the Year and Futsum Zienasellassie the Mountain Region's Athlete of the Year.

When the awards section of the evening ended, a band played a few songs to round out the night. As the band set up, all but two teams departed the auditorium—leaving only the Oklahoma State University women and the NAU men.

Although slightly deterred by the lack of attendees, the band struck up a tune and the OSU women started dancing. Andy Trouard and Day joined in the festivities at the front of the stage while the rest of their team and coaching staff watched with amusement from twenty rows back. It was harmless fun in the tiny mosh pit until Trouard boldly climbed onto the stage with the intention of jumping off into the crowd.

"Don't do it . . . don't do it," Heins muttered under his breath as he watched Trouard leap from the stage.

The NAU team held their collective breath as one of their historically injury-prone athletes tested his durability just two days before nationals.

The next day, Trouard appeared to have survived the jump as he plodded around the LaVern Gibson Championship Cross Country Course during the team's pre-meet jog.

It was shorts and T-shirt weather on this beautiful seventy-degree day in Terre Haute. Everyone appreciated the unusually warm weather for November in Cross Country Town USA. They also understood that pleasant conditions weren't in the forecast for race day.

One silly pre-meet ritual the NAU team had adopted was to run the first mile slower than ten-minute pace. While other teams blew past the Lumberjacks, they

The top seven looking to make history were, clockwise, from lower left: Matt Baxter, Geordie Beamish, Tyler Day, Cory Glines, Andy Trouard, Nathan Weitz, and (middle) Futsum Zienasellassie.

jogged along at what was, for them, a walkable pace, calling out anyone who accidentally picked it up to anything resembling a run.

The mood of the team was light, as though they were ready for what was to come but hadn't yet taken the time to think about exactly how they should feel about it. A shared nervous energy wouldn't set in until the team assembled in Heins's hotel room the evening before the race to hand out numbers.

As each athlete sat silently staring at the number in their hands, Heins spoke. Before every race, Heins always had words of encouragement for his team. This time, he kept it short.

"You guys know what to do," he said before kicking everyone out of his room.

"You might want to pack a jacket," Baxter told Zienasellassie as he looked out their hotel window.

At midday, when more than 200 young men would fill the starting boxes awaiting the gun, it was going to be thirty-six degrees. Wind gusts of thirty-one miles an hour would create a windchill temperature below freezing.

Baxter and Zienasellassie left the safety of their room and headed out to join their team in the lobby prior to departing for the course. As the elevator doors slid open, the two athletes were greeted by a couple of NAU supporters.

"Are you guys looking forward to the race?" one of the women asked as the doors closed.

"We sure are," replied Zienasellassie, smiling between the visible nerves.

The woman smiled back as she introduced herself. "I don't think we've met. I'm Coach Heins's mom."

Baxter stood in the corner, taking in the bigger picture of this elevator ride. "All season, we knew that trying to win in Terre Haute was a big deal to Heins. I never even considered the fact that his family was equally invested in this," Baxter said. "It added another layer of pressure, seeing the excitement and confidence on his mom's face—I wished I had that."

Heins's family members weren't the only ones who made a long trip to watch the Lumberjacks compete. NAU President Dr. Rita Cheng and her husband, Thomas Cheng, were there, along with NAU Athletic Director Lisa Campos, Senior Associate Athletic Director Robyn Sharp, and Ron Mann, driving in from Louisville. NAU had also invested in a videographer to follow the team all weekend.

With the team assembled in the lobby, the guys piled into a van with Heins at the wheel and Mike Smith riding shotgun. The nervous energy in the van was almost unbearable; if it hadn't been so cold outside, every window would have been rolled down to let it escape.

Most of the guys were looking out the van windows, lost in their own worlds, when an ad came on the radio that drew everyone's attention. It started by posing a question, "What is this sound?" Puzzled faces listened to the cracking and crunching noises coming from the radio, trying to decipher what it was.

"That's the sound of your neck breaking in a car accident," said the voice from the radio.

The team audibly cringed as the ad continued.

"What is this sound?" said the voice as a squishing noise played.

"Turn it off, turn it off!" yelled Beamish from the back.

Smith had clearly dropped the ball on his DJ duties. The team laughed as he fiddled with the radio stations to find a less grotesque pre-race playlist.

The athletes' seriousness eased slightly, if only for a second, but straight faces returned as the van pulled into the parking lot.

Standing by the kilometer-to-go mark, Heins took a deep breath as he surveyed the setting for his last race as NAU program director. The mixed emotions he'd carried since the spring filled his eyes with unshed tears. The last long run was bearable, as was the last Lumberjack workout and the last pre-meet with his athletes. But nothing compared to the feelings simmering before the impending last race.

This moment of reflection wasn't solely focused on the finale. "Leading up to the race, I remember it being a fun year," said Heins. "It took me a long time to realize how to focus on the process, not just the end result."

When Heins had downtime during the season, he made trips to Durango, Phoenix, and Houston to see his family. This time away from Flagstaff kept him relaxed and enjoying the season more than he had in previous years.

With the team expected back from its warm-up any minute, Heins regained his composure as he walked to the tent. The energy he left at the start of the final kilometer might fuel the Lumberjacks soon, as they dug deep to survive the home stretch.

Before the team could embrace the pain of the finish, however, they had to endure the nerves of the start. With their starting box wide enough to fit four at the front, NAU put their expected top finishers with their feet on the white paint. Numbers 394, 399, 393, and 390 would lead their teammates into the unknown.

The starting pistol raised, Baxter's eyes fixated on the barrel, ready to see a puff of white smoke that would give him permission to recruit every fast-twitch muscle fiber in his body.

Then . . . smoke.

With elbows coming from Georgetown University on the left and the University of Texas to the right, the Lumberjacks did a modest job of holding two spots on the front line down the opening straight. Texas was forcing them left, although the pack needed to eventually merge right. While Baxter and Zienasellassie claimed spots near the front, the rest of the NAU team disappeared into the sea of 251 men canned like sardines.

The front pack was fourteen people wide as it barreled through the first kilometer in 2:50. This wasn't a scorching pace, but considering the blustering side wind and moderate incline of the starting straight, it was decent.

Once the pacers out front found their rhythm, the runners behind could take a deep breath for the first time since the crack of the gun. So too could Heins, as he saw Baxter and Zienasellassie out front, with the rest of the team positioned appropriately within the pack. The only Lumberjack he couldn't find was Glines.

"Where's Cory?" Heins asked his graduate assistant, Jarred Cornfield.

Trouard could answer that question: he had hurdled Glines as he lay on the ground just after the one-kilometer mark. A fall in front of him had taken Glines down with a nasty hit to the head in the process.

"Get up!" Trouard shouted at his friend.

By the time Glines regained his feet, he'd lost significant ground on his target position. This course wasn't extremely narrow, but it was going to be very difficult to get back to an All-American spot awarded to the top forty finishers. And even if he got there, the chances of holding on when the race inevitably picked up in the last couple of miles was slim, considering the energy he had already expended in the tussle. It was safe to say the Lumberjacks had just lost one of their top five.

At the front, Baxter was getting itchy feet, so he decided to pick up the pace. By the three-kilometer mark he had a step on the field.

"I was used to running out front in most races in New Zealand. The lead didn't scare me. However, I was aware that at some point the field would swallow me up, and I had to be prepared to hang on for dear life when that happened."

The three-kilometer team scores showed a surprising early challenger for the national title. The University of Texas at El Paso was leading with 135 points, with NAU in second with 136, and Stanford University in third with 169. The difference between the point totals among the top three teams represented just seconds within the closely bunched pack. There was no clear favorite yet.

The leaders reached four kilometers in 12:04 with Baxter still leaning into the pace at the front. A few minutes later, as the pack came into the long starting straight to begin their second lap of the course, Baxter was engulfed by the other runners.

Zienasellassie asserted himself as the lead Lumberjack in the field—with Baxter desperately holding onto him.

The NAU team came through the five-kilometer halfway point in good position: Zienasellassie and Baxter in the top ten, Day and Weitz in the top thirty. Updated team scores showed the Lumberjacks making progress, but still not enough. Stanford led with 117 points, NAU held second with 125, and Syracuse was overtaking third with 150 points.

The new individual leader was Villanova University's Patrick Tiernan, who introduced the field to his fifth gear as they came through six kilometers. He didn't want to give the three-time NCAA cross country champion from the University of Oregon, Edward Cheserek, or Syracuse University's Justyn Knight the opportunity to run him down in the final few hundred meters. Quick to respond to this move was Zienasellassie, who positioned himself within the breakaway pack.

For the first time since the gun fired, Baxter saw Day out of the corner of his eye. He knew they had to go with this move or be left behind. Baxter reached his arm across the chest of another athlete, pointed at Day and said, "You and me, let's go!"

And they went.

The eight-kilometer team scores were more promising for the Lumberjacks. NAU led with 110 points, ahead of Syracuse (123) and Stanford (150). Stanford's fade over the last three kilometers was helping NAU, but these final two kilometers were vital.

Coming past the kilometer-to-go mark, where Heins had been reflecting just an hour before, Zienasellassie, in fourth place, desperately chased Cheserek in third. Next past the mark was Baxter, followed by Day, and then Weitz. This was a solid top four, but Weitz's legs were starting to falter.

The final 400 meters is a brutally long straight—the finish line a mirage that never seems to get closer. The wind, cold, and energy-sapping footing of the previous miles meant there was no telling how an athlete would handle this final stretch.

Tiernan was dominating the battle for the individual title with Knight on his tail. They crossed the finish line in first and second, respectively, Knight securing valuable points for Syracuse.

Unable to close the gap on Cheserek down the home straight, Zienasellassie finished fourth as NAU's first runner across the line. Thirteen seconds behind was Baxter in eleventh and then Day in twenty-third. They gathered to see who would be next.

Trouard met shocked faces as he powered through the line in thirty-seventh to earn NAU its fourth All-American honor of the day. After an up-and-down season, Trouard turned in his best day when it mattered most. Seeing his good friend and teammate on the ground early in the race had ignited a fire that pushed him to his most important collegiate performance to date.

Hordes of athletes came through in the twenty-three seconds it took for NAU's fifth man to appear in the finish chute. Somehow, after running most of the race with a concussion, Glines came across the line in eighty-fourth—a few seconds ahead of Weitz and then Beamish.

The exhausted teammates came together before asking the most important question, "Did we win?"

That question was met with blank faces and doubt. NAU had a strong top four, but Stanford's fifth man had finished eleven spots ahead of NAU's. It didn't look good. The Lumberjacks had lost vital places in the last two kilometers, finishing with 125 points. Since the first edition of these championships in 1938, only three men's teams had won with a higher point total.

"It looks like Stanford got us," Heins speculated to Smith as they waited for their guys to leave the finish chute.

The Lumberjacks emerged from the carnage of exhausted athletes and began a long, silent walk back to their team tent.

The team changed out of their uniforms, removed their spikes with frozen hands, and took occasional bites from the cold pizza in one corner of the tent in overwhelming quiet. The videographer, camera pointed at the floor, stood in another corner.

Trouard broke the silence to encourage his comrades. "Guys, I'm really proud of you all no matter what." A couple teammates looked up to acknowledge the gesture, but most shrugged it off.

Day and alternate runner Harvey Nelson decided to stay outside the tent to avoid being suffocated by the tension inside. It was hard to breathe in there.

It had been twenty minutes since the race finished, and there were still no official team scores. Heins and recent NAU graduate Caleb Hoover were walking back to the team tent with Mann, Cheng, and Campos not far behind when the announcement finally came over the loudspeaker.

"In fourth place with 193 points is Mississippi …

"In third place with 164 points is Syracuse …

"In second place with 158 points is Stanford …

"And your 2016 NCAA cross country national champions with 125 points is Northern Arizona University."

With tears in his eyes and quavering voice, Mann shouted, "Damn! We finally did it!"

Day and Nelson sprinted back to the tent to share the news.

"We won! We won!" they shouted.

Their teammates looked up with hesitation, having gone what seemed an eternity thinking they'd lost.

"I'm serious," Day assured them. "We won!"

The tent erupted as the guys started jumping all over each other. There were tears, hugs, and feelings of disbelief that they'd managed to pull this off. The shift from agonizing loss to stunning victory led to an overwhelming release of pure joy. The videographer raised his camera to capture the magical moment.

Coach Eric Heins holds the trophy he had worked a career to achieve, surrounded by Futsum Zienasellassie (left) and Nathan Weitz.

The NAU men's cross country squad had just won their school its first NCAA national team title for any sport, during the team's fiftieth-anniversary season, in Heins's last race as director. It was the fairy-tale ending they had all dreamed about—the very top of the mountain the Lumberjacks began climbing with Red Haberlack.

The celebrations took a momentary pause as the team realized, almost in unison, the man of the moment was missing.

"Where's Heins?" Trouard asked.

Heins was nowhere to be seen. Then, just as the team started to drop back down to Earth, Heins ran into the tent screaming and was immediately surrounded by his athletes, jumping in the air while chanting, "NAU! NAU! NAU!"

"That's the only reason I lost my voice," Heins told a reporter. "I wasn't screaming during the race. I was screaming after."

Eric Heins (left) and Tyler Day acknowledge their achievement.

When asked how it felt to win NAU its first national team title, Heins responded, "It's an unbelievable feeling. Just so proud of these guys putting it together like this. 'Cause, you know, a lot of pressure on them, a lot of expectations, and to top it off, 'Coach Heins's last race.' What are they going to do? Well, they come out and win the dang thing. Just so proud of them."

Another coach with pride written across his face and in every tear that rolled down his cheek was Smith. The person primed to take over the program was in the perfect place to understand how much this title meant to the team. But Smith still had a job to do. With the season now over, Smith put on his coaching hat and asked Heins, "You want me to get these guys cooling down?"

Heins grabbed a set of van keys, handed them to Smith, and said, "Coach, you're in charge now. If you want to get them to cool down, then let them cool down. You're driving."

What Smith would do with the program in the future was unknown, but his first decision as head coach was one his athletes approved of—don't bother cooling down, just keep celebrating. △

Chapter 15
A Rivalry Is Born

THE FIRST THING MATT BAXTER NOTICED WHEN HE WALKED INTO the student-athlete center after winter break in January 2017 was a five-foot-tall NCAA championship banner hanging from the second-floor railing. While this represented a historic moment in NAU athletics history to most, for Baxter it was a vivid reminder of hours spent grinding through workouts with his teammates to make that day possible.

It had been a year since Baxter and his girlfriend, Emily Roughan, had taken an Arizona Shuttle bus from Phoenix Sky Harbor International Airport and been dropped off in the Dome parking lot. The couple from New Zealand felt fortunate to be given the opportunity to study and compete in the United States.

While Roughan and Baxter were racing at the 2015 Australian Cross Country Championships, Ben Ashkettle—a 2010 NAU graduate who was born in New Zealand but resided in Australia—had called Heins to give his endorsement of Baxter as a recruit. Although Baxter had been talking with Heins already, that conversation had sealed the deal for Roughan, who hadn't been actively looking at college options.

Baxter and Roughan's shuttle was the last one up the mountain before the interstate closed due to a heavy snowstorm. "I remember we couldn't see the Dome from where we parked because of how dark it was and how heavily the snow was coming down," said Baxter. "Thankfully, one of my new teammates was there to pick us up. But I remember getting this awful feeling in my gut as I realized this was where I would spend the next three years of my life. I felt so far from home in that moment."

Baxter's first-day jitters stood in stark contrast to his feelings as he stared at the championship banner a year later. Flagstaff had come to feel like a second home. And six months later, the banner would make Baxter feel even more at home, when teammate and roommate Andy Trouard was given permission to take the banner down and display it in their O'Leary Street house.

Waiting upstairs for Baxter, Mike Smith was now comfortably settled in his new office. After enduring the windowless space across the hall for a semester, Smith had finally claimed his permanent spot with a view of the outdoor track at Lumberjack Stadium. Smith didn't rearrange much in Heins's old office to make it his own, although it did resemble more of a greenhouse, and the copy of *Daniels' Running Formula* was a new addition.

"Come in and take a seat," Smith invited Baxter. "And shut that door behind you."

While Baxter took note of the subtle changes Smith had made, what stood out most was the thing that hadn't changed. On the wall facing Smith's chair hung canvassed photos of every podium finish from the NAU men's and women's cross country teams over the years.

Smith had arranged to meet with Baxter, as he had all his athletes. After spending a semester sitting in the back seat and letting Heins do his job, Smith was taking charge. The purpose of these meetings was for Smith to get to know them on a more personal level. He asked about their families, their interests outside of running, and anything that helped shape them as a person. Some meetings would run more than two hours, which seemed like an incredible commitment, but Smith managed to build the kind of rapport with each athlete in those few hours that other coaches struggle to establish in four years.

This empathetic approach was developed through lessons Smith learned from his mom, a physical education teacher of thirty-five years.

"She would come home from work and tell me about people who were bullied, left out, or didn't have nice clothes," Smith said. "The greatest gift from my mom was teaching me about how other people might be feeling. That's one of the most powerful ingredients in coaching—imagining what someone else must be feeling like. Watching out for people on the fringes who are feeling left out. When you tap into the empathy then speak to the empathy, this leads to a lot of listening. When you respond to them, you meet them where they are. When they know the person in control understands, it changes everything."

While Smith was learning more about each athlete, the athletes were curious to hear more about Smith's expectations for the program moving forward. For the men's cross country team, standing on top of the mountain, it seemed like there was little room for improvement, but that wasn't how Smith saw things. Aside from training changes he intended to introduce, Smith sought to solidly instill his belief that, "If one person isn't doing well, then the whole team isn't doing well."

For the women's program, team culture and helping the runners see a bright future were the major focus. The NAU women had been on the podium before, and Smith made it a priority to get them back to that level.

"We have to do better," said Smith. "I'm not comfortable with the men succeeding and not having the same standard for the women's team."

Having coached a successful women's program at Georgetown University, Smith knew he had the skills to do the same at NAU. With the help of assistant coaches Jarred Cornfield and Becca DeLoache, NAU looked to be entering a new era. And as one era begins, often another one comes to an end.

On March 17, 2017, Leo "Red" Haberlack passed away in Flagstaff at age eighty-four. The man who had planted the seed for the NAU program made sure to stick around long enough to see his roots come to fruition with a national champion team.

Many of Red's family, friends, and former athletes gathered at the Elks Lodge the evening before his funeral to share "Red" stories. Even more attended his funeral at the Catholic Church on McMillan Mesa while the sun highlighted the San Francisco Peaks that Red fondly referred to as "The Mountain."

Red Haberlack, shown here in 1975, made it great to be a Lumberjack.

At the start of every year, Red handed out a packet to his athletes that outlined his expectations for the team. These packets would always conclude with the same phrase, which has never ceased to be true: "It's great to be a Lumberjack."

The NAU men's cross country team was used to taking aim at the best teams in the country, but it was a new feeling for the Lumberjacks to have a target on their backs. They were the defending national champions heading into the 2017 fall season. With five of their top seven returning from 2016, this team had every right to be confident, but so too did their emerging rivals, who didn't hesitate to voice their desire to prevent the Lumberjacks from going back-to-back in November.

While NAU was in Madison, preparing for the Nuttycombe Wisconsin Invitational, the Brigham Young University team was gearing up at Pre-Nationals in Louisville, Kentucky. Running in Louisville gave BYU a taste of the national course, something NAU had also received two weeks prior at the Greater Louisville Classic, where they won with nineteen points. That was also the first time the Lumberjacks employed their "gas" strategy. Smith had told his athletes, "Whenever you have a decision to make in a race, what do you do? . . . Gas."

When Tyler Day and Baxter came through the first mile at Louisville with a healthy lead on the field, a coach shouted to his athletes in the chase pack, "Don't worry, they'll come back."

They didn't.

While "gas" became the chief coaching instruction of the season, the men's team motto was coined during a goal-setting conversation on their annual camping trip at a spot off Lake Mary Road south of Flagstaff. After expressing his excitement for what was ahead and the special group of guys working together to get ready for Louisville, Cade Burks looked at his teammates and blurted out, "We got some *Boys*," an acknowledgement of the special group of friends who were fortunate to also be teammates.

Being the number-one-ranked team in the country carries pressure, and Smith sought to relieve that where he could. So when Day shouted from the back of the van in Madison, "Dude! They have laser tag here. Can we go?" Smith thought back on what he learned from the 2016 cross country team.

"The ways that they were goofy was ultimately what allowed them to execute," Smith acknowledged. "That was one of the greatest lessons for me. For that to all be put together for them to execute in 2016 was affirmation about the absence of tension."

"Let's do it," Smith replied to Day's request.

The night before the Lumberjacks were due to compete in the second-biggest race of their season, they ran around playing laser tag for over an hour. This didn't help lower anyone's heart rate before bed, but it did burn calories from the dessert wheel they downed at dinner.

At the Iowa State Classic earlier in the year, Smith inadvertently started a team tradition by ordering what he thought was going to be a few desserts for the table. The waiter took it upon himself to bring out multiple variations of every sweet on the menu until everyone had something in front of them. Each person took a spoonful, passed it to the person on their right, and continued the wheel until everything was gone.

Geordie Beamish (427) at the 2017 national meet.

Most teams wouldn't opt for laser tag and a dessert wheel the night before a big race, but neither sugar nor exercise was going to inhibit an athlete's preparations more than nerves would. It was impossible to be anxious about a race when half of your team and your athletic trainer—who served two tours with the U.S. Marine Corps—were trying to shoot you with lasers.

This laidback approach to race prep continued to benefit the Lumberjacks as they won the Nuttycombe Wisconsin Invitational with fifty points—twenty-eight lower than they scored in 2016. Trouard, Day, and Baxter all finished within a second of each other to get third, fourth, and fifth, respectively. Not far behind was Geordie Beamish in seventeenth and true freshman Luis Grijalva in twenty-first.

This strong performance from the top five impressed Smith, but he was even more excited about the team's depth. Peter Lomong finished forty-third, while Cory Glines finished seventh in the B race, making a conservative start to racing after nursing an injury. Every one of these guys had shown their capability of being an All-American on the grass. Even after losing a guaranteed low stick and valuable leader in Futsum Zienasellassie, the team was looking better than ever before.

Before leaving Madison for Flagstaff, the NAU team got in their long run on a flat dirt path. When they arrived back at the team vans, Cornfield had the Pre-Nationals race up on his phone. The guys watched as BYU—led by Rory Linkletter, using his thumbs to pop out his singlet and show off the letters "BYU" on the front as he celebrated his individual win—took the team title with just forty-one points.

Peter Lomong gave NAU's 2017 squad depth.

When asked in his post-race interview about his team's motivation heading into the meet, Linkletter replied, "After seeing what Northern Arizona was able to do yesterday, we knew we had to come out and make a bigger statement than that. I don't know if we did, because they did pretty dang good. But we put it out there."

There was a silence in the van before Baxter asked his teammates, "Do they really think that was a bigger statement? He's joking, right?"

Day started having flashbacks to an encounter with some BYU athletes in the hotel elevator after NAU won the 2016 NCAA Cross Country Championships. While holding the national trophy, one of the BYU athletes told Day, "We're coming for that next year."

"It shouldn't have felt personal, but it did," said Baxter of Linkletter's comments. The men may have established NAU as the king of the mountain, but now they had to defend the summit from teams looking to plant their own flag.

NAU's performance at the Nuttycombe Wisconsin Invitational was arguably more impressive than BYU's Pre-Nationals performance based on the depth of the respective fields, but without the two teams going head-to-head, there could only be speculation over which team was better.

At the Western Athletic Conference two weeks later, BYU dominated a strong University of Portland team with a perfect-score performance. Connor McMillan crossing the finish with a line of four other BYU athletes popping their jerseys behind him was the statement Linkletter wanted.

Over at the Big Sky Cross Country Championships, NAU employed their "gas" strategy once again, with Burks serving as a sacrificial lamb to take the Lumberjacks through their first kilometer in 2:49. Baxter and Day once again ran side by side for the entire race, often clipping elbows, until Day won the final sprint for the line. NAU swept both the men's and women's titles, with the men accumulating only nineteen points despite sitting out three of their top seven.

The suspense and hype building around an NAU-BYU showdown at nationals intensified when the two teams faced each other for the first time at the NCAA Mountain Regional Championship. For both teams, this was more of a formality in their season, since they'd already done enough to secure their spots at nationals in eight days. BYU held out Casey Clinger and Daniel Carney, while NAU held out Grijalva. With both teams treating the race as a glorified workout, the result wouldn't be an accurate predictor of the final in Louisville.

While the Lumberjacks won the race with forty-nine points—thirty ahead of BYU—a statement made by BYU athlete Clayton Young in the first hundred meters of the race ramped up the rivalry between the two teams. From four boxes over, Young sprinted off the starting line and cut straight into the middle of the NAU pack.

"I don't know how Clayton got off the line that fast, but that was a bold move to insert himself in the middle of a group of guys who really didn't like the singlet he was wearing," said Baxter.

The race in Louisville was set to be one for the ages. Isaac Wood of The Wood Report said, "This is going to be one of the better showdowns that we've had at NCAAs in a while. I don't think there has been two teams of this level and running this consistently headed for a duel at nationals in a long time."

From the start of the season, Baxter and Day knew what was expected of them at the 2017 NCAA Cross Country Championships. Their job was to take the race out hard while their teammates hung back to pick up the pieces as athletes started to die off. Baxter and Day had practiced this tactic during tempos at Buffalo Park and during their four recent races, where they had finished within two seconds of one another each time. The plan was foolproof.

Then came the wind.

The scheduled start was moved up because of thirty-mile-per-hour winds with gusts of forty-six mph expected by early afternoon. Even with the time change, the Lumberjacks stepped off their bus at Tom Sawyer State Park on race day to fifteen-mile-per-hour winds blowing through the trees. At their tent, Smith pulled Baxter aside to ask if he thought they needed to adjust their tactics.

Baxter watched the leaves dancing behind Smith before replying, "I think we should stick to the plan. If people don't go with us at the start, it'll be even harder for them to catch up in this."

The risk of employing this tactic in wind lay in how the field would respond to the honest effort from the gun. NAU could lose vital points at the end of the race if Day and Baxter were used as glorified pacers while the wind exacted its toll. That was a real fear, but one Day wasn't concerned with. He also agreed the plan should remain in force.

Once that decision had been made, Baxter and Day rejoined their teammates inside the tent. Burks had been designated as the morning's official DJ, and he took his job of keeping the mood light very seriously. The environmental science and philosophy major had also been the catalyst for the biggest team debate of the season, following a question he had posed on the locker room whiteboard: "Who would win in a fight between a trillion lions and the sun?"

The BYU team whiteboard wasn't interested in such musings. At the start of the season, the Cougars wrote "Let's win this flippin' thing" on theirs. BYU wanted nothing more than to spoil the NAU party happening in the tent next to them. With a videographer following their every move and their school mascot, Cosmo, in attendance, they were ready to make program history.

Twenty minutes before race start, the Boys—dressed in all black—made their way over to the starting line. If you were to ask the team why they wore black that day, they'd tell you it was because they were going to a funeral. And if you're the one going to the funeral, then it's not yours.

On this walk, there were no more jokes, no more laughs, and no more smiling faces. Just before reaching the starting line, the team passed BYU's Cosmo holding a sign that read "NAU shortcut," with an arrow pointing away from the course.

"That was possibly their biggest mistake," said Baxter. "I had never been so angry heading into a race before. I already wanted to beat BYU up to that point, but after seeing their mascot holding that sign, I just wanted to make them regret that."

Standing on the starting line in striped blue, white, and yellow adidas singlets that had arrived the night before, the Lumberjacks took a last collective breath while looking out to the long starting straight. It was easy for them to feel confident heading into this championship, but once the starting pistol was raised, confidence had to translate into execution. The first step was surviving the stampede.

The team had split into two lines to fit everyone inside the starting box. How quickly the first line reacted to the gun would dictate the second line's chances for a good position. If a fall was going to happen, it would usually claim someone from the second line who couldn't find space, got squeezed into the pack, and then was taken down by someone who couldn't stay on his feet.

After fighting through injuries to reach the starting line healthy and ready to perform for his team, Glines got caught in a fall at the start. The senior athlete, running in his last collegiate cross country race, suffered a gash to the shin and a cruel flash of déjà vu as he came through the first 400 meters in dead last. In 2016, Glines had recovered from a similar fall and scratched his way back to a scoring position. This time, that wasn't possible. The Lumberjacks had to rely on six athletes to get the job done.

The all-out sprint into position finally settled as the field, hugging the left side of the course, stretched beyond 100 meters in length. While everyone took a deep breath after the initial shock to the system, Day and Baxter asserted themselves at the front and began their painful journey together.

"It's just another tempo at Buffalo Park," Baxter said to Day as they came through the first kilometer shoulder to shoulder.

Matt Baxter (426) and Tyler Day (429) inflict "gas, gas, gas" in the early going of the 2017 NCAA national meet, while the NAU flag waves behind them.

The first team points to be displayed were going to be a good indicator of which teams had positioned themselves well in these early stages. Although Glines had a tough start, the rest of the team was exactly where they needed to be. The Lumberjacks led at two kilometers with 151 points, ahead of Portland in second with 183 points, Syracuse in third with 219, and BYU in fourth with 239. Even though BYU hadn't positioned themselves well, the main pack was dense enough that a few hard moves could change that.

A challenge to the NAU push at the front came at the eleven-minute mark, when Alabama's Gilbert Kigen got tired of NAU controlling the race and made a hard move to leave the field. Day instinctively responded to this challenge before looking back at Baxter, who had chosen to let it go.

"That was a defining moment of the race for us," said Baxter. "I was so confident that if Tyler and I maintained the effort we were already pushing then we would catch Kigen at some point. I didn't know when it would happen, but I knew it would happen. We had to run our race, not his."

Day dropped back to his teammate and the two continued their strategy, albeit from what had become the chase pack. The priority for Baxter and Day was to prevent their pack from settling for a slower pace, so athletes would eventually fall off the back. That would help their teammates in the second chase pack, who were looking for lone runners to hunt down.

There was excitement and concern for the Lumberjacks when the four-kilometer team scores came through. NAU had continued to move up and was still leading with ninety-one points, but BYU had made significant progress to climb into second with 135 points. The Cougars were on the prowl.

The field had split into three main groups at the five-kilometer halfway mark. Kigen was still out on his own with a four-second lead on a chase pack that included Day and Baxter at the front and seven others tucked in behind. The second group contained Lomong, and the third, stretched-out group had Trouard, Grijalva, and Beamish all within a few seconds of each other.

Excited about how his teammates were positioned, Trouard decided to let one of his rivals know about the Lumberjacks' advantage. When passing Linkletter, who was having an off day, Trouard turned and said, "We have five in front of you."

NAU's good position coming into the last big lap didn't mean they were going to ease off. The race plan was "gas," and that was a pedal they intended to push to the finish line.

Day and Baxter kept their heads down and continued to push a steady effort until they closed the gap on Kigen at seven kilometers. The Lumberjacks reasserted themselves at the front of the race and pressed the pace until Kigen fell off the back and only Syracuse's Justyn Knight was left on their tails.

Race strategies don't always go to plan, but the strategy of having Baxter and Day break the field from the front was working better than anyone could have imagined.

Lomong had moved up to a top-ten position, while Trouard and Beamish were sitting in All-American spots. The eight-kilometer team scores showed how the Lumberjacks had continued to move up as other teams began to falter. NAU was leading with sixty-eight points, ahead of BYU in second with 165 and Portland in third with 169. It was going to take a spectacular blowup from NAU or an unbelievable last two kilometers from BYU for the team standings to change.

In 2016, the Lumberjacks waited an agonizing twenty minutes to find out they had won. In 2017, Smith knew the result with one kilometer to go. After all seven athletes had passed him, Smith texted his mom to meet him at the starting line.

"You mean the finish line," she replied.

"No, meet me at the start," he texted back.

A few hundred meters away from the noise and swirling emotions that characterize the finish line of a big cross country meet, Smith and his mom stood where chaos had reigned thirty minutes ago. This time it was desolate, and the only sounds were the wind blowing through the trees and faint screams coming from the distance. Smith wanted to take this moment of calm to thank the person who had supported his success on this day, the days before, and the ones that would come.

"I told my mom how much she was a part of my coaching," said Smith. "How when I was a kid, she taught me how to think about how other people were feeling and that was the lifeblood of my coaching. And I just got to say thank you."

Over at the finish line, an excited group of athletes couldn't wait for their coach to arrive. After a battle up the home straight, Knight took the individual title ahead of Baxter in second and Day in third. Lomong was twenty meters out from the finish when he popped his jersey, poked his tongue out, and then crossed the line in eighth, while his brother, Lopez Lomong, waved an NAU flag from the sidelines.

Trouard was next across the line in thirty-fifth before Beamish with his hands in the air—knowing the team had won—finished in fortieth. Rounding out the team's efforts were Grijalva in sixtieth and Glines in 102nd.

The NAU team camp had already started celebrating before the official scores came through announcing they had won with seventy-four points, ahead of Portland (127) and BYU (165). Smith reached his athletes in time to congratulate them before supporters mobbed them as they exited the finish chute.

It was a perfect day for the Lumberjacks as they successfully defended their title to bring home another national trophy to Flagstaff. The party peaked back at the

Repeat champions, 2017.

Defending the title. Front row, from left: Luis Grijalva, Geordie Beamish, Cade Burks, Matt Baxter. Back row: Athletic Trainer Jeff Trudo, Assistant Coach Becca DeLoache, Andy Trouard, Peter Lomong, Ryan Wolff, Cory Glines, Tyler Day, Harvey Nelson, Graduate Assistant Coach Jarred Cornfield, Head Coach Mike Smith.

team tent, when everyone sang Neil Diamond's "Sweet Caroline" at the top of their lungs while their rivals next door pondered what had gone wrong. It wasn't the day BYU was hoping for, but they weren't going to stop chasing victory. And thanks to an Instagram post from Beamish after the race, the rivalry would only intensify as both teams attacked the spring season. △

Chapter 16
Mounting Pressure

LISTEN UP
Talk, talk, talk
Talk is bullshit
Let those little boys talk …

While Geordie Beamish hadn't weighed in on the team's rivalry with BYU during the 2017 season, after the Lumberjacks returned to Flagstaff he decided to antagonize them with this Instagram post. The comment was intended to be a dig at BYU for vocalizing their desire to win in Louisville without following through on their words. What it became was a rallying cry for the BYU athletes as they headed into the spring season.

The NAU team radiated confidence after their Louisville win. Although the Lumberjacks were the defending champions going into that race, a lot of uncertainty had surrounded how the team would perform under new leadership. Navigating a coaching change isn't easy, especially when the program is on top. Not only did the team make it through the transition, they came out the other side as a stronger and more cohesive unit, something Eric Heins was pleased to see.

"I didn't need to stay for them to keep winning," Heins said. "Coach Smith came in, picked it up, and made it even better."

One of the core reasons Mike Smith was able to come in and make the program better was the way he carried himself. "Mike was such an impressive young man out of the gate," said HYPO2 founder Sean Anthony of his time working with Smith. "He was so thoughtful, insightful, sensitive, inquisitive, and not afraid to show his emotions. Such a genuine person, a gifted listener, and good with people in a way that I've hardly known. The thing that stands out to me most about Mike is how much he cares about developing people. He thinks good running comes from developing good people."

This core tenet of Smith's character began to shine through the NAU team's culture. Smith would tell his athletes, "You don't have to be best friends, but you do have to be good teammates." He set expectations that the athletes would enforce, making them resolve any conflicts internally unless it was necessary for him to step in. This forced the team to take accountability for their collective actions, which put the responsibility of getting along on the athletes themselves.

Any conflicts that arose had to be dealt with immediately before they infiltrated the group. Among the potential threats lurking for any program: cliques, a lack of trust in teammates, an individualistic outlook on training and racing, and a lack of belief in the team's collective goals. Any of these could start as a small fire that, if not extinguished, would engulf the work put in by athletes over decades.

The hardest challenge for the 2018 team was maintaining their blue-collar underdog mentality when they were no longer either of those. NAU was attracting some of the country's finest recruits, support from adidas was noticeably increasing, and the university was located at what was now undeniably recognized as one of the best endurance-training sites in the world.

With the team's changing position in the college athletics pecking order came confidence that expressed itself as cockiness. Andy Trouard's 2018 NCAA Indoor Track and Field Championships' 3000m race was a perfect example of the mood inside the NAU team camp. In the lead with 100 meters to go, Trouard, who had the powerful kicker Justyn Knight on his shoulder, took his eyes off the bend to poke his tongue out at Smith—a gesture to say he knew the title was his. Trouard then clipped the inside rail, but somehow stayed on his feet to hold off Knight for the win.

The team's confidence came to a head when met with the confidence of BYU's Rory Linkletter. After Linkletter won the 10,000m at the 2018 NCAA West Regional Preliminary Round with a flex of his bicep at the line, he took to Instagram to post a photo of the three other BYU athletes who qualified for nationals in the event, provocatively captioning the post #Letthelittleboystalk.

While Baxter wasn't in any place to snap back at Linkletter's post, considering NAU had only qualified two athletes for nationals in the 10,000m, he poked fun at Linkletter's bicep flex in his own Instagram post after winning a qualifying round.

The childish back-and-forth between the two squads resulted in a heated clash at the 2018 NCAA Track and Field Championships in Eugene, Oregon, a week later. Some members of the NAU cross country team who road-tripped to Eugene from Flagstaff antagonized Linkletter with a "flex" chant during most laps of his 10,000m and 5000m races.

What began as a fun rivalry between the two schools was getting personal. Linkletter and Baxter stood out as the main vocal opponents of each other's programs. While the building tension between the two teams quieted down over the summer, it was destined to reignite again as they prepared for battle in the fall.

The scene inside the NAU starting box at the 2018 NCAA Cross Country Championships was organized chaos. With snow covering the course in Madison, Wisconsin, and freezing temperatures expected during the race, the Lumberjacks were doing everything they could to stay warm before the gun went off.

Blaise Ferro, a freshman during NAU's 2016 cross country season, was finally healthy and ready to race in his first national championships. The New Jersey athlete had opted to don just about every article of clothing he could for the race. He wore the insulated underwear Smith handed out the night before, along with the long-sleeve thermal, gloves, and headband.

For some athletes, extra layers of clothing weren't enough. Baxter had experimented in the week leading up to nationals with using Vaseline as an extra layer of insulation on exposed skin. While the results from this experiment were inconclusive, the team was willing to try anything to preserve warmth. The Lumberjacks emptied the tub of Vaseline in their starting box, lathering plenty on their legs to create a thick goo that didn't penetrate the skin.

The cold hit some athletes harder than others. Luis Grijalva had stayed warm in the team tent by standing next to a space heater. It was a logical decision—until he got too close, and his pants caught on fire. The sight of Grijalva running out of the tent to douse the small flame in the snow offered some much-needed comic relief.

When it came time to strip off every layer the athletes wouldn't race in, Baxter realized a mistake he had made. "I overdressed on the warm-up to avoid getting cold, but this meant I ended up sweating a lot. Then when I took all my extra layers off, my racing kit was wet, and I got cold right away. Unsurprisingly, dipping myself in Vaseline didn't solve that problem."

Four Lumberjacks, led by Tyler Day (556), can be seen in this photo of the early going of the snowy 2018 national meet in Madison, Wisconsin.

While the Lumberjacks prided themselves on their ability to perform under any conditions, racing in the snow was something most of them were not accustomed to. Although Flagstaff can experience harsh winters, conditions had remained mild in the buildup to nationals that fall.

During the pre-race athlete press conference, Baxter alluded to the team's race plan looking different than it did in 2017. In reality, the plan was the same. The difference was that Baxter and Day expected a group to go with them. The other

athletes had made a mistake in letting them run away from the field last time, and it was safe to assume their competitors wouldn't make that mistake twice. It was a solid plan based on each athlete's strengths, but the day's wintry conditions would make implementation much more difficult than in 2017.

"After the first kilometer I already knew I was in trouble," said Baxter. "I went to the front as I was supposed to do, but I couldn't relax my breathing after the fast start. The cold air was burning my lungs every time I inhaled. Just when I started to compose myself, Conner Mantz took the pace, and it broke me."

For NAU's plan to dissolve within the first few kilometers was a concerning sign. Day was still sitting comfortably at the front of the field, but Baxter had drifted to the back of that pack, where he found Grijalva. The saving grace for Baxter at this early stage of the race was that three more of his teammates were close by. Ferro, Peter Lomong, and Beamish were all situated toward the front of the chase pack. Everyone was within a few seconds of where they needed to be, a position reflected in the first lot of team scores.

At four kilometers, NAU was leading with fifty points, ahead of Portland in second with 122 points and BYU in third with 149 points. To be leading by this much was not overly surprising, based on the depth NAU had shown during the regular season. After perfect-scoring the George Kyte Classic, the team won the Nuttycombe Wisconsin Invitational with forty-six points (four points better than their 2017 result). Two weeks later, the team went back to Wisconsin for Pre-Nationals.

Due to an excessive number of team entries, the field was divided into two even races. NAU won their race with forty-one points, while BYU won theirs with twenty-nine, leaving fans to once again speculate how the two teams would look in a head-to-head battle.

While the back-and-forth comments between NAU and BYU had remained dormant since the spring, Day reignited the rivalry heading into the NCAA Mountain Regional Championship being held on BYU's home course. In an interview with FloTrack posted a few days prior to the race, Day said, "We are going to get booed by people's grandmothers." The humorous remark was met with a sign in the first kilometer of the race that read, "I'm not booing @ Tyler Day."

Looking to further spice things up heading into nationals, Baxter took a jab at BYU during an NAU team interview at the NCAA banquet two nights before the race.

When asked if the Lumberjacks could say something nice about BYU, Baxter leaned into the microphone and said, "They're good at letting us win."

Baxter's words may not have helped his own race efforts, but they didn't hurt the overall positioning of his teammates. Although BYU had made up ground on NAU by the eight-kilometer mark, the Lumberjacks were still in control and holding their positions. Seeing Lomong smile and Ferro laugh as they rolled into the hardest part of the race was enough evidence for Smith that his squad was doing fine.

Standing at the kilometer-to-go mark was a proud Heins, letting his Lumberjacks know they were about to win their third national title. The joy was evident on his face, as five athletes he recruited were sitting in All-American positions.

It was a fierce battle to the finish up the home straight for the front pack. The University of Wisconsin's Morgan McDonald edged out Stanford University's Grant Fisher to take the win on home soil. Coming in sixth place to lead the Lumberjacks as their first scorer was Day. Although the team couldn't manage three in the top ten like they'd done in Louisville, they did the next best thing and put six in the top forty: Baxter finished in fifteenth, Grijalva twenty-third, Ferro twenty-sixth, Lomong twenty-ninth, and Beamish thirty-ninth.

A third straight national championship warmed up the NAU men on a frigid day in 2018. From left: Ryan Raff, Kyle Havriliak, Geordie Beamish, Tyler Day, Luis Grijalva, Jack Shea, Peter Lomong, and Matt Baxter.

In the immediate aftermath of the 2016 race there was disappointment; in 2017, there was elation; in 2018, relief. The mounting pressure and expectations the Lumberjacks carried throughout the season showed on their faces when they were told they had won. Even their coach wasn't immune to this weight.

"The moment [of winning in 2016] was so special," Smith said. "Since then, some of the feelings afterwards have been relief. I hate saying that, and that's where it gets complicated when you start winning. But that one in 2016 was just emotion and joy. It had the absence of have, must, should."

The expectation that NAU would get it done that day no matter what was one reason Lomong described this win as "the hardest one." It was also why no one gave up. No matter how hard it got, everyone put their head down and kept going because there was no option to quit. "I wasn't doing it for myself. I was doing it for my brothers," said Grijalva.

Winning back-to-back-to-back national titles was an incredible feat for the NAU team. Only five men's teams had accomplished it since the first NCAA Cross Country Championships in 1938. Only twice had a team won four in a row, and no team had maintained a longer streak. The Lumberjacks were knocking on the door of being one of the best collegiate cross country programs ever. Reaching such heights would mean learning to handle pressures and expectations that would only grow as their winning streak continued.

Ed Eyestone was given, in his words, the "keys to the Cadillac" in fall 2000 when he was hired as head coach for the men's cross country team and assistant coach for the men's track and field team at BYU. A four-time NCAA champion during his tenure as a BYU athlete as well as a two-time Olympian, Eyestone had the experience to continue the school's strong distance legacy as its newly minted coach.

"We have a great chance to contend for the national title in a few years," Eyestone told a reporter when he took the job. While not an unrealistic goal, contending for a national title did take a little longer than Eyestone originally thought. "When we finally made it on the podium, the difficult thing was to stay there while also trying to climb it."

A quote from the comedian Steve Martin resonated with Eyestone as he watched the strength of his roster change from year to year: "Perseverance is a great substitute for talent." With three of his top athletes having graduated in spring 2019, Eyestone believed it was perseverance the program would have to rely on for their 2019 cross country season.

It was unfortunate timing for BYU's cross country program to become national title contenders right when NAU hit a hot streak. There were a lot of years when BYU's 2017 or 2018 teams would have carried off a national title, but it was looking like they might have to wait another year, since the 2019 Lumberjacks were on track to be NAU's best contingent yet.

"In 2019 we didn't worry about what NAU was doing," said Eyestone. "It was a foregone conclusion that they were going to win by the media. We didn't get caught up in that because we wanted to get on the podium and there were other really good teams."

Anybody paying attention would have agreed with Eyestone that NAU was a shoo-in to run away with another national title. Although the Lumberjacks had lost three top veterans in Day, Baxter, and Lomong, a talented freshman class would take their places, joining a team that only knew winning. Presumably, the young runners would absorb that positivity and simply "rinse and repeat" the tradition.

FloTrack was one of the media outlets that anticipated the Lumberjacks striking gold a fourth time in November. They contacted the NAU athletic department over the summer for permission to film a documentary about the NAU cross country team's 2019 season. While some athletes felt hesitant because of the unnecessary distractions cameras at practice can bring, the team eventually agreed it would be good exposure for the program and that having cameras around wouldn't change how they went about their business.

The Lumberjacks won the 2019 George Kyte Classic after a strong challenge from visiting Tokai University—the defending champions of the prestigious Japanese race, the Hakone Ekiden. "We decided to participate in the race because we thought it was a rare opportunity for the Hakone championship team and the U.S. cross country championship team to compete," said Tokai assistant Nori Nishide.

NAU's winning streak continued at the John McNichols Invitational at Terre Haute where the Lumberjacks put four athletes in the top six—three of whom were freshmen. A month later they dominated the Nuttycombe Wisconsin Invitational by seventy-four points, with the whole team packing the front of the race. They won the Big Sky Cross Country Championships in miserably cold conditions.

The NAU and Tokai teams took a group photo after the 2019 George Kyte Classic before the Japanese runners ended their altitude camp in Flagstaff and headed home to Tokyo.

The NCAA Mountain Regional Championship further solidified the NAU dynasty coronation. With nationals coming up the following week, NAU vanquished the toughest region in the country with just twenty-one points by putting five athletes in the top ten—first, second, third, sixth, and ninth. Beamish's convincing regional win provided an exciting glimpse into his range, since he'd won the mile at the 2019 NCAA Indoor Track and Field Championships earlier in the year.

As had been the case throughout the history of the NAU program, success breeds success. Still operating with the blue-collar underdog mentality that the men had outgrown, the NAU women were hoping to finally break their ten-year streak of not making nationals.

The hardest part of this journey for these Lumberjacks was reviving their belief that they belonged at nationals and then accumulating the numbers to validate their ambition. Time and time again, they got their hopes up about a season, only to be on the outside looking in, denied a spot at the national meet by a small margin once results from around the country were all tabulated. The guys enjoyed the luxury of approaching regionals as a formality, even holding back their strongest runners. The women had to treat it as the season's biggest race if they wanted any hope of advancing out of their rugged region to compete one more week.

By 2019, Smith had assembled a group of women who were ready to break the streak. At the Nuttycombe Wisconsin Invitational, they finished sixth after coming into the meet with a goal of breaking the top ten. They went on to win their conference meet with thirty-six points before arriving at the always-tough NCAA Mountain Regional Championship in Salt Lake City, Utah, ready to earn their spot at nationals.

After the race, the same uncertainty filled the team that had prevailed in previous years. The Lumberjacks finished in sixth place with 146 points, putting themselves on the dreaded "bubble." Had they performed well enough to win the points for a coveted at-large bid? As the women stood around discussing the race, a nonchalant Smith walked over and shared what he'd just been told. "You're good," he smiled. "You're gonna go to the NCAA meet."

The entire NAU program reveled in this moment of jubilation, as most of the athletes had either experienced the heartbreak or seen it on their teammates' faces when the news hadn't been as encouraging in previous years. For the first time in more than a decade, NAU would be sending a full team to nationals, and Smith was excited about bringing the entire roster along for the ride.

"Live, Laugh, Love."

At the start of the 2019 season, those were the words written on the whiteboard in the NAU men's cross country team's locker room. The sappy personal-growth affirmation resonated with the Lumberjacks—always looking for a bit of twisted humor. Eventually, though, there comes a time when the jokes get put on hold. No matter how foregone the sport's collective conclusion of an NAU four-peat, on the morning of November 15, they still had to perform. All the pressure was on them. As Eyestone said, "It was NAU's to lose."

Smith knew the mounting expectations of his athletes, mixed with their own assumptions that everything would come together on the day, had the potential to be problematic. "The best thing about this team is that they have been there before and done this before. And the worst thing about them is they have been there before and done this before," he said.

It didn't matter how much fun the Lumberjacks had during their regular season; the nerves that accompanied the season's biggest race existed in them the same as anyone else. And, perhaps overlooked by the experts . . . even if NAU had been-there-done-this three times before, the same could not be said about the racing hearts of the four freshmen in their top seven.

The last time NAU had run nationals in Terre Haute was in 2016. A lot of things went wrong that day, but they still managed the win despite a high point total. The team that lined up to try for NAU's fourth national title would have dominated the 2016 team. And as Smith pointed out, they would have likely beaten many other national title–winning teams as well.

"In 2017 I wasn't sure we had the best team; in 2018 I wasn't sure we had the best team; in 2019 I was sure we had the best team," he said.

On a cold and wet Saturday morning in Terre Haute, all eyes were on NAU to see what the best team in program history would do. △

Part 4 – The Dynasty (2019–2021)

Chapter 17

"Let's See How NAU Responds"

IN THE MUDDY MESS OF LAVERN GIBSON CHAMPIONSHIP CROSS Country Course, the scoreboard stated clearly what had been unthinkable all season to the NCAA cross country world: 1. BYU, 109 points; 2. NAU, 163 points; 3. Colorado, 164 points.

The rain had finally settled down, as had the wind. All of the NAU men's team were respectfully dressed for the awards ceremony. Underneath their clean outer layer were legs covered in mud and goosebumps that had yet to subside.

Mike Smith tried to compose himself as he prepared for one of the most important interviews of his coaching career. After taking a deep breath, Smith fronted the FloTrack film crew to address tough questions about a loss he and his staff were still trying to wrap their heads around:

> Our guys are obviously disappointed. We just never got in position. With conditions like this you're not gonna be able to just hit the button and zip forward. Why that happened, I'm not sure. It will require some debriefing when they're not hypothermic.
>
> One of the things I'm unsure of is maybe we've just had a good stretch of easily working into the spot we've wanted to get into, and we just weren't ready for how hard that was going to be today.

The things that get me are some of those guys come up to me and say, "Sorry" ... Only one team can finish second and feel like they let down the country ... That's another part of coaching I look forward to taking on right now and working with these guys. The thing that they have to understand is that this equally comes with the championships and the winning and all the joy they've had the last couple of years. This equally comes with it; it's always come with it, whether they know it or not. This is an important part of their journey.

The whole time I've been here, I've had this file in my head of this fork in the road of our story. It's not just this charmed path of everything we touch turns to gold. It was never gonna be like that. This to me is ultimately the real sign of a team. It's not what you do when you're on top of the mountain forever. It's moments like this. So, let's see how NAU responds.

Each athlete on the NAU team dealt with the loss differently. While most left town within a few days of arriving back in Flagstaff to spend Thanksgiving with their families, Drew Bosley sat in an empty campus dorm room. He was haunted by endless thoughts of the race; there was still a lot of decompressing to do.

Teammate Jimmy Fitzgerald had stayed in Flagstaff too. He offered Bosley a time-honored way to work out his emotions.

Emerging from opposite holes in the fence of Cardinal Field, Fitzgerald and Bosley met up to get in some easy laps. Named after the Arizona Cardinals NFL football team, who used it as summer training camp to escape the Phoenix heat for more than two decades, these two grass football fields on NAU's south campus are the best place to log easy miles in Flagstaff. The luscious grass gets a modest watering from the university sprinklers, making it perfect for athletes who want to kick off their trainers and enjoy the most natural way of running. The unofficial NAU team rule of Cardinal Field is that running must be easy.

During the football season, the NAU band uses the turf field below where Bosley and Fitzgerald were jogging to practice their on-field routines. Often, a run around Cardinal is accompanied by the same thirty-second drumbeat played over and over, as if to emphasize the mindless repetition of doing countless laps.

The emotions Bosley felt prior to and during the race in Terre Haute were still raw in his body as he opened up to Fitzgerald on their run. Lying in bed at night,

Bosley's brain would replay a movie of how he'd felt at the start of the race. "I was going through waves of being super calm and composed and then feeling like I was going to shit my pants," he said.

Talking out loud about the race proved therapeutic for Bosley. Throughout the entire cross country season, he had been diligent about filling out his log—a private online document each NAU athlete completed daily to track how they felt during and after training sessions, how they slept, and their mileage that day. This document is only visible to their coaches, so athletes are free to be open, knowing their thoughts escape the eyes of their teammates. After nationals, Bosley's log for that day was left blank.

"I didn't know how to put how I felt into words," Bosley said. "Maybe if we won, then I would have had something to say."

Drew Bosley was the top overall freshman finisher in the 2019 NCAA national meet in which NAU finished second as a team.

Of all the NAU athletes who lined up in Terre Haute, Bosley should have been the least disappointed with his effort. The top scorer for NAU, the top freshman in the race, he handled the conditions better than any of his teammates. But the group's pain dampened his ability to appreciate any personal accomplishment at the time.

After a few days of processing his memories, Bosley began to see the positives in feeling so down when the team got second. He realized how much people care about NAU cross country and are invested in seeing the program succeed. That was something Bosley could appreciate, considering it wasn't the case for all college programs around the country.

"I am proud to be on one of the programs that people care about," expressed Bosley. "It is a privilege for people to care about what you do."

The biggest learning curve for Bosley and the other Lumberjacks following their 2019 season was that regardless of the outcome at nationals, a season could still be viewed as a success based on other metrics. Hard though it may be to swallow, getting outclassed by a strong team at one race didn't negate the enjoyment of the rest of the season. The ability to embrace this view reflected the continuing improvement in team culture under Smith's leadership. Chasing team titles on the grass requires athletes to be selfless and always put the team first. This was clear in the work ethic the team showed on Bosley's recruiting visit to NAU.

"Everyone seemed in sync when working out together on my visit. It was an inviting feeling. Something that you want to be a part of," he said.

Bosley was impressed by the genuineness of the team's interactions with him on that first visit—another sign that NAU was the right place for him. Everyone on the team came up to him at one point or another to introduce themselves, express their appreciation for him coming to check out their school, and say they hoped he would enjoy his trip.

As Bosley and Fitzgerald finished off their last lap around Cardinal, both felt better about the weekend's experience and the future of the NAU program. They knew one second-place finish would not define the team. It took the NAU program more than half a century to reach the point where second place was an unexpected disappointment.

As Bosley jogged back to his dorm room, he acknowledged there was nothing he could do to rewrite history. NAU's winning streak came to an end on a miserable day in Terre Haute. But any winning streak begins with a single win. Next fall, they could begin the streak once more. With that in mind, Bosley finished his run with a quiet smile on his face.

The indoor season comes at an awkward time for teams that put a lot of energy into cross country. After taking a deserved break for the remainder of November, athletes have December to get back into reasonable fitness before the condensed racing block that runs from January through late February. During this racing block, the focus for top-tier athletes is to run fast times to qualify for the NCAA Indoor Track and Field Championships in mid-March. Unlike the outdoor season that progresses from a preliminary round to nationals, indoor season qualification for nationals is solely based on time.

After an emotionally draining end to the cross country season for the NAU men's distance crew, it was hard to tell if they would be ready to attack an indoor season or if it would take the spring outdoor schedule for their motivation to return.

For Tyler Day, excitement about a big track season had been brewing since he last raced in an NAU singlet during spring 2019. Unable to compete in Terre Haute because he no longer had cross country eligibility, Day had to endure the team's loss from the sidelines, feeling helpless as he watched his friends struggle through the mud. When the opportunity to race in an NAU singlet again finally came around, he was more fired up than ever.

It's unusual for the team to travel to the East Coast for an indoor race due to the high cost, but Smith knew Day, Luis Grijalva, and Geordie Beamish were in great shape and needed to be pushed in a race set up to go fast. Lining up on the famous Boston University track for the John Thomas Terrier Classic on January 24, the three NAU athletes were looking to get their NCAA indoor qualifiers done and perhaps walk away with some nice personal bests at the same time.

The decision to send this trio to Boston ended up being one of the best decisions Smith ever made during an indoor season. Day rewrote the history books with a stellar performance, challenging Paul Tanui, 2016 Olympic Games silver medalist in the 10,000m, for the win. Although Day finished just short of the 5000m gold, his time of 13:16.95 shattered the NAU school record held by David McNeill and was the fastest time ever by an American collegian—the previous best was 13:18.13 by Oregon's Galen Rupp.

Grijalva joined Day in securing his spot at NCAA Indoors with a time of 13:29.74—a new Guatemalan national record. Beamish narrowly missed earning a spot at the NCAA Indoor Championships in Albuquerque, running 13:51.14.

NAU had come out of the gates flying, and they weren't even close to being done. Inspired by their teammates, Abdihamid Nur and Ryan Raff wanted to secure spots on the starting line in Albuquerque. But they weren't going to try for it on one of the fastest tracks in the world. They were going to try and qualify the hard way.

Taking a deep breath in the Dome can be more stressful than relaxing. With every door closed to the frigid temperatures outside, the ventilation system saps nearly every ounce of moisture from the already dry air. If the rolling door is open, runners experience an uncomfortable blast of cold air every time they come into the final bend. There's no such thing as perfect conditions in the Dome, only differing degrees of challenge.

NAU teammates Nur and Raff were coughing as they warmed up for the 5000m at the Mountain T's Invitational on January 31. Moistening their throats with frequent sips of water after every seventy-meter pick-up stride, they tried to delay the inevitable dry mouth that would lead to a hack-like cough affectionately dubbed "Dome lung." Countless hours spent training on this track gave them the advantage and disadvantage of knowing the kind of pain that awaited them over this fourteen-minute race.

Embracing each other one last time, Nur and Raff took their spots on the starting line. As a single goal united their minds—qualifying for NCAA Indoors—the gun fired. The two NAU athletes exploded off the line, undeterred by being the only participants in the race. It isn't uncommon to have limited fields for early-season home track meets, but just two people was exceptionally small by any standard.

There are two benefits to racing in the Dome for the NAU team. First, it is close and therefore saves traveling out of state to find another adequate indoor facility. Second, times run at 800m or more are granted an altitude conversion. Since the NCAA Indoor Track and Field Championships were due to be held in Albuquerque, New Mexico, on March 13–14, there was real merit in trying to qualify for the championships through a race in the Dome. Albuquerque's 5,312 feet of elevation meant that even if an athlete qualified for the championships at sea level, there was no telling how they would handle racing at altitude if their body wasn't used to it.

The NCAA adjusts times run at elevation using a chart that equates a raw elevation time to a time run at sea level. The Dome's position at 6,900 feet gifts a healthy conversion for anyone who races there. The conversion given to an altitude time is based on elevation, distance, and the time it takes to cover that distance.

For example, a male athlete running a mile in the Dome will get an approximate nine-second conversion. Therefore, a 4:09 mile in Flagstaff is equivalent to a 4:00 mile at sea level.

Nur and Raff wanted to make the most of the altitude conversion available to them. All they had to do was run a time that would keep them ranked in the top sixteen by the end of the qualifying period. The plan was to go out at 14:10 pace (unconverted) and hang on for as long as they could. If they finished anywhere close to that time, they should be safe.

Racing in an NAU singlet meant a little more to Nur than it did for most. His journey onto the team was filled with hurdles many others in his position wouldn't bother to jump. Born in Somalia, Nur had an unusual transition into the sport of running. After moving from Somalia to Kenya to Egypt, Nur arrived in the United States as a sixth-grader with a passion for soccer. "Soccer was my life," said Nur. "My whole family played soccer." With seven siblings, it wouldn't have been hard for Nur to find someone to kick a ball around with.

After spending time in New Mexico and Minnesota, Nur moved to Phoenix his freshman year of high school, where he continued to play soccer, but the high level of competition made it difficult to stand out. In his sophomore year, Nur was in a car accident that required him to hang up the soccer cleats for six months. His soccer coach assured him if he competed in cross country during the fall, he would be ready for soccer again come spring, and it would be a good way to maintain his endurance.

Nur wasn't sold on the idea. "I hated cross country," he said. "I hated the shorts, turning up to practice, and I didn't understand the idea of going for an eight-mile run."

It was on a trip to Flagstaff when Nur started to show potential. Over a tough Buffalo Park loop, he placed third in an early-season high school race, running seventeen minutes for 5000m. Afterward, Nur's coach said he had potential to be very good. Nur didn't buy it.

Once spring rolled around and Nur rejoined soccer, he hurt his knee in practice, and his dreams of pursuing that sport drifted away. It was a tough choice, but Nur decided to give this running thing a real go.

"I came up to Flagstaff for a camp in my senior year, and by this point I loved the city, as I had been up there a few times before," said Nur. He met Smith at that NAU camp. Special guests and speakers included two-time Olympic medalist Nick Willis, four-time (eventually five-time) Olympian and fellow Somali-born Abdi Abdirahman, Olympian Kim Conley, and legendary coach Ron Warhurst. It was at this camp that Nur fell in love with running.

After a successful senior year highlighted by a state cross country title, Nur set his eyes on joining a college team. There was only one problem. After neglecting his schoolwork, Nur didn't have the grades necessary to get into any of the colleges he applied for. "I didn't know I was messing up my future doing this," Nur said about frequently skipping class in his early high school years. "Had I just gone to class, I would have got into college."

Despite the challenges, Nur desperately wanted to join the NAU team. Undeterred by the possibility that his attempt might be futile, Nur moved to Flagstaff in fall 2017 and began studying at Coconino Community College. With the encouragement of his family and Smith, Nur made it through his first year at CCC and was accepted into NAU as a student. However, an NCAA rule required Nur to complete a year of schoolwork at NAU before he could be eligible to compete. "I never had any idea if I would actually make the team," said Nur.

In fall 2019, after two years of trying, Nur finally earned his spot on the NAU track and field and cross country team. To say Nur was grateful to get this far would be an understatement. The beaming and infectious smile he brought to practice every day told his teammates more about how happy he was to be on the team than words ever could.

The work didn't stop for Nur once he made the team. Originally not planning on racing Nur in his first season with the Lumberjacks, Smith saw the progress he was making and placed him on the starting line in Terre Haute for the 2019 NCAA Cross Country Championships.

Nur had fought to make the NAU team like it was something he needed in life, when—in reality—it was the NAU team that needed him. Being the second Lumberjack home in Terre Haute was an unexpected result for Nur, but it was also a sign of things to come.

A roar of support engulfed Nur and Raff as they came down the home straight with one lap to go at the Mountain T's Invitational. In the lead and starting to put some ground on his teammate, Nur could hear Smith's voice inside his head, telling him, "What are you going to respond with?" After the tough second place finish for the team in Terre Haute just two months prior, Smith rhetorically asked his athletes how they planned on responding to that loss. This became a key source of motivation for the men as they moved toward the indoor season. "I didn't think we were going to respond as fast as we did," laughed Nur, thinking about his teammates' efforts in Boston.

The team cheered as Nur crossed the finish line in 14:18.07 with Raff close behind in 14:19.31 (both times unconverted). The two had successfully secured their spots as first-time NCAA indoor qualifiers and brought the number of NAU athletes who had qualified for the 5000m up to four.

NAU's 2020 indoor season was far from over after a great racing block in January. Next on the schedule was the Millrose Games in New York City, where Beamish secured his spot at NCAA Indoors in the mile by running 3:56.90. Before Beamish silenced them by winning the mile at the NCAA Indoor Championships the year prior, his teammates teased him about being the only athlete in the field who hadn't broken four minutes. Since he had qualified in the Dome, it was a converted sub-four effort that got him there. That wouldn't be the case this year for the defending champion.

Beamish's performance in New York helped the team receive its first ever top-ten indoor ranking by the U.S. Track & Field and Cross Country Coaches Association. NAU was used to being ranked in cross country, but they'd always been left out of the conversation when it came to track because of the program's lack of depth across all event groups.

A top-ten ranking was nice, but the NAU team wasn't done yet. Beamish stretched the NAU school budget to stay back East for another week after the Millrose Games until Day and Grijalva joined him in Boston for a fast 3000m. This time, Grijalva experienced the true magic of the Boston University track at the David Hemery Valentine Invitational by winning the race in 7:43.73, earning him a new school record and another Guatemalan national record.

Beamish backed up his mile performance with a 7:44.67 result—just half a second off the New Zealand national record, with Day coming in a close third running 7:45.70, which safely secured his spot at NCAA Indoors alongside Beamish and Grijalva for the 3000m.

On the other side of the country, Blaise Ferro put together a great 5000m performance at the Husky Classic in Seattle, Washington, running 13:39.58 and becoming the fifth NAU athlete to qualify for NCAA Indoors in that event. This performance meant NAU would make up nearly a third of the 5000m field in Albuquerque.

Joining Ferro in Washington was Theo Quax, who lined up in the mile. His time of 3:58.13 originally ranked him seventeenth—just outside of qualification—but with three eventual scratches from the mile, he squeaked in as the fourteenth qualifier and the final NAU athlete to qualify for the championships.

Quax's performance was special not only because it was his first sub-four performance but also because it put him in the history books with his dad. They became New Zealand's first father-son duo to break four minutes in the mile. Quax's dad, the legendary Dick Quax, was no stranger to the record books. In 1977, he broke the world record for the 5000m in Stockholm, running 13:12.9 a year after getting second in the 5000m at the 1976 Montreal Olympics. This was the perfect way to round out the group representing NAU in Albuquerque.

During NAU's three-week hot stretch of racing, the U.S. Track and Field and Cross Country Coaches Association ranked the Lumberjacks as the number-one team in the country for two weeks straight. Getting ranked tenth was a special recognition; getting ranked first was almost unbelievable. No one ever predicted that an all-distance-qualified squad could contend for an indoor national team title. The schools that usually win are programs that place people in nearly every event on the track and in the field, not in just three.

For the first time in school history, the Lumberjacks could approach NCAA Indoors in a similar way to how they approach cross country—as a team.

"We joked about eyeing up a long jumper or talking trash at the high jump mats," laughed Quax.

The idea of challenging the country's most well-rounded programs was fun to entertain. Quax didn't see any reason why the NAU team couldn't make the podium if the guys performed as expected in their events.

What better way to respond to a tough cross country season than that? △

Chapter 18
A Short Trip to Albuquerque

MIKE SMITH WAS SMILING AS HE PULLED THE WHITE PASSENGER VAN into the Dome parking lot. By now he was used to the sight of giddy athletes congregating here; the excitement of a road trip with friends was too much for any of them to hide. Athletes who were forward-thinking enough to get on top of their schoolwork had earned this break from the stressors of normal college life. On this trip to Albuquerque, they would live like professional athletes for a few days, which was fitting considering they'd been training as such the whole season.

A childlike enthusiasm filled the air as the guys joked back and forth about anything but running.

A few roommates/teammates who had served as Uber rides that morning lingered well after their drop-off duties were complete. They wanted to see their friends off and wish them well on a trip all of them wished they could take themselves. The NCAA Indoor Track and Field Championships is usually an intimate trip for the select few who qualify. However, after an outstanding couple of months for the NAU men's middle and distance runners, the traveling squad resembled a cross country team more than it did a track team.

After Geordie Beamish won the mile at the 2019 NCAA Indoor Track and Field Championships at the Birmingham CrossPlex, those who didn't qualify for the 2020

Championships had vowed to go to Albuquerque to watch their teammates compete. Nobody wanted to miss a moment like the one that went down in Alabama. Coming into 270 meters to go, Beamish unleashed a monster kick. With his luscious locks fanning out behind him, reminiscent of a young Sir John Walker—the legendary former world record holder from his native New Zealand—Beamish never relinquished the lead. Crossing the line with his arms out to his sides and a stunned look on his face, Beamish stamped his name in the history books.

Aside from Blaise Ferro, none of the guys standing outside the Dome could relate to what it was like to battle constant injuries during their collegiate career the way Beamish could. Hurt immediately after the 2018 cross country season, Beamish hit a real low point, unmotivated to endure another season he felt would undoubtedly end prematurely on the sidelines. It had happened every other track season, so why would 2019 be any different?

Overcoming the self-doubt eating away at him was Beamish's only option as he approached the 2019 indoor season. This incredibly talented athlete with wicked closing speed could endure the pain of a mile better than most. When he crossed the finish line in Alabama, it wasn't a surprise to his teammates. They knew the engine hidden inside, having seen it at workout after workout.

Beamish's finishing flourish over the last 200 meters in Birmingham was a thing of beauty. It was not panicked or outrunning demons so much as it was opening his stride and running free, as if to finally punish the years of ailments that had tormented him.

With one NCAA individual title already under his belt, Beamish was looking to add two more to his résumé during his final season as a Lumberjack. For the 2020 indoor and outdoor seasons, it appeared nothing could stop a healthy Beamish from claiming what was his.

Of the seven NAU athletes who would compete in Albuquerque, three were favorites for an NCAA individual title. Tyler Day held the NCAA leading time in the 5000m (13:16.95), as did Luis Grijalva in the 3000m (7:43.73). Beamish was the defending mile champion with a season best of 3:56.90. At this unmissable championship, NAU would be a dominant force with a genuine chance at making the podium as a team, solely on the legs of their distance crew. If things broke right, they might reach the top of the mountain in early spring as they had done three times in the fall.

Smith jumped out of the driver's seat and opened the back doors of the van. "Time to load up," he told his athletes.

One by one, the guys picked up their duffels and tossed them in the back. With Smith at the wheel, athletic trainer Jamie Spicuzza in the passenger seat, and seven excited athletes on board, the van exited the Dome parking lot to begin the five-hour trip straight east on Interstate 40 to New Mexico.

For the teammates left standing in front of the Dome, it was a tough goodbye. They wanted so desperately to jump in their cars and convoy to Albuquerque to support their teammates over the weekend. But despite their vow after Beamish's Birmingham win, they couldn't. The NCAA had released a statement just two days prior saying only family members of athletes would be allowed to attend this year's championship due to concerns of a strange, novel coronavirus beginning to make its way around the world.

No matter how much this team felt like a family, that wouldn't be enough to get these athletes in the doors at the Albuquerque Convention Center to watch their brothers compete. If Beamish set the track on fire with another stellar finish, those left behind would have to enjoy that moment together in front of a screen, as they did the year before.

The road trip to Albuquerque was filled with mixed emotions for everyone inside the van. Before departing the Dome, the team already felt that external forces were trying to put a damper on their trip, even if their demeanor didn't hint at that. They'd spent the past few weeks trying to ignore constant news coverage about the virus and focus on their training, so a few more days of exactly that shouldn't have been an effort. But as parts of the globe became hot spots for the virus, the news was inescapable. The horror they'd been trying to ignore was soon knocking at their door.

The guys knew how lucky they were to leave the Dome parking lot; not everyone was fortunate enough to get that far into their trip to NCAA Indoors. Ten minutes before they were due to head for the airport, Harvard athletes Anna Juul, Abbe Goldstein, and Kieran Tuntivate were informed their school had scratched them from their events. They would not be allowed to travel to Albuquerque because of safety concerns.

Devastated, all three athletes took to Instagram to express their frustrations at how the situation was being handled. Tuntivate posted a photo of himself finishing an indoor race with the caption, "I didn't know it at the time, but this was my last race for Harvard."

By midday March 11, not long before an excited NAU crew left Flagstaff, the Ivy League Conference announced that all their spring sports were canceled. Some institutions within the conference also told students not to return to campus after spring break, as their classes would be online for the remainder of the semester.

The situation with the coronavirus disease, also referred to as COVID-19, was evolving so rapidly that a decision to take a van full of athletes to Albuquerque went from being a good idea on Tuesday to a questionable one on Wednesday. It became even more so just hours before the team left the Dome.

The difficult part was that most questions didn't have answers. Without NAU or the Big Sky Conference forcing Smith to turn the van around, it made sense in the moment to continue with the journey and not force these athletes to miss one of the biggest athletic opportunities of their collegiate careers.

In the weeks leading up to this trip, there wasn't much talk among NAU athletes about COVID-19. This was not an attempt to dismiss its severity and the growing devastation it caused. Rather, to talk about COVID-19 was to acknowledge that all the training these guys had logged during the season, and the big goals they were in position to achieve, may not come to fruition. To talk about COVID-19 was to accept that an external force may dictate the outcome of their hard work. To talk about COVID-19 was to risk losing a race before it even started. No one wanted to speak into existence their worst fears.

Not until the Big Sky Indoor Track and Field Championships two weeks earlier in Pocatello, Idaho, did the coaching staff meet to discuss concerns about the spread of COVID-19. That same weekend at the U.S. Olympic Marathon Trials, President Donald Trump interrupted the live stream of the race to report the first death of an American from COVID-19. It had been a little over a month since the first confirmed case of the virus within the country.

"Things started to change every day leading up to the championship in Albuquerque," said NAU Assistant Coach Jarred Cornfield. "We talked about protocols a bit, but not much."

Partway into their drive, in the middle of nowhere on I-40 heading east, Ryan Raff came across a concerning video on his phone. Utah Jazz basketball player Rudy Gobert had just tested positive for COVID-19, and the NBA announced it would be suspending the remainder of the season.

As Raff continued scrolling through news stories, he began to think to himself, "Can we run this one race and still be safe? And get home safe?" Eventually he came across a statement by the World Health Organization, declaring COVID-19 a pandemic.

"How serious the team took the virus lasted about the length of the van ride," said Theo Quax. What had started out as a low-level concern quickly escalated to a high-level threat.

What should have been a fun drive quickly turned into one filled with fear and uncertainty for what might happen beyond this weekend. None of the team's sessions with HYPO2 sports psychologist Shannon Thompson could prepare them for competing while the world around them was crumbling. Staying focused on just the race ahead would prove nearly impossible.

It was a beautiful fifty-two degrees in Albuquerque when some of the guys left their hotel for a French breakfast spot across the street. Absent from the meal were Beamish, Day, and Grijalva, who were driven by Smith to their ESPN media commitments.

"We were so carefree at breakfast," said Quax, acknowledging the stark contrast to the team's demeanor the day before.

At around 12:30 p.m. on March 12, the Lumberjacks arrived at the Albuquerque Convention Center to begin their pre-meet warm-up of an easy run followed by hurdles, mobility, drills, and strides. This would be only the second time racing on a banked track for some. It was helpful to get a feel for the sharp corners and short straights before race day.

Mastering the banked track wasn't the only challenge awaiting them as they walked into the facility. Right away, Abdihamid Nur could tell something was off. "As soon as you got into the building you could feel the tension," he said. "People were scared and not talking much." After a morning break from the realities of COVID-19, the team was once again forced to deal with its existence.

With the situation surrounding COVID-19 evolving so rapidly, coaches were scrambling to develop protocols to keep their athletes safe. Teams were kept away from one another, elbow bumps replaced the usual handshake, and athletes awkwardly sidestepped each other in the restrooms.

Undeterred by the weirdness around them, NAU set up camp on the infield of the track and began their usual warm-up. With just enough space each, the guys grabbed their team-issued ropes out of their backpacks and began active isolated stretching (AIS), which opened every warm-up for them as surely as the sun rose each morning.

After a three-mile run outside, the guys headed back to the convention center. On their way in, the Lumberjacks passed groups of athletes leaving. Nur thought they were going back to their hotels after finishing their pre-meet; in actuality, they were heading home. The Atlantic Coast and Big Ten conferences had pulled their athletes from the championships.

"There is no way the Big Sky Conference will pull us," joked Quax. "We love them, and they love us."

Standing next to the NAU team was a Louisiana State University athlete who felt similarly about his own conference. "The SEC is still here," he shouted. "Don't you worry, the SEC is still here!"

After finishing their hurdles and drills, Grijalva, Day, and Beamish threw on their spikes to do an 800m tempo on the track before some hard strides. Cornfield stood on the infield with his phone out to record the three athletes as they came flying by at a controlled effort.

Nur could tell that the focus on his teammates' faces was different from what he had seen before. "Smith was trying to keep everyone relaxed, but I could see Geordie and Luis were looking really antsy. It was like someone popped the happiness bubble in the room."

The Lumberjacks had been dreaming about this weekend since they started to set the indoor season ablaze. They tried so desperately to maintain tunnel vision that none of them realized the light they'd been moving toward was slowly fading into darkness.

The guys were in the middle of doing strides when Gordon Mack from FloTrack came over to tell them that the meet—and the upcoming outdoor track season—had been canceled.

As this news circulated through the team, everyone splintered. Beamish retreated to a corner of the arena to digest the fact that his time as an NAU athlete was over.

After endless setbacks during his career, to finally be in a good place and never get an opportunity to show it was crushing.

"We were devastated," said Raff. "It sucked the energy out of everyone."

Raff joined athletes from other schools in running a few hard efforts, reflexively, to blow off steam. He was soon followed by Quax, Grijalva, and Nur. Nobody knew how to handle the situation. The way some of these guys had dealt with tough moments in the past was to run, so run they did.

Once all the adrenaline had drained from their bodies, hopelessness settled in. "I felt horrible," said Quax. "But some of these guys had put themselves in positions to win their event. If I felt this bad, I couldn't imagine how bad they felt."

Mack approached Smith for a comment. When asked about his reaction to the entire spring season being canceled, Smith answered in his usual optimistic way. "It's a privilege to have sport be the biggest thing in your world," he told Mack. "If we're worrying about games, our lives are pretty good."

As Smith answered these questions, his eyes continued to monitor his athletes sitting beside the track. Smith guided Mack's camera to the situation and highlighted Grijalva. "That's a guy who is in tears right now because of how badly he wants to do this."

For Day, his college career had been a fairy-tale story of a mediocre high school athlete transformed into a star. Eric Heins took a chance on recruiting an outgoing, red-haired goofball from Gilbert, Arizona, and it was one of the best coaching decisions he ever made. Day was integral to the NAU cross country three-peat, became a school record holder in the indoor 5000m, and was on the verge of winning an individual national title. Instead of capping off his unexpected college career in glory, he sat alone. The endless energy that was always his trademark was now nowhere to be seen.

"I grinded for five years and I was starting to really hit my stride," Day said. "This was the first time in my life that I felt like I had a chance and I really believed in myself. The one thing that was missing for me was an individual national title, and I was so confident that I could do it. After hearing the news, I knew my days as an NAU Lumberjack were over."

Smith let the guys take time to come to terms with the situation before he told them to collect their things and head to the van. Just four months earlier, when Smith posed the question of "What are you going to respond with?" to the guys at the end of the 2019 cross country season, no one could have foreseen this—leaving the NCAA Indoor Track and Field Championships, heads held low, lumps in their throats, and not even stepping on the track in competition.

The dark and empty expanse beyond the headlights was a perfect match for the silence inside the van as it retraced the miles driven less than twenty-four hours earlier, back through Grants, Gallup, Winslow, and the wide-open spaces of the Navajo Nation and Painted Desert. Ferro curled up with his head against the cold window listening to music through his headphones, bathing in a different emotion than the rest of the team. Having dealt with a sore back for most of the season, a canceled meet came as a relief in some ways. But that didn't encompass Ferro's full spectrum of feelings.

Failing to make it to the end of multiple seasons because of injury, he had developed a coping strategy of quickly moving on from disappointment to accepting the situation and switching his focus to what would come next. This was helpful at times in projecting a sort of resigned optimism and calm resolve in the face of external factors, yet it didn't always match how he truly felt on the inside.

"I was hiding from myself about how much I loved the sport," he said.

For his part, Nur was at the opposite end of the coping spectrum: struggling with the uncertainty ahead, he was blind to any light at the end of this long tunnel. After working harder than anyone else in the van just to earn a spot on this team, Nur considered whether the journey had been worth it.

"I felt like I waited so long to compete for the team, just to wait again and not know how long it'd be," he said.

For a team starting to reach unprecedented heights, the musings during this van ride would determine the program's future. The questions swirling in the young men's heads weren't yet formulating into decisions that had to be declared right now. But the downward spiral in Nur's mind was indicative of the larger cause for concern when it did come time to make them.

"Maybe this isn't worth it," Nur thought to himself. "If this goes on and I don't compete this fall, I don't see any reason for me to keep running. I'll just get my degree, find a job, and head back home. If COVID is going to do this, maybe it wasn't meant for me." △

Chapter 19
One Last Effort

A TIRED THEO QUAX SCOURED THE FRY'S GROCERY STORE FOR SOMETHING to satisfy his hunger. Hunched over the shopping cart, pushing reluctantly, he couldn't find anything that piqued his interest until the candy aisle.

After a late night of driving back from Albuquerque, and an even later night to blow off steam once the team arrived in Flagstaff, it was surprising that Quax had the energy to haul himself to the supermarket even by late morning the next day. He was ready to drown his sorrows in chocolate and ice cream, even though he knew the impending sugar high was only going to eventually make him feel worse.

As Quax was making his way to the checkout, a call came through from Luis Grijalva.

"Hey, what are you doing right now?" Grijalva asked.

"I'm just at the supermarket," Quax replied. "You wanna play video games?"

"Nah, I'm doing a hard mile. Do you want to come pace me?"

Quax was quick and blunt with his response. "No, I don't."

Smith had given the team an opportunity for one last effort before everyone headed home for the remainder of the semester. Quax saw little appeal to such an offer. His mind had been fixed on performing for the team in Albuquerque. Without a team title to fight for, he was willing to call it a season and start looking toward the next goal—whatever . . . and whenever . . . that may be.

Not everyone felt the same way. Grijalva bought into the idea of rounding out the season. "We can do a hard workout, a mile time trial, or even a 3k," Smith told the team. A hard workout wasn't going to give Grijalva the stimulus he was looking for, and a 3000m time trial seemed too long.

"Let's do a mile," Grijalva told Smith.

With Smith in agreement, Grijalva tried to recruit some teammates as pacers. If Grijalva knew how little sleep Quax was operating on since the team had arrived back in Flagstaff, perhaps he would have called someone else—possibly someone who would have said yes.

It wasn't as if Grijalva was giving Quax a lot of notice. He was planning to start his warm-up that same afternoon with an estimated 4 p.m. start time for the mile. That way, he would be racing when the 5000m final would have taken place at the now-canceled NCAA Indoor Track and Field Championships.

Although Quax couldn't think of anything worse than what Grijalva was asking, he got a sense from his friend's tone of voice that this meant a lot to him. "It seemed like he was pretty crushed by me telling him no," said Quax.

After their conversation ended, a brief text exchange ensued before Grijalva called Quax once again.

"I need your help," pressed Grijalva. "It would mean a lot to me if you came out. I don't want to do this solo."

Quax may have mentally checked out from all things running by this point, but the desperation in his teammate's voice was too much to ignore.

"Sure man, I'll be there," he told Grijalva. "I just have one question—what pace are we going at?"

Grijalva's teammates couldn't quite understand his burning desire to extend his season to one more race. A near-solo effort in the Dome with no crowds, no media, and no official timing would render a result no one else saw the point in chasing. COVID-19 was stirring so much uncertainty about the future that people were struggling to think beyond the day they were in.

Uncertainty about the future was a weight Grijalva had carried his entire life. He'd been brought to New York City from Guatemala as a one-year-old so his dad could find better work opportunities. When he was three years old, his family moved to California, where he spent the rest of his childhood.

Without proper documentation for his presence to be considered legal within the United States, Grijalva applied for DACA (Deferred Action for Childhood Arrivals) status, which provides recipients with administrative relief from deportation. DACA is not a pathway to citizenship, and recipients have their applications reviewed every two years. Without the protections DACA provided, Grijalva could be subjected to deportation to Guatemala, a country he has pride in but hadn't been to since he was a baby.

After the disappointment of a season cut short, Luis Grijalva was determined to prove to himself that he was championship-ready.

The American political landscape casts stressful uncertainty on someone like Grijalva. Simple changes in administration and issues at the southern border ignite passionate backlash that keeps most DACA recipients understandably quiet about their status. The one constant for a person in Grijalva's position is that, aside from some special circumstances, they will be denied re-entry at the border if they leave the United States. COVID-19 restrictions would soon do to the world what Grijalva had dealt with his entire life.

DACA is a label that carries the weight of restrictions and stigmas, but none that ever altered Grijalva's evolving passion for running. The young people affected by DACA are often referred to as "dreamers" (after the Development, Relief and

Education for Alien Minors—DREAM—Act legislation that has failed to pass Congress numerous times). It's a fitting moniker for Grijalva.

Since high school, Grijalva's lofty aspirations were quite evident even if the pathway to reach them was less so. His 2017 high school recruiting class was lighting the track on fire. Although Grijalva could claim a 4:07 mile and sub-nine 3200m, he was overlooked by blue-chip programs across the country. His options for running at the collegiate level were soon narrowed down to Sacramento State University (where his high school coach had just accepted a coaching position) and NAU.

NAU had just won its first national team title in cross country by the time Grijalva visited Flagstaff in winter 2017, but he wasn't automatically sold on the school. He had loved working with his high school coach and felt that staying close to home might be his best option. It certainly didn't help that Grijalva's official visit to NAU occurred during a snowstorm. Smith began to have serious doubts about whether the mountain town would be the right fit for the Californian after that.

If the below-zero visit jeopardized the possibility Grijalva might someday wear an NAU singlet, Smith's coming out to California for a home visit reeled him back in. "I liked everything he had to say," said Grijalva.

Smith's character and lack of ego resonated with Grijalva and convinced him that he would feel at home at NAU. For Grijalva, it didn't matter that NAU was the national champion. What mattered was that he trusted Smith.

During his first semester with the Lumberjacks, Grijalva was struck by the expectations that came with being on the best cross country program in the country. "All you know is winning. It's a bad mindset to have," he admitted.

Coming in as a high-caliber freshman meant Grijalva was thrown into the deep end. He raced his first NCAA Cross Country Championships in 2017; Grijalva's sixtieth-place individual finish was a modest contribution to the team's win. He qualified for the 2018 NCAA Outdoor Track and Field Championships in the 1500m. Unfortunately, he struggled in Eugene and ended dead last in his heat.

Things were picking up as Grijalva headed into his junior year with a twenty-third-place finish at the 2018 NCAA national cross country meet—the third man on NAU's three-peat in Wisconsin. He went on to place fourteenth and fifteenth in the 5000m at the NCAA indoor and outdoor championships, respectively. His trajectory seemed right, but then a disappointing fifty-second-place finish at the 2019 NCAA Cross Country Championships forced Grijalva to reassess his mindset.

"It hurt a lot getting second [as a team]. We were all really confident that we were going to win. We didn't expect it when things went wrong," said Grijalva. "Learning how to lose was one of the hardest things I had dealt with at NAU."

This defeat, mixed with his individual poor performance, lit a fire. Grijalva didn't want to go another season feeling like he underperformed when it mattered most.

After setting two Guatemalan national records in the space of two weeks during the 2020 indoor season, Grijalva looked unstoppable on his mission to show the world what he was capable of. Then suddenly, it was over. His season ended with tears and feelings of devastation on the side of a track in Albuquerque.

Grijalva could have accepted the reality that circumstances beyond his control had ended his season. He could have reset his expectations to perform his best when it mattered most at the next championship. But that wasn't enough for him. Grijalva needed to prove to himself that on the day he was supposed to race in Albuquerque, he would have been ready.

It was 2:30 p.m. when Grijalva arrived at the Dome to start his warm-up for the mile. Joining him on the infield was Tyler Day, Geordie Beamish, and Quax. All three had agreed to either race Grijalva or be a pacesetter. Unfortunately, not all of them were excited to be there.

"Let's go home," Beamish said as the four NAU athletes jogged around the concourse above the track.

Both Beamish and Day were understandably bummed since arriving back from Albuquerque. Grijalva had his season canceled, but for these two, their careers at NAU had been cut short. They had been on the verge of cementing their names in the NAU history books one last time before venturing off to run professionally. Their college careers ended three months early, and soon they would find out most brands were putting a hold on signing athletes as the pandemic sent the corporate world into retreat mode and companies steeled themselves for financial fallout.

After a few more laps, Beamish and Day decided the right thing to do was support their teammate from the sidelines instead of digging themselves into a deeper mental hole.

This left Grijalva and an unenthused Quax to get the job done.

As the boys made their way back down to track level, they were joined by three teammates who'd gotten a tip-off about the mile race through a message in the group chat. With a Little Caesars pizza to share between them, Ryan Lanley, Joey DeFeo, and Brodey Hasty loudly awaited the start. Just as Grijalva had pent-up emotions he needed to get out, so did they.

By the time Smith arrived, forty minutes late, the support crew had grown impatient. "Come on, are you going to do it or not?" joked DeFeo. "We didn't come all this way and pay for parking to not see you race."

With the smell of pizza in the air and the noise of a restless, albeit limited, fan section bouncing around the emptiness of the Dome, the stage was finally set.

Jarred Cornfield and Smith had their fingers hovering over the start button of their stopwatches. Both wanted to make sure to record Grijalva's time as accurately as possible.

With a little jog to the line, Smith shouted "Go!" and the two were off.

They ran the first straight and bend before disappearing behind the basketball court and bleachers. The Dome was still a multipurpose facility, as it had been when first built. The ice-skating rink had been removed because of plumbing issues, and NAU no longer had a softball team, but when the turf was rolled up at the end of each football season, a basketball court was always laid down at the same time the track was unveiled. Large bleachers around three sides of the court made it impossible to see Quax and Grijalva on the back stretch from where everyone was standing on the home straight.

Quax led Grijalva through the first 700 meters right on pace before peeling off into lane two to let his teammate go by. "I'll catch you on the next lap," Quax shouted.

This unorthodox pacing method wouldn't fly under usual circumstances, but Smith allowed it.

Making a running start as Grijalva came flying toward the line to signify 600 meters to go, Quax reclaimed the lead and put his already struggling body through another quarter mile of pain for his teammate. When he pulled off once more, Grijalva would have just 200 meters left to run.

At the finish line, Cornfield and Smith eagerly awaited Grijalva's arrival. With their view obstructed, both wondered whether his wheels were coming off.

As he came off the last bend, the enthusiastic support crew erupted with cheers. Grijalva came hurtling through the line as Smith and Cornfield intently pushed the stop buttons. They looked down and then at each other. The final time averaged across their watches was 4:02.07—an unofficial Dome mile record.

The boys sprinted over to their exhausted teammate, who lay sprawled out on the track. The emotions had taken more of a toll than the race itself. A slight smirk crept across Grijalva's face because he knew on the day when it mattered most, he was ready. "This was one of the easiest races ever," he said.

In the immediate aftermath of this truly momentous effort, no social media posts or videos surfaced online to show the incredible achievement. There was simply a rumor that circulated around Flagstaff and a satisfied Grijalva, who could end his season a little happier than most.

As the Dome cleared out, Grijalva was the last to leave. Walking up the steps, he didn't know when his next race would be. Campus was about to shut down, and soon everyone would be told to go home. When they were finally allowed back, the world would be a different place.

"Come home now, or soon you won't be able to."

That was the message being pushed by the New Zealand government to all citizens temporarily based overseas. Quax and teammate Mitchell Small were forced to immediately evaluate their situation.

International students in similar circumstances filled American colleges. The pandemic was clearly getting worse, but if students left the U.S. for their home countries, no one knew how long it would be before they could return.

As the situation with COVID-19 rapidly deteriorated, countries enacted drastic measures to protect their citizens. Lockdowns in Wuhan, China, at the beginning of the outbreak seemed extreme at the time, until similar policies became the only apparent option to slow the virus's worldwide spread.

An unnerving fear swept the globe about the deadliness of COVID-19 if unprecedented measures weren't taken. Countries around the world, including New Zealand, were making plans to close their borders. Unless there was a disincentive to travel, and soon, more people would bring the virus to previously unaffected areas.

"We have to go home," Small told Quax.

In Quax's mind, there was still time to see how things would play out before jumping on the first flight. With few cases in Flagstaff and its being a small town compared to Auckland, the big city he called home back in New Zealand, it was logical to consider staying. On the other hand, Small wasn't prepared to risk getting stuck in the U.S. and riding out the unpredictable coming months there. He booked a flight home and made it just before the border officially closed.

With Quax's decision now made for him, he could shift his focus to his online classes and the eight-week training plan Smith had sent. Lacking any confirmed races on the horizon, he'd approach this training block as an extended summer buildup for the fall.

Theo Quax continued the running legacy of his record-setting father.

After finishing his final exam, Quax headed out the door of his house in Rio Townhomes and made it a mile before a searing pain shot through his foot. Unable to continue the run, he walked home. Quax arranged with the NAU medical staff to get booked for an X-ray, and the result made him wish he'd gone back to New Zealand. A stress fracture in the second metatarsal of his right foot put an immediate end to Quax's training and made the impending isolation period in Flagstaff feel a lot more daunting.

What was supposed to be six weeks in an orthopedic boot turned into eight, then ten, then twelve. Each time Quax tested his foot, the pain of an unhealed bone returned. It became a frustrating routine that toyed with him through the entire summer.

Losing fitness due to injury was an inevitable consequence of getting hurt during the pandemic. Without access to the usual cross-training methods due to pools and gyms being closed, Quax could do little but let the hard work he'd put in slip away.

Ever since Quax was a kid, running had played a special role in his life. As an eight-year-old, he would go for runs with his superstar dad, Dick Quax. "We made it a point to stop at two playgrounds," the younger Quax said. Even though Dick was an Olympic silver medalist and prior world record holder in the 5000m, his son didn't feel pressure to pick up the sport. Up until the age of sixteen, Quax played rugby. It wasn't until a hard head knock that he started to reevaluate whether a contact sport was right for him.

Once Quax set his sights on running as the sport for his future, he began to seriously investigate the possibility of going to the United States for college. He was already familiar with the big-name schools when his dad directed his attention toward a university he'd never heard of.

"Come and watch this," Dick shouted to Quax from the next room. "This team has two New Zealanders and they're winning!"

Quax joined his dad in watching the 2017 NCAA Cross Country Championships. "That was when I decided I wanted to go there," said Quax.

Without having even taken an official visit, Quax signed his letter of intent to attend NAU in fall 2018 and planned to move to Flagstaff in the summer. Everything was set for Quax to embark on this next adventure of his life. But when his dad, who had been battling cancer for some time, passed in the early hours of May 28, 2018, the decision to up and leave felt unimaginably hard.

Overnight, New Zealand lost a running icon, but Quax lost a rock in his life.

After reflecting on his situation, Quax concluded that his dad would want him to do this. "He would want me to go to NAU, get fit, and carry on with my life."

Now, sitting in his Flagstaff home two years later in a moon boot, feeling farther from home than ever before, memories of his dad reminded him why he embarked on this journey in the first place.

By the time the fall season rolled around, Quax would be physically and mentally ready to return to the sport that had always connected him to his father. He couldn't wait to join his teammates on their playground at Lumberjack Stadium. △

Chapter 20
Training Through a Pandemic

THE COVID-19 TESTING LINE AT THE NAU FIELDHOUSE STRETCHED to the front door. There were not a lot of people waiting to get tested, but the required six feet of separation to observe social distancing guidelines made the line appear much longer. Like a doctor's waiting room, not knowing why people were in line was sufficient reason to allow plenty of space.

NAU required weekly testing of all student-athletes arriving back on campus for fall 2020. While the PCR nasal swab that consisted of a Q-tip reaching the nasopharynx (where your nose meets your throat) was common at the beginning of the pandemic, the Fieldhouse offered saliva tests as a less invasive alternative. This made the weekly testing regimen more bearable.

Once Drew Bosley reached the front of the line, he was greeted by a clinic staff member in a hazmat suit sitting behind her desk. She pointed an infrared thermometer at his forehead to see if he had a fever—he didn't. She gave Bosley his instructions.

"Follow these arrows and find an empty cubicle. Then you will sit in the chair, unscrew the top from the tube, and use the straw to spit into the tube until it reaches the line. Once you're done, screw the top back on the tube, throw the straw in the trash, and use the wipe on the chair so it's ready for the next person. Any questions?"

"Nope," replied Bosley, who had heard these instructions several times before. He grabbed the sample kit and followed the arrow stickers on the floor to an empty cubicle.

Bosley sat down in a chair still slightly damp from the sanitizing wipe used by the person before him. While removing the straw from its wrapper, Bosley looked down and noticed a groove in the floor that ran under his chair and beyond the curtain in front of him. He didn't know it, but this groove was one of the last pieces of evidence that the Fieldhouse used to be home to the NAU track and field team.

The Activity Center that housed NAU's first indoor track had become University Union Fieldhouse, a cavernous space occasionally used for special events, recreational sports, or temporary storage. There were no more sprinters creating sparks at the end of the track or baseballs flying down lane one. After the track was torn up, all that remained was the extended groove in the floor below Bosley's feet where the inside rail used to be.

Once Bosley's saliva had reached the minimum line on the tube, he gave the chair another wipe down and handed his sample to the clinic staffer sitting by the exit. He used the large hand-sanitizing pump before exiting the Fieldhouse and walking the few hundred meters to Lumberjack Stadium.

Stationed at the back entrance closest to the team's locker rooms, Assistant Coach Jarred Cornfield stood watch, an infrared thermometer in hand. Although Bosley had just had one of these guns pointed at his forehead ten minutes prior, his temperature had to be checked once again to gain access to the outdoor track.

While there were no stickers on the ground to indicate six feet as there had been in the Fieldhouse, the Lumberjacks gave each other adequate space as they congregated on the track. After months of practice, everyone was pretty good at gauging this distance.

The temperatures were still warm during those last few days of Flagstaff summer. Soon, the city would enter its best time of the year for runners. During the fall, temperatures are moderate, the wind dies down, and the leaves on popular trails turn golden. A dirt trail that looks like a high-elevation yellow brick road surrounded by beautiful aspen trees is enough to take your breath away.

The thin air of Flagstaff felt a little thinner from behind the surgical masks the Lumberjacks wore to practice. Masks were only one of many changes as Bosley and teammates returned to campus in fall 2020. The team had stopped meeting for long runs. They were not allowed access to the locker rooms unless a coach let them in to use the restroom. Weights had been relocated to the infield at Lumberjack Stadium. And for the first time since 1982, the men and women practiced at separate times.

Strict protocols at practice were necessary to abide by all the requirements set forth by the university and the NCAA, but to ensure athletes weren't bringing COVID-19 to practice, these protocols extended into the Lumberjacks' personal lives as well. Going to crowded places where social distancing would be difficult was discouraged, and hanging out with people outside the team was only allowed in well-ventilated spaces, preferably outdoors, and while masked. Even when carpooling with roommates, masks had to be worn and windows rolled down. All of this was intended to prevent a positive test that would shut down practice for one or both teams for an undetermined amount of time.

College students weren't alone in navigating unprecedented lifestyle changes, priorities, and decisions since the pandemic began. From the mundane to the tragic, the world was reeling. Restaurants only offered takeout, while social distancing became second nature. Toilet paper, hand sanitizer, disinfectant wipes, and flour were in limited supply. Debates raged over what types of masks were best, while surgical gloves and face shields were common sights.

The threat to the elderly and the immunocompromised required diligence, as did the unknown impact of the virus on children and those who were pregnant. News reports and social-media videos from around the world supplied shocking footage of people on ventilators and in mass graves amid the exponential growth in COVID-19 cases and deaths.

With a focus on personal health and that of others, fear was palpable. Touching another person, being breathed on, sitting together in a car, or even running past someone on a trail was believed to carry some level of risk. On a university campus, which thrives on community and is built to serve thousands in a relatively small space, the adjustment was significant, even if its population on the whole was not as vulnerable to the worst effects of the virus.

Spanning the globe, billions of people made daily choices about what was important to them, what was safe, and what responses were appropriate. For student-athletes in America, this meant deciding how motivated they were to follow their sporting passions in a world where, as Coach Mike Smith had said at the moment his track team's spring season ended five months earlier, "worrying about games" was a luxury.

For Smith's Lumberjacks, cross country practice was their outlet to escape the isolation that dominated their lives as an entirely new kind of school year got underway. The team provided an opportunity to not only socialize, but also to feel like they were still moving forward after the world had stopped spinning. Even so, the toll social distancing was taking on the NAU team's closeness presented a direct challenge to its culture. The freshmen felt it acutely from the moment they arrived on campus.

Rio Townhomes had become the accommodation of choice for the majority of the NAU cross country team. The 153-unit community consisted of modest, connected family homes with large communal living areas, ideal for college students, especially from its location southeast of downtown Flagstaff, a convenient five-minute bike ride to both north and south campuses. One house being rented by a group of NAU distance athletes became another up the street, and then another within the same cul-de-sac. Being in the same place made it convenient to share rides and spend time together outside of practice.

When Nico Young moved into a house in Rio during his freshman year, the close environment had significantly changed. "Outside of practice, we couldn't get together much," said Young. "It took a long time to get to know people because of this."

Freshmen were usually required to stay in the dorms their first year, but the pandemic had loosened those rules. There was no point forcing students to live together in a building COVID-19 would certainly rip its way through. "I didn't feel like I was missing out on anything," Young said, acknowledging that having a room to himself was certainly a perk of living off campus.

Adjusting to life as a student-athlete typically takes time, but it was unusual to have the whole team going through a similar transition period at once. Seniors, freshmen, and everyone in between were getting used to the protocols at practice and in their online classes.

Young could empathize with his new NAU teammates who had been left devastated on the side of a track in Albuquerque when they found out their season was canceled. He, too, had his stellar high school career end in dramatic fashion. After an impressive junior year in which he ran 4:08.82 in the mile and 8:40.0 in the 3200m, the Californian looked unstoppable going into his senior track season in spring 2020.

Coming off an individual and team win at the Nike Cross Nationals in fall 2019, the Newbury Park High School athlete had set his sights on the record books. On February 8 in New York, Young broke the U.S. high school 3000m record by running 7:56.97. Then, before he could get another fast time under his belt, the remainder of the spring season was canceled.

COVID-19 restrictions made the transition to college life more difficult for high school phenom Nico Young once he arrived in Flagstaff in fall 2020.

"I was really upset to lose my season," said Young. "I was going to run a 1500m and was in a good spot before it got canceled."

Young was determined to get in at least one more race before concluding his high school career. The difficult part of trying to race in spring 2020 was finding a facility willing to host one. COVID-19 restrictions meant that meets were shut down, but Young found a track in Portland, Oregon, that would allow him to run a time trial with pacers.

After a month of delays, Young took to the track to chase Galen Rupp's high school record of 13:37.91 in the 5000m. Rupp, whom Smith was coaching, was originally going to be a pacer for this race, but injury issues prevented him. Instead, Young found a couple of guys who were planning to stick with him for two miles—they made it just five laps. It was a long final 3000 meters for Young in the eighty-degree heat after that.

Young ran a hard-fought 13:50.55 to round out his high school career in bittersweet fashion. While still a great time for a prep athlete, Young knew if he'd raced a normal spring season, the record books could have included his name a few more times.

A lost season didn't make Young any less sought-after among colleges interested in hosting his considerable talent. He could have gone anywhere in the country but decided on NAU. Aside from Flagstaff's preeminent running location, Young was lured by the team's culture. "I had the most fun on this visit," he said. "I watched a workout in Sedona and a long run on Woody Mountain Road. I loved the team. They were the closest team by far from any of the visits I went on."

NAU athletes have long prided themselves on giving recruits an enjoyable and honest experience while in town, but what Young saw during his first trip to Flagstaff was impossible to replicate in the upturned landscape of fall 2020. It's hard to bond when you're perpetually six feet apart.

Despite many differences in college life during a pandemic, the expectations to perform were as big for Young as they were for other high school standouts who came before him. Given his credentials, likely even more so. With that came a heavy burden to prove himself right out of the gate. Young and Smith discussed that when he first arrived.

"We addressed the pressure a little bit," Young said. "There were no outcome-oriented goals that compared my upcoming performances to high school. I did worry about the pressure a bit. I had an injury in the fall and didn't run for five weeks. And I was wanting to show people that I was just as good of an athlete. I didn't want people saying I peaked in high school."

While Smith and the team refrained from applying additional pressure, Young's own drive to succeed was a difficult weight to carry, especially since he didn't know when he would race next. It was hard to prove himself without a concrete opportunity to do so.

On September 22, the NCAA Division I Board of Directors announced the 2020 NCAA Cross Country Championships would be held in the winter instead of the fall. The new date was March 15, 2021, two days after the conclusion of the NCAA Indoor Track and Field Championships.

The schedule change meant the Lumberjacks had to choose whether to focus on getting on the podium at an indoor championship, as they had wanted to do in March 2020, or go all-in on cross country, chasing redemption for their 2019 second-place finish. Although it would have been great to try for the podium at NCAA Indoors, it was a no-brainer to focus on cross country. For the first time, two cross country titles would be up for grabs in the same calendar year—one in March and one at the usual time in November. In the year 2021, NAU saw an unprecedented opportunity to achieve something no school had ever done before and perhaps could never do again.

Brodey Hasty was eight days into a break between training blocks when it was announced that the team would compete at the Oklahoma State University Invitational on October 17. The eight-kilometer race provided the Lumberjacks with an opportunity to get familiar with the same course they would be running on at nationals in March.

Having a race on the schedule was exciting, although the thought of driving thirteen hours to Stillwater, Oklahoma, wasn't. This was the team's first trip since the new COVID-19 restrictions had been put in place. To avoid unnecessary exposure to the virus, the safest mode of transportation was a private bus.

Ryan Raff chose NAU over his beloved home-state team and Lumberjack archrival, BYU.

This drive to Oklahoma was a test run for how the team would handle travel in March. Unfortunately, the test run included the team's getting stuck in crawling traffic on I-40 and only making it to Albuquerque instead of the Texas Panhandle on their first day. The second day of travel just got that much longer.

The Lumberjacks faced numerous unknowns as they headed into the race. While Luis Grijalva and Ryan Raff were both healthy and ready to roll, Bosley, Hasty, and Abdihamid Nur were not in their best shape. The team would also be relying on two freshmen to fill the gaps in the top seven.

Raff was looking forward to lining up against the college he almost went to after high school. Having grown up in a Mormon home in Utah, it was a given that he'd consider BYU as one of his top options. BYU is a great program, consistently one of the country's best. "Culture-wise and family-wise, the easy option was to go twenty minutes from my house to BYU," said Raff. In the end, the easy option wasn't what he was looking for. "I wanted to challenge myself and go somewhere that I wasn't always comfortable."

The trails in Flagstaff and NAU's distance dominance tipped the scales for Raff in deciding to leave Utah. Having grown up supporting BYU athletics, it was a strange transition to align himself with a rival of their cross country program. While some of his teammates were vocal in feeding that rivalry, Raff stayed quiet, having a unique perspective and appreciation for both schools.

The decision to come to NAU ended up being the right one for Raff. Not only did he thrive at 7,000 feet, but he also found the love of his life at a local church in Flagstaff. While 2020 wasn't a good year for most people, Raff appreciated what it had brought him. In January, he met Sarah and they soon started dating—things were moving quickly. "We both felt like this was it," Raff said. By March he had proposed, and in June they got married in a small ceremony at Sarah's grandparents' place.

Raff was in a happy spot in his life when he lined up on the starting line at the OSU Invitational, ready to beat the team that he might have run for. Even though the Lumberjacks were fielding a half-strength team, they still pulled off a narrow win, ahead of OSU in second and BYU in third. It was great to get a win under their belt, even knowing these early results weren't necessarily an accurate prediction of the strength of any team.

The most eye-catching part of NAU's performance was Grijalva's individual win. He had been working hard and training consistently since the spring. Grijalva had proven himself a dominant force on the track, and it was looking like he might be a force to be reckoned with come nationals in March.

The race signified both the start and end of the season for the Lumberjacks. They wouldn't race again until the turn of the calendar year. "Usually when you're coming off a meet you have a clear path, but we don't have that right now," said Smith. "We want to get back to campus safely, and we'll be back to training when it's safe to do so, and we'll just be looking ahead for the next opportunity. We're really fortunate to have the chance to compete, and we look forward to the future."

If there was one positive about finishing their season when they did, it was holding on to their number-one ranking. For the thirtieth consecutive week, NAU was ranked as the number-one cross country program in the nation by the U.S. Track & Field and Cross Country Coaches Association. This was a streak the team was proud of, but it would soon come to an end.

Blaise Ferro started to run again the week of November 20, 2020. The fall season had come and gone while he continued to deal with the back problem that first gave him issues during the indoor season. The injury got worse, until Ferro was no longer able to bend without experiencing a lot of pain. He sought help from a chiropractor who told him, "I can't let you run. Your body is not good at all."

In Flagstaff over the summer, Ferro kept busy by working at a local bike shop. He was putting in eight-hour days while bike sales were particularly brisk. The pandemic had motivated a lot of people to start exercising outdoors, and purchasing a bike became a natural first step. The high demand for bikes and bike repairs meant Ferro's days in the shop were intense.

Without the ability to run, Ferro biked a lot. These rides were supplemented by skateboarding on the ramp Ferro and a couple of teammates built in his garage. Skateboarding wasn't helping his back problems, but he continued to spend hours on the ramp. That went on until the team began training together in the fall and Smith told Ferro he might need to take a break from skateboarding in order to heal.

By the time the new year rolled around, Ferro was finally running consistently and putting in decent miles. In January, he got up to fifty miles a week, and that continued to climb until he maxed out at eighty miles.

When Ferro couldn't run good mileage, he knew the importance of supplementing with cross-training. Ferro laughed as he thought back to his days in middle school, when he did a project on whether aqua jogging would improve a person's mile time. The conclusion of his amateur research was that it would, but he admitted he didn't control his variables very well—time trialing a mile every week might have been a confounding factor that skewed his promising results. Ferro became all too accustomed to time in the pool as multiple injuries plagued his college career. "Obviously, this project has come full circle," he joked.

It was good that Ferro could see the humor in a place that was also very dark for him. Injuries are a tough reality of the sport, and for those who deal with them frequently, they can completely alter the relationship an athlete has with running. After a long road back to doing what he loved, Ferro appreciated feeling healthy heading into the final cross country season of his college career.

The Lumberjacks' winter 2021 racing schedule consisted of a condensed six-week block comprised of two Las Vegas meets, conference, and nationals. Teams were used to racing from the start of September to late November, so this short season forced Smith to get creative with preparing his athletes for each race.

The first race on the schedule was the Silver State Collegiate Cross Country Challenge on February 1. As would be the case for all their races that season, the Lumberjacks made the four-hour trek to Las Vegas by bus. Notably absent were Grijalva and Bosley, both dealing with injuries.

While the team had enjoyed a good showing at their race in October, this time BYU came out ready to roll. The Lumberjacks were solid though their fourth runner, but a drop-off to their fifth hurt the team in the standings. BYU took the win with forty-nine points, ahead of NAU's fifty-four for second. The meet ended NAU's thirty-two-week streak of being ranked the best team in the country.

Two weeks later, NAU looked more like themselves as they raced with a full-strength squad for the Battle Born Collegiate Challenge. Nur and Young put in incredible performances at the front, going one-two and running 22:30 for the eight-kilometer course. Ferro and an almost-fit Grijalva were not far behind in fourth and fifth. Hasty took thirty-one places off his performance two weeks earlier and finished eighth to round out the top five. Although BYU was absent this time, NAU's twenty-point total against Stanford in second and Colorado in third was still an impressive feat.

With no NCAA Mountain Regional Championship that season, Smith had to be strategic in deciding whom to hold out from conference to keep fresh for nationals. The first one was Young. An injury popped up right before conference that interrupted his training, adding another layer of stress for the freshman leading up to nationals.

The second athlete held out was Ferro. He had a history of issues with injury, and for him to be fit and healthy by this point of the season was a gift to protect. The final athlete held out was Grijalva. He was still coming around after the hamstring injury he picked up in January and could benefit from avoiding another long drive.

Each athlete was held out for legitimate reasons, but when the Lumberjacks came in second to Southern Utah University by three points at conference, it didn't look good having three of the top seven at home in Flagstaff. The team thought they still had the strength to pull off the win, but they couldn't quite make up the difference at the back end. Winning the conference meet is always a priority for NAU, and it stung to take second just before nationals.

As the guys had learned from their 2019 season, no matter how prepared they may be and how many races they might win during the season, on the starting line at nationals, anyone is still vulnerable. For the 2020 season, they had only won once out of the three times they showed up.

The Lumberjacks would have to pass one more test before boarding the buses for nationals. What started as a rumor circulating around the team was confirmed once they arrived back in Flagstaff after conference weekend. Smith was pulling out all the stops to ensure nothing prevented his squads from toeing the starting line at nationals. △

Chapter 21
Emerging From the Bubble

"HEY MAN, WHAT DO YOU WANT?" ASKED ABDIHAMID NUR FROM HIS bed across the room.

A confused Brodey Hasty was awakened by the strange question from his roommate at two in the morning. Unsure how to respond, Hasty simply replied, "Huh," to which he was met with silence from Nur.

Hasty tried again. "Abdihamid, what?"

Annoyed by the fact that Hasty was asking him questions at this hour, Nur replied, "Why are you talking to me?"

"You woke *me* up," Hasty snapped back.

"Bro, I'm not dealing with this right now," said Nur, who rolled over and went back to sleep.

While that was the end of their late-night conversation, it wasn't the end of Hasty's confusion. The NAU team had barely begun their bubble stay when Hasty learned Nur was a sleep talker. It looked like this might be a long two weeks for the new roommates.

Aside from occasional sleep deprivation, the bubble was an enjoyable experience for most. NAU rented four houses—two for the men and two for the women—for the top seven and alternates who would be traveling to the upcoming 2020 NCAA

Cross Country Championships now being held in March 2021.

The bubble's purpose was simple. "We put the team in Airbnb houses for the two weeks before the meet because we were afraid of people being taken out," said Mike Smith. Having side-stepped catastrophic run-ins with COVID-19 up to this point in the season, it would have been devastating to squander all the team's hard work with a positive test right before nationals.

Rooming with teammates wouldn't be enough to prevent any possible exposure to COVID-19 during these two weeks, so life inside came with rules attached. The most obvious one was that athletes weren't allowed contact with anyone outside the bubble. Runners were also separated by gender during their bubble stay.

Leaving the bubble was only approved for training sessions. The team couldn't even go to the grocery store. Only contactless deliveries were permitted for food and necessities. If an athlete had forgotten something at their house, a roommate could drop it off on the driveway of the rental house, but they had to leave before the athlete came to collect the item.

The rules may have seemed strict, but they were necessary to ensure the bubble worked. And as Ryan Raff found out, there were benefits to being isolated during this time. "We didn't have to worry about COVID for two weeks," he said. "It felt like we were living a pro's life—eating, sleeping, running."

On top of that, the men would meet up at the bigger Airbnb to play pool or air hockey and cook dinners together. For Nico Young, the bubble provided something COVID-19 had robbed him of since his arrival in the fall. "The bubble was a big step in me getting to know my teammates," he said.

While the athletes inside the bubble were mostly enjoying the experience, that wasn't always the case for those excluded from it. One special thing about being on the NAU team is how every athlete is valued. Whether an athlete is on the travel squad or not, they're a part of the team's success. The bubble challenged that. It became a clique created by Smith, which went against a fundamental piece of NAU team culture and Smith's own coaching philosophy.

"Smith admitted this could devalue what people do outside the bubble, and it could put too much pressure on those in the bubble," said Theo Quax, one of the athletes on the outside.

The decision to isolate the travel squad was purely to ensure there would be a travel squad. Temporary damage to team culture could be repaired; however, a missed trip to Oklahoma would always be a lost opportunity to make history. In this uncertain time, drastic decisions had to be made. Their consequences were never going to be favorable to everyone.

In the end, the bubble more than justified its own existence. "We got to the last couple of days and felt like it had been a waste," said Quax. "Then someone outside the bubble tested positive, so it was a saving grace."

Had both teams not isolated for two weeks, then at least one of them wouldn't have been getting on the bus to Oklahoma. The coaching staff could breathe a sigh of relief, knowing the investment in the bubble was worthwhile. And the athletes could get on the bus feeling safe around each other, knowing COVID-19 wasn't coming along for the ride.

Hasty stared at the ceiling of "some dirty NAU bus" from his uncomfortable position lying in the aisle. The NAU team had yet to reach the halfway point on their thirteen-hour trip to Oklahoma, and the boredom of travel was already taking its toll. Though it could be argued that the Lumberjacks had lost touch with their hardscrabble roots in recent years, taking a bus to nationals revived some of that lost identity.

Barreling toward Oklahoma in various states of discomfort, these Lumberjacks were, unbeknownst to them, channeling their early predecessors. Back in 1969, Coach Red Haberlack had made the same drive, his team squeezed into a nine-passenger station wagon on loan from the local Babbitt Ford dealership. His squad's ninth-place NAIA nationals finish would mark an impressive accomplishment for the young program. Fifty-two years later, NAU was chasing a return to the mountaintop.

Aside from the occasional teammate walking over the top of him, the bus floor proved a relatively relaxing space for Hasty. By not glancing out the window, he missed the steady flow of mile markers, cows, and highway exit signs, frequent indicators of how far the team had traveled. It also gave his mind the opportunity to wander.

Eyes closed, Hasty thought back to his recruiting visit in fall 2017, where he witnessed the toughest back-to-back days the NAU team would endure that season. It began with a Friday evening run to the top of Mount Elden, which trashed every athlete's legs. Fourteen hours later, the team stood at the base of Snowbowl Road for an easy long run. The term "easy" is used loosely, as the run started with a 1,500-foot climb up to Aspen Corner, then some descent before ending on the rolling Hart Prairie Road.

A young and excited Hasty had joined the Lumberjacks for a portion of this long run. He managed to survive the climb but took a hard fall on one of the sweeping downhills. While he was quick to get back on his feet and continue the run, it was a concerning sight for the athletes who were guiding him through the uneven trails.

"I was pretty sure he wasn't going to come here after that," laughed Matt Baxter, who was behind Hasty when he fell.

Baxter's prediction turned out to be correct. Hasty committed to the University of Oregon a few months later.

The University of Oregon boasts one of the best and most well-rounded programs in the country, continuously producing athletes who succeed in college and, often, as professionals. For someone like Hasty, who had been focusing on the mile, Oregon was the perfect fit. It wasn't until Oregon's distance coaches, Andy and Maurica Powell, left for positions at the University of Washington, that Hasty reevaluated his decision.

Hasty based his original choice on where he believed he would excel as an athlete. As time went on, he started to think more about where he could excel as a person, not just as a runner. Although Hasty knew he could have found success at Oregon, and he appreciated the program's support and understanding during his difficult process, he knew that working with Smith and the NAU team was ultimately the right choice for him. After Oregon released him from his letter of intent, Hasty signed with NAU and arrived on campus in summer 2018.

Since Hasty had raced late into the summer, Smith wanted him to rest before starting a buildup. "He told me, 'We don't need you,' but in a good way," said Hasty. The Lumberjacks had four returning All-Americans from the previous cross country season and would do just fine that fall even if the high school standout redshirted.

Hasty's time to compete in an NAU singlet came in spring 2019, when he qualified for the NCAA Outdoor Track and Field Championships in the 5000m—an incredible effort for a freshman. Aside from an Achilles flareup over the summer, Hasty continued his momentum into the fall, placing forty-sixth at the 2019 NCAA Cross Country Championships before spending the next three months dealing with another injury.

Although his teammates were disappointed to have their 2020 indoor season end in dramatic fashion and Hasty could empathize with them about that, on a personal level he was more relieved. "I got to start from zero," he said. "We had no races. I didn't have to rush anything. By the time I got healthy, it felt like I had a summer-plus just to run."

Taking the time to hit the reset button and run without the pressure of impending races was exactly what Hasty needed. It meant he got on the bus to Oklahoma for the 2020 NCAA Cross Country Championships feeling fit and in a great headspace.

"Excuse me, do you have any earplugs?" Blaise Ferro asked the starter.

"I'm sorry, I only have a used pair," he replied.

"I don't care, I'll take them," said Ferro. The starter thoughtfully gave them a quick wipe on his shorts before handing them over.

The howling wind and screams from the crowd were distractions Ferro was looking to avoid. Having earplugs in meant he could hear the voices in his head singing Eminem's "Go to Sleep" a little louder. Coincidently, the song's title was the same advice Smith would give his athletes during the middle of longer races. When conserving energy and relaxing as much as possible was vital to have anything left over the final kilometers, Smith would shout "Go to sleep" as his runners came by.

Unfortunately, the earplugs only amplified the tense silence within the Lumberjacks' starting box. The air was thick with a nervous energy that was equal parts fear and confidence—sometimes it was hard to decipher between the two. COVID-19 had made athletes more appreciative of an opportunity like this, but it also added another layer of pressure. Fifteen long months had passed since they felt this kind of sickness in their stomachs.

The nerves of the men's team had been slightly alleviated by watching the women's race. The Lumberjack women had qualified for their second nationals in a row and hadn't come to Oklahoma to mess around. At the first kilometer they were leading with fifty-nine points—nearly fifty points ahead of North Carolina State in second place. From there, they dropped back one spot every kilometer to find themselves in fifth with just one kilometer left to run.

Everything was looking good for the Lumberjacks as Taryn O'Neill led the team with a sixth-place individual finish, but a tough last kilometer saw NAU fall back to

Left: The reality of COVID-19 was on display as NAU teammates (from left) Jessa Hanson (358), Pipi Eitel (357), Delaney Rasmussen, and Taryn O'Neill (361) line up for the 2020 NCAA Cross Country Championships in March 2021. Right: O'Neill celebrates her sixth-place individual finish and the Lumberjacks' eleventh-place team showing from the podium.

eleventh place. While this wasn't the dream result, considering the position they'd attained early on, it was still the best effort by the NAU women's team since their seventh-place showing in 2007. For the men, watching this gutsy performance by their teammates lit an even bigger fire inside as they prepared to go to battle over the same course.

The long journey to the starting line in Stillwater motivated every single one of these Lumberjacks.

Ferro was injury free after having been told he was too broken to even consider running during 2020.

Nur had bounced back from thoughts of giving up the NAU singlet he had spent two years fighting to wear.

Luis Grijalva still wanted to redeem himself after missing his shot at an indoor NCAA title, but a cold he picked up from a teammate on the bus ride to Oklahoma was threatening to once again upend his preparations.

Young was ready to prove he was more than just a high school standout.

With just four weeks of training under his belt because of injury, Drew Bosley didn't know how this race would go.

Hasty was determined to help his team now that he was finally fit and healthy.

Raff was excited to be back on a nationals starting line for his first time in over two years.

The Lumberjacks were filled with hope, determination, and a strong will to succeed. Though the 2019 loss, pre-COVID, had occurred in a very different world, it stood fresh in their minds. So did the agony of finding out their season had ended in Albuquerque, which had occurred almost a year ago to the day. No matter what motivated the guys as individuals on March 15, 2021, the one thing that gave them tunnel vision for the race ahead was the thought of bringing that number one trophy back to Flagstaff.

The cropped, brown grass carpeting the starting straight resembled a track in look and feel, highlighting what the team already knew: it was going to be a fast start. Just how fast would be determined by one man—Iowa State University's Wesley Kiptoo.

Though prospective frontrunners—from NAU and every other school—had chosen to focus on just one of the two national competitions being held in the same week of this unusual spring schedule, Kiptoo was attempting an unprecedented double. Fresh off his indoor title in the 5000m, Kiptoo was ready to push a hard opening kilometer like the one that had established his seven-second lead in Fayetteville, Arkansas, just three days prior. While a 2:32 first kilometer on an indoor track was a tough way to start a race, a 2:31 first kilometer on the grass set a blistering pace, even considering the fast Stillwater terrain.

Raff, Bosley, and Hasty all looked at each other in shock as they heard a coach yell 2:37 when they came through the first kilometer deep in the pack. They knew how hard this course was, having run it in October. The footing might have been fast, but the front runner's effort seemed unsustainable over the hills yet to come.

The NAU men employed a different tactic than the women and came through the first kilometer in a more conservative position. While this was what lost them the race in 2019, the openness of the Greiner Family OSU Cross Country Course meant that moving up wasn't going to be the issue it had been in Terre Haute. They were happy to let BYU lead this early section of the race while they sat back in fourth.

As the pace settled, with Kiptoo easing off to a 2:52 second kilometer at the front, the Lumberjacks started to move through the field and create a pack of their own within the top ten. Grijalva, Nur, Young, and Ferro found one another and began running as a cohesive unit, with just a couple other athletes along for the ride.

While things looked promising for NAU at the front of the race, their fifth man found himself a little farther back than anyone liked. Hasty was sitting in seventy-third with Bosley two spots behind at two kilometers. They were running together, which was a positive sign, but if they wanted to close the eleven-point gap with BYU, at least one of them had to move up.

Nico Young (675), Abdihamid Nur (672), Blaise Ferro (667), and Luis Grijalva (669) work together at the 2020 national meet.

A battle raged at the front of the race, with Hofstra University's Alex Masai and BYU's Conner Mantz joining Kiptoo for a fight to control the pace. Meanwhile, the pack of four NAU athletes had no interest in making a hard move to close the gap on the leaders. They were happy to get in sync with one another and ride the course as a team.

Bosley knew the team was depending on him to move up, so he spent two kilometers making his way through the field until he found the position he wanted. He managed to drop forty-eight places to get himself into twenty-seventh. This helped NAU take the lead, as the University of Notre Dame positioned themselves in second just forty-six points behind.

The early fast paces and impending hills on the course made it hard to get too excited about this positioning, however. A lot of the field was still close together, meaning it wouldn't take much of a move to shave off team points. As the fast opening kilometer took its toll, there was no telling who might suffer over the second half of the race.

Brodey Hasty pushes to the finish in Stillwater.

At the seven-kilometer mark, Ferro made his move. Having his teammates to run with for most of the race was helpful, but there comes a time in the race when each athlete has to play to their strengths. Ferro was winding up the pace far enough out that he wouldn't have to rely on a kick to the finish to hold his position. The consequence of this move was that it split up the NAU pack. Ferro's decision was an individual effort with a team goal in mind.

The eight-kilometer team scores gave NAU cause for concern. Although they still had four in the top ten, Bosley was fading. He had lost fifteen spots over the last kilometer and looked like he might fall back even more. This allowed Notre Dame to cut their gap on the Lumberjacks, who were holding onto the lead by only sixteen points.

With the team title on the line and the top four unable to gain more than a point or two in the last two kilometers, it was all on Bosley to hold his position even as the wheels came off.

Ferro had continued to press the pace as he sat in fourth place with Young right on his shoulder in fifth. They had opened a healthy gap on Nur and Grijalva, who were in eighth and twelfth, respectively, at the nine-kilometer mark. A lot of people would have predicted Grijalva to be fighting for the individual title. But coming into

Masked or not, the smiles of Coach Mike Smith (left) and Abdihamid Nur were bright enough for all to see after NAU's victory in Stillwater, Oklahoma, to cap the 2020 cross country season.

this race with a cold meant he suddenly found himself slipping outside of a top-ten position.

The battle for the individual title was fiercely fought, with BYU's Mantz taking home bragging rights over Florida State University's Adriaan Wildschutt in second and Iowa State workhorse Kiptoo in third, his second podium in less than a week. Not far behind, a wave of NAU athletes were running the best team race in school history. They put four athletes in the top ten, with Young finishing fourth, Ferro sixth, Nur seventh, and Grijalva clawing his way back to ninth. Usually an effort like this would secure the team title, but the grind to the finish for NAU's fifth man wasn't looking promising.

Bosley was running on fumes as he came into the last kilometer. He had lost another three spots and was continuing to go backward. The lack of training leading into this race had finally overcome him. "I was losing my eyesight," he said. "It was getting foggy, and I didn't know if I was running in a straight line or not. I was fully lactic. I was panicking."

For most of the race, Bosley knew he was NAU's fifth man, aware his teammates were depending on him to pull through and hold off any challenges down the homestretch. All five Notre Dame athletes had already crossed the finish line. Every spot he lost in the final few hundred meters dragged NAU further from their goal of getting back on top of the mountain.

As his body shut down, Bosley slipped back to fiftieth and then sixtieth, all while the finish line was in sight. Then, somewhere in the chaos, the weight Bosley was carrying as the fifth man was lifted. "Brodey passed me, and I didn't even know," he said.

While Bosley had made hard moves early in the race and fartleked to hold onto positions, Hasty had moved slowly through the field until he had Bosley in his sights by eight kilometers. When Bosley entered the final three hundred meters,

Hasty passed him and kicked in for home to cross the line as NAU's fifth runner in forty-fourth place.

Collapsing across the finish line in sixty-second place might have been a disappointing conclusion for Bosley, but he managed to sneak out a smile when he heard the news. NAU had won their fourth national title with sixty points—the lowest any team had scored since 2005.

The March 2021 championship signaled a return to the mountaintop for NAU cross country—its fourth national title in five seasons.

Going from NAU's top scorer in 2019 to their sixth man in 2020 would rattle a lot of athletes. For Bosley, there was joy in knowing that even if Hasty hadn't passed him and he'd been the team's fifth man, they still would have won by eleven points. Bosley had done his job, as had his teammates, and their efforts would be forever remembered by the trophy that sits in its glass case on NAU's campus—a trophy that signified the most difficult climb the Lumberjacks had ever made … one that ended where a dynasty began. △

Epilogue
Beyond the Mountaintop (2022 –)

LUIS GRIJALVA RUMMAGED THROUGH HIS BACKPACK, LOOKING FOR the striped white and blue rope Mike Smith had given him in his freshman year at NAU. Even though Grijalva had graduated nearly two months prior, he and his coach continued to work together as Grijalva transitioned from college athlete to professional. This rope had traveled with Grijalva to workouts, races, and to his home in California over the summers. It was a core instrument to his active isolated stretching warm-up routine, which consisted of eight different exercises. The first was a simple knee-to-chest while lying on the ground.

"Whether you're at the George Kyte Classic or the Olympic Games, every warm-up starts the same: with knee-to-chest," Smith told his team at the start of each season.

Lying on the infield of the warm-up track before the 5000m final at the 2020 Tokyo Olympic Games, Grijalva pulled the rope from his backpack and began the AIS regimen, just as he'd done before every race for the past four years.

It was a miracle that Grijalva was in Tokyo for these Games, which were postponed a year due to COVID-19. After earning his spot on the Guatemalan team following his runner-up finish at the 2021 NCAA Outdoor Track and Field Championships, where he ran under the 13:13.50 Olympic standard, Grijalva submitted his application for an advanced re-entry document to leave the country.

This application, which allows a DACA recipient to return after leaving the United States, typically takes ninety days to process. Grijalva had just over a month from the time he hired a lawyer to help with the paperwork until the heats of the 5000m on August 3.

The story of Grijalva trying to get to the Olympics went viral as people discovered his situation through social media posts. "When people saw my story, I got so much support," said Grijalva. "It's insane when people rally behind you. Someone's post blew up and got lots of attention, putting the USCIS under pressure."

In a final effort to obtain the advanced reentry document, Grijalva took a trip to the U.S. Citizenship and Immigration Services office in Phoenix on July 26 and contacted Arizona Senator Mark Kelly. After an agonizing month of not knowing whether he would be competing in Tokyo, Grijalva's application was approved, and his agent booked his flight for July 30.

For the first time since he had arrived in the United States as a one-year-old, Grijalva was allowed to leave the country and legally return.

Grijalva arrived in Tokyo on July 31 and lined up for the 5000m heats three days later. With little time to mentally prepare for this race and having done zero heat training because he didn't think his application would be approved on time, Grijalva somehow dug deep enough to secure a spot in the final as the second-to-last qualifier.

Against all odds, Grijalva stood on the starting line of his first Olympic final proudly wearing his Guatemalan singlet and feeling like he had nothing to lose. As had been his goal for the past two years, Grijalva simply focused on giving his all when it mattered most. And he did just that. Grijalva ran a personal best and a Guatemalan national record of 13:10.09 to finish twelfth, an effort the humble athlete wasn't afraid to say he was proud of.

"Get your positioning and fight hard."

That was Smith's advice to the NAU men's cross country team as they headed to the starting line of the 2021 NCAA Cross Country Championships.

After graduating Blaise Ferro and Grijalva in spring 2021, speculation swirled. Would the Lumberjacks secure their second national cross country team title of the calendar year? The pandemic had made this unprecedented opportunity possible, but NAU would be losing two of their top-ten finishers from the 2020 championships held in March 2021. Could NAU's fourth and fifth men pick up the slack?

"There's a case to be made that NAU, who enters Saturday's 2021 NCAA Cross Country Championships in Tallahassee ranked number one in the nation, is not even the favorite," read the LetsRun.com race preview. "In cross country, NAU, OK State, and BYU are the blue bloods. It's time for some new blood: Notre Dame will win their first NCAA XC title since 1957."

The University of Notre Dame had finished second behind NAU at nationals in March, and their clear goal was to do one better in Tallahassee. By now, the Lumberjacks had gotten used to being the target of other teams' ambitions. It didn't bother them because they didn't acknowledge it.

"We didn't care about what anyone else was doing," said Theo Quax. "We never talked about another team the whole season."

When the gun went off in Tallahassee and the stampede was let loose, NAU ran like a team that wasn't concerned about anyone else's race tactics. They showed patience through a fast opening kilometer and trusted their ability to move through the field once the pace settled. By four kilometers, the Lumberjacks had established their lead, while other teams were already struggling.

NAU maintained that position through eight kilometers with their point total fluctuating by just single digits at each kilometer split. Historically NAU had a knack for turning up the heat in the final minutes of big races. In fall 2016, Smith had first glimpsed how the Lumberjacks thrived over the last two kilometers at nationals. He liked to say this was the part of the race where his athletes set up their desks and chairs and got to work.

Leading the Lumberjacks across the finish line was Abdihamid Nur in seventh; the same place he finished as NAU's third man in March. Nur was coming off a big spring season, running a school record of 27:42.73 for the 10,000m. Close behind Nur was Nico Young in tenth and Drew Bosley in thirteenth.

The question of how NAU's fourth and fifth runners would perform lingered for just sixteen more seconds after Bosley crossed the line. George Kusche, who had recently transferred to NAU from the University of Nebraska, was the next Lumberjack across the line, followed by Brodey Hasty less than a second later.

The agony and the ecstasy. Abdihamid Nur gutted out seventh place to lead NAU scorers at the 2021 NCAA national meet in Tallahassee, Florida, then celebrated on the podium.

With so many athletes coming up the finishing straight together, Hasty was confused about where he had placed. "When I crossed the line, I thought we had lost," he said. "I thought George and I were in the fifties."

That feeling of defeat lasted just a split second before Nur ran over to give Hasty a big hug. Hasty had underestimated his placing. He had finished thirty-ninth, with Kusche two spots ahead in thirty-seventh. Hasty looked up at the scoreboard while continuing to hug Nur and saw NAU in first place with ninety-two points, ahead of Iowa State University in second and Oklahoma State University in third. This was NAU's fifth title in the space of six years, and it moved them to fourth on the all-time list, equal to the University of Wisconsin and the University of Colorado.

In the team's post-race interview, Nur was asked where he had seen the most growth in the team since March.

"Our bond together," Nur told the interviewer. "The doubts and all of the extra talk, all the noise, we're used to that. When you're at NAU you know that's what comes with it. A headline can't look exciting without our name on it."

Three years had passed since NAU athletes competed at the NCAA national indoor meet. After the meet was canceled in 2020 and the team opted to focus on cross country instead of indoors in 2021, it was finally time to bring a team trophy back to Flagstaff. The only problem: in 2020 NAU qualified seven male athletes but just three in 2022.

The three Lumberjacks who would represent NAU at the 2022 Indoor Track and Field Championships in Birmingham, Alabama, were Nur, Young, and Bosley. All three were entered in the 5000m after they ran 13:22.24, 13:22.59, and 13:26.19, respectively, at Boston University in December 2021. Nur would also be competing in the 3000m, having run 7:40.66, joined by Young after a last-minute 7:59.02 (unconverted) at the Big Sky Indoor Track and Field Championships held at elevation.

Nur had also qualified in the mile with a 3:55.94 time, as had Young after running 3:56.00, but both decided to scratch from the event. Among all the impressive performances during this indoor season, Young's 4:02.89 (unconverted) mile in the Dome, breaking Diego Estrada's record, was a definite highlight.

On March 11, 2022, Nur, Young, and Bosley lined up for the 5000m on the first day of competition. Iowa State's Wesley Kiptoo took the race out in a blistering fifty-eight-second opening 400 meters. Nur wisely held back from the quick early effort and stayed relaxed until it was time to make his move late in the race.

With five laps to go, Nur took the lead and began to slowly squeeze down the pace. With daylight between himself and second place as he came into the bell lap, Nur maintained his lead through the finish to bring home his first individual national title in a meet record 13:19.01. Young was the next Lumberjack across the line in third, with Bosley finishing as the last scoring athlete in eighth.

On the second and final day in Birmingham, Nur backed up his win in the 5000m with a win in the 3000m. He became the first NAU male athlete to complete this double. Adding Young's seventh-place finish in the 3000m to the team's total, NAU concluded the meet with twenty-nine points for fourth place—earning the first podium finish for the track and field program.

This team trophy would get a new home in Smith's office, while the array of cross country trophies moved from their display case in the Dome, directly across San Francisco Street, to NAU's shiny new $46 million Student-Athlete High Performance Center a month later.

The momentum the Lumberjacks had built during the indoor season continued into the outdoor schedule, where Nur and Young lined up for a 5000m at the Sound Running Track Meet on May 6. With NAU alum Geordie Beamish as the first pacer, the two Lumberjacks boarded a train that included 2020 Tokyo Olympic Games 1500m champion Jakob Ingebrigtsen. Nur kept himself in the front pack as the field started to separate and hung on for fourth in 13:06.32—a new NCAA 5000m record. Young wasn't far behind in fifth, running 13:11.30.

Nur and Young went on to qualify for the 2022 NCAA Outdoor Track and Field Championships, with Nur taking third in the 10,000m and Young third in the 5000m. The duo extended their season to the 2022 U.S. Track and Field Championships, where Nur finished third in the 5000m to earn a spot on Team USA, which would compete at the 2022 World Athletics Championships in Eugene, Oregon.

One characteristic of a successful college program is how it sets its athletes up for future successes once they graduate. After Nur signed a professional contract with Nike before his heat at the World Championships—forgoing the remainder of his college eligibility—he became one of five NAU alumni to compete at these Championships. Joining Nur in the 5000m was Grijalva representing Guatemala and Beamish representing New Zealand. In the hammer throw, Brooke Andersen represented Team USA and Adam Keenan represented Canada.

Andersen kicked things off for the NAU alumni group in outstanding fashion by launching an enormous 78.96m throw. That effort earned the 2020 Olympian a new title: world champion.

On the starting line of the 5000m final, Nur and Grijalva stood side by side. It had been a long journey to get to this spot. In an interview after the heats, Grijalva was asked about his friendship with Nur. With tears filling his eyes, Grijalva responded,

"Where he came from and where I come from, it's pretty special honestly. We've been through a lot together and we're brothers, you know, best friends…I'm sure he told you he's staying in Flagstaff."

A brotherly bond that started on the NAU team would continue in Flagstaff with Smith as their professional coach. The adversity in their lives helped them develop a common understanding for one another. It helped them work together as teammates, to live together as roommates, and to push each other to become World Championship finalists.

As the camera panned to Grijalva standing on the starting line, he grabbed Nur's arm and lifted it in the air—the last overt display of their friendship until the race was complete.

To round out an incredible event from the NAU alumni group at Eugene's Hayward Field, Grijalva finished fourth and Nur eleventh in their first World Championships. This impressive showing will likely only be the start for these two as they continue pushing each other to their limits at Lumberjack Stadium for years to come.

Multiple Olympians and World Championship qualifiers. A fifth cross country title. A first-ever podium finish in track. A new facility on par with any in the country. The state of the NAU program seemed to be getting brighter every day in the year-plus since March 2021, when the Lumberjack men returned to the mountaintop and avenged their 2019 runner-up showing.

But living through a dynasty means that even when you're in the middle of it, you know there's no guarantee it will continue. Times change, but the best course of action is to respect the traditions and history that got you there and keep pushing beyond the summit.

On any given Tuesday night in fall 2022, Smith could be found standing on the infield of Coconino High School's track in east Flagstaff. Often coming straight from an afternoon workout with the NAU cross country team, Smith made it a priority to fit Team Run Flagstaff practices into his busy schedule.

"If you only work with elite athletes and on high performance, you can forget about what is important," Smith said. "I can't do a lot of it, but I get an hour a week to get back to the grassroots of the sport. This is a reminder that NAU is a part of the running community, but it isn't *the* running community."

Indeed, *the* running community is as robust as the college program. During summer months, the weekly Bagel Run, a tradition that has been going on for nearly two decades, can bring more than 100 runners to Biff's Bagels. The Flagstaff Urban Trail System has grown to fifty-six miles and, based on the city's master plan, will continue growing to 130 total miles. HYPO2 continues to support some of the best athletes in the world. From 2009 through the 2020 Games, athletes from forty-four countries who had trained in Flagstaff and used HYPO2 services earned a total of 356 Olympic and Paralympic medals.

And there stood Smith, having left and returned to his beloved mountain town, in a much more prominent position in the sport than when he founded Team Run Flagstaff more than a decade earlier, yet still, in a fundamental way, standing in the center of both successes. In between shouting splits or "time" at the end of each rep as runners young and old passed by, Smith considered how the NAU season was progressing.

The women were off to a great start. After finishing second at the Cowboy Jamboree in Oklahoma and third at the Nuttycombe Wisconsin Invitational, they were ranked fourth in the country by the U.S. Track & Field and Cross Country Coaches Association.

The men, however, were struggling to build their usual momentum by the middle of the season. After a third-place finish at the Jamboree, the Lumberjacks got third once more at Nuttycombe—ninety-one points behind Stanford in first.

As a result of an increase in intensity and some tough hilly runs added to his training plan for the 2022 season—based on his understanding of how challenging the nationals course would be—Smith had dug a hole that his athletes ran themselves into. Once the fatigue set in and the Lumberjacks struggled to recover between workouts, it was too late to have them feeling anything close to fresh for the mid-season races.

Somehow, amid all the negative press the team had received, Smith maintained a quiet confidence about the remainder of the season—provided some immediate adjustments were made to their training.

The TRF practice came to an end, with the sun lost somewhere behind Buffalo Park, and Smith finally headed home. His coaching job would continue long into the night while his athletes slept, giving their bodies time to recover, so the training their coach was putting together could be put to maximum use.

Elise Stearns led the charge for the Lumberjacks at the 2022 NCAA Cross Country Championships in Stillwater, Oklahoma. The sixth-ranked team in the country coming into the race was hoping to significantly improve upon their twenty-third-place showing in 2021.

The familiar firm brown grass on the Greiner Family OSU Cross Country Course felt like it had been manicured and pressed, providing fast footing for the athletes. The turf gave good energy return from each stride over the rolling hills, and a bite to the air was felt deep in each runner's lungs.

The Lumberjack women held onto fourth place until the race pace started to ramp up over the last two kilometers. They ran with the intention of getting on the podium—confidence they had worked hard for.

Running the race of her life with the front of the field, Stearns crossed the line in fourth place, with Annika Reiss in forty-sixth, Jesselyn Bries in sixty-third, Bryn Morley in eighty-fifth, and Alexis Kebbe in ninetieth, earning themselves a sixth place to match their ranking coming in. This was their best team result in thirty-one years and second best in program history.

There was a moment of calm as fans got back into their positions and eagerly awaited the start of the men's race. The spike of adrenaline felt from the sidelines had settled, but soon it would inject itself into the crowd once more.

Young was quick to get everyone's hearts racing again as he made a decisive move at the one-kilometer mark to open a gap on the field. This move had been planned a month in advance. It was the best strategy to give the Lumberjacks a shot at another team title.

Bosley, who made the decision to go with Young, helped share the load of dictating the pace at the front, with Charles Hicks of Stanford coming along for the ride. With only a kilometer to go, Hicks pulled away from the two Lumberjacks. The pack was charging, but Young held onto second place and Bosley third in a scene reminiscent of Baxter and Day's front-running efforts in 2017.

Next across the line for NAU was Santiago Prosser in nineteenth, Hasty in twenty-fifth, and Kusche in thirty-ninth.

The leaders emerge. NAU teammates Nico Young (right) and Drew Bosley (center) set a blistering pace from the first kilometer at the 2022 NCAA meet. Stanford's Charles Hicks went with the Lumberjacks.

The celebrations from the NAU supporters were instant, as the results listed NAU as the winners the moment Kusche crossed the line.

But when the results refreshed, Oklahoma State University, racing on its home course, jumped to the top with a thirty-three-point margin on NAU.

The local crowd erupted.

The results refreshed again.

The cheers were short lived.

NAU and OSU had both scored eighty-three points. The winner would be decided by a five-man, head-to-head tiebreaker.

ESPN got the whole NAU team when it asked for the championship perspective in 2022. Left to right: Ryan Raff, Santiago Prosser (partially obscured), George Kusche, Drew Bosley, Colin Sahlman, Nico Young, Brodey Hasty (obscured), and Theo Quax.

When the scorers of each team were compared against each other, numbers one through five, NAU won three of five battles. The Cowboys then protested to confirm the placing of one of their athletes—understandable considering the mad dash of runners crossing the line at a big meet. The wait for the decision just added to what seemed an eternity between the first displayed results and the eventual winner being declared.

Bosley had been handed the first-place team trophy prematurely while the protest was still ongoing. His hands held it tight, close to his chest, unwilling to lift it above his head until a final decision was made.

After a long and challenging season, with endless doubts to overcome, Bosley, with his Boys by his side, finally hoisted the trophy to the sky. ∆

Drew Bosley (center) celebrates a repeat three-peat with his Boys.

"I hope NAU track and cross country is a part of the sport forever. I hope that 100 years from now the team is still a part of the local community. I hope that despite having success we never forget about our roots, and we never get so big and fancy that we get away from the purity of what we do here. The bottom line is that we still pile athletes in a van and drive to Bellemont or A-1 and run down a dirt road and back. As we get big and win things, we need to remember that is the heart and soul of what we do."

—Mike Smith, NAU Director of Cross Country and Track and Field, 2021

Appendix A

NAU Team Results from National Cross Country Championships

Men, NAIA
1969 – 9th

Men, NCAA
1971 – 9th
1984 – 17th
1986 – 10th
1987 – 8th
1988 – 2nd
1990 – 19th
1991 – 19th
1994 – 4th
1995 – 2nd
1996 – 12th
1998 – 7th
1999 – 12th
2000 – 7th
2001 – 4th
2002 – 7th
2003 – 3rd
2004 – 24th
2007 – 4th
2008 – 6th
2009 – 4th
2010 – 9th
2011 – 14th
2012 – 4th
2013 – 2nd
2014 – 4th
2016 – 1st
2017 – 1st
2018 – 1st
2019 – 2nd
2020* – 1st
2021 – 1st
2022 – 1st

Women, NCAA
1987 – 11th
1988 – 14th
1989 – 13th
1990 – 14th
1991 – 3rd
1992 – 9th
1996 – 10th
1998 – 17th
1999 – 11th
2001 – 12th
2002 – 10th
2003 – 15th
2005 – 12th
2007 – 7th
2008 – 23rd
2019 – 14th
2020* – 11th
2021 – 23rd
2022 – 6th

*National meet postponed until March 2021 due to COVID-19

The jubilant 2016 national champion Lumberjacks. Front row, from left: Jeff Trudo, Matt Baxter, Andy Trouard, Futsum Zienasellassie, former coach Ron Mann, Coach Eric Heins, Athletic Director Lisa Campos, NAU President Rita Cheng, Assistant Coach Leah Rosenfeld, Senior Associate Athletics Director Robyn Sharp, Assistant Coach Mike Smith. Back row: Nathan Weitz, Tyler Day, Cory Glines, Geordie Beamish, Blaise Ferro, Peter Lomong (obscured), Cade Burks, Harvey Nelson, Graduate Assistant Coach Jarred Cornfield.

NAU alumni and 2022 champions celebrate the repeat three-peat together. Everyone in the photo had a hand in at least one of the six crowns.

Appendix B

NAU Individual Top 40 Finishers, NCAA Cross Country Championships

Men

2nd	Nico Young	2022
2nd	Matthew Baxter	2017
2nd	David McNeill	2009
3rd	Drew Bosley	2022
3rd	Tyler Day	2017
3rd	Futsum Zienasellassie	2014
3rd	Lopez Lomong	2007
3rd	Bo Reed	1988
4th	Nico Young	2020
4th	Futsum Zienasellassie	2016
4th	Futsum Zienasellassie	2013
4th	Lopez Lomong	2006
5th	Jordan Chipangama	2009
6th	Blaise Ferro	2020
6th	Richard Sliney	1971
6th	Tyler Day	2018
7th	Abdihamid Nur	2021
7th	Abdihamid Nur	2020
7th	Diego Estrada	2011
8th	Peter Lomong	2017
8th	Milfred Tewawina	1988
9th	Luis Grijalva	2020
9th	Larry Chumley	1984
10th	David McNeill	2007
10th	Henrik Ahnström	2003
10th	Travis Laird	2001
10th	Dave Tocheri	1972
11th	Nico Young	2021
11th	Matthew Baxter	2016
12th	Richard Sliney	1970
13th	Drew Bosley	2021
15th	Brian Shrader	2012
15th	David McNeill	2008
15th	Matthew Baxter	2018
16th	Diego Estrada	2010
18th	Seth Watkins	2002
19th	Santiago Prosser	2022
19th	Ahmed Osman	2010
20th	Jama Bile	1995
21st	Travis Laird	2003
21st	Richard Sliney	1972
22nd	Drew Bosley	2019
22nd	Tim Martin	1996
23rd	Tyler Day	2016
23rd	Theo Martin	1994
23rd	Luis Grijalva	2018
24th	Jama Bile	1994
24th	Kim White	1991
25th	Brodey Hasty	2022
25th	Matt McElroy	2013
25th	Bruno Mazzotta	2001
25th	Bo Reed	1986
25th	Milfred Tewawina	1987
26th	Blaise Ferro	2018
27th	Henrik Ahnstrom	2001
27th	Mark Souza	1985
28th	Brian Shrader	2013
29th	Peter Lomong	2018
30th	Tim Martin	1995
31st	Matt McElroy	2014
31st	Futsum Zienasellassie	2012
31st	Kevin Koeper	2000
32nd	Theo Martin	1995
33rd	Abdihamid Nur	2019
33rd	John Howell	1995
35th	Andy Trouard	2017
36th	Caleb Hoover	2014
36th	Seth Watkins	2003
36th	Web Shelley	1997
37th	George Kusche	2021
37th	Geordie Beamish	2019
37th	Andy Trouard	2016
37th	Richard Selby	1971
38th	Billy Herman	1998
39th	George Kusche	2022
39th	Brodey Hasty	2021
39th	Geordie Beamish	2018
40th	Geordie Beamish	2017
40th	Juwan Nuvayokva	2001
40th	Billy Herman	1999

Appendix B *Continued*

NAU Individual Top 40 Finishers, NCAA Cross Country Championships

Women

1st	Johanna Nilsson	2005
1st	Angela Chalmers	1986
4th	Elise Stearns	2022
6th	Taryn O'Neill	2020
8th	Ida Nilsson	2002
8th	Angela Chalmers	1985
9th	Ida Nilsson	2003
9th	Rikke Ulslev Pedersen	1996
10th	Johanna Nilsson	2003
10th	Amy Swier	1997
12th	Ida Nilsson	2001
16th	Veronica Pohl	2008
21th	Kendra Versendaal	1999
21th	Tracy Jarman	1991
21th	Larah Treadwell	1989
22th	Tracy Jarman	1992
25th	Martha Wood	1988
26th	Kristi Klinnert	1991
30th	Ilsa Paulson	2007
33th	Emily Allison	1998
36th	Nikki Toms	1987
37th	Larah Treadwell	1991
38th	Veronica Pohl	2009
40th	Tracy Jarman	1990

Swedish sisters Johanna (658) and Ida Nilsson (659) were key figures in the NAU running story.

Appendix C

NAU School Records in Distance Events, Track and Field (through Summer 2023)

Men

Indoor

Ray Chavez	*600m*	1:11.35	1979
Lopez Lomong	*800m*	1:48.80	2007
Abdihamid Nur	*Mile*	3:55.94	2022
Drew Bosley	*3,000m*	7:36.42*☆	2023
Drew Bosley	*5,000m*	13:13.26*	2022–23
Nathan Weitz, DeShon Norris, Andy Trouard, Futsum Zienasellassie	*Distance Medley Relay*	9:39.19	2016

Outdoor

Lopez Lomong	*800m*	1:45.79	2007
Abdihamid Nur	*1,500m*	3:36.33	2022
Billy Herman	*3,000m Steeplechase*	8:26.12	2000
Abdihamid Nur	*5,000m*	13:06.32*☆	2022
Abdihamid Nur	*10,000m*	27:42.73	2021

Women

Indoor

Charlotte Reeves	*600m*	1:31.45	1982
Ashley Taylor	*800m*	2:03.66	2018
Johanna Nilsson	*Mile*	4:32.49	2006
Johanna Nilsson	*3,000m*	9:06.61	2006
Elise Stearns	*5,000m*	15:33.74	2022–23
Katja Rosenplaenter, Monique Young, Elin Wilk, Johanna Nilsson	*Distance Medley Relay*	11:13.18	2006

Outdoor

Angela Chalmers	*800m*	2:03.52	1987
Johanna Nilsson	*1,500m*	4:10.72	2003
Ida Nilsson	*3,000m Steeplechase*	9:43.25	2004
Ida Nilsson	*5,000m*	15:33.18	2004
Jessa Hanson	*10,000m*	32:55.24	2021

**Big Sky Conference record*

☆NCAA record

Alumnus Luis Grijalva lifts national runner-up Nico Young off the ground as Lumberjacks past and present acknowledge the dynasty in 2022 after their sixth national title in seven seasons.

Appendix D

NAU Distance Athletes/Coaches in School Hall of Fame (through 2023)

Induction Class of 1982
Richard (Sliney) Lawrence, cross country 1969–73

Induction Class of 1984
Leo "Red" Haberlack, track and field coach 1964–82

Induction Class of 1987
1971 men's cross country team

Induction Class of 1991
Richard Selby, cross country, track and field 1969–73

Induction Class of 1992
Angela Chalmers, cross country, track and field, 1982–86

Induction Class of 1993
1988 men's cross country team

Induction Class of 1995
Mark Souza, cross country, track and field 1983–86

Induction Class of 1997
Art Menchaca, cross country, track and field 1979–80;
Nikki Toms, cross country, track and field 1988–90

Induction Class of 1999
Ron Mann, cross country, track and field coach 1980–2005

Induction Class of 2005
1995 men's cross country team

Induction Class of 2006
Dave Tocheri, cross country, track and field 1969–72

Induction Class of 2010
Ida Nilsson, cross country, 2001–04; track and field, 2002–05;
1967 track and field team

Induction Class of 2011
Johanna Nilsson, track and field, 2003–06 and cross country 2002–03, 2005; 1991 women's cross country team

Induction Class of 2013
Lopez Lomong, cross country, track and field 2005–07

Induction Class of 2015
David McNeill, cross country, track and field 2007–10

Induction Class of 2016
Rikke Ulslev Pedersen, cross country, track and field 1994–99

Induction Class of 2019
2003 men's cross country team

Induction Class of 2022
Eric Heins, cross country, track and field coach, 2007–16
Diego Estrada, cross country, track and field, 2008–13
Kristi Klinnert, cross country, track and field, 1989–93

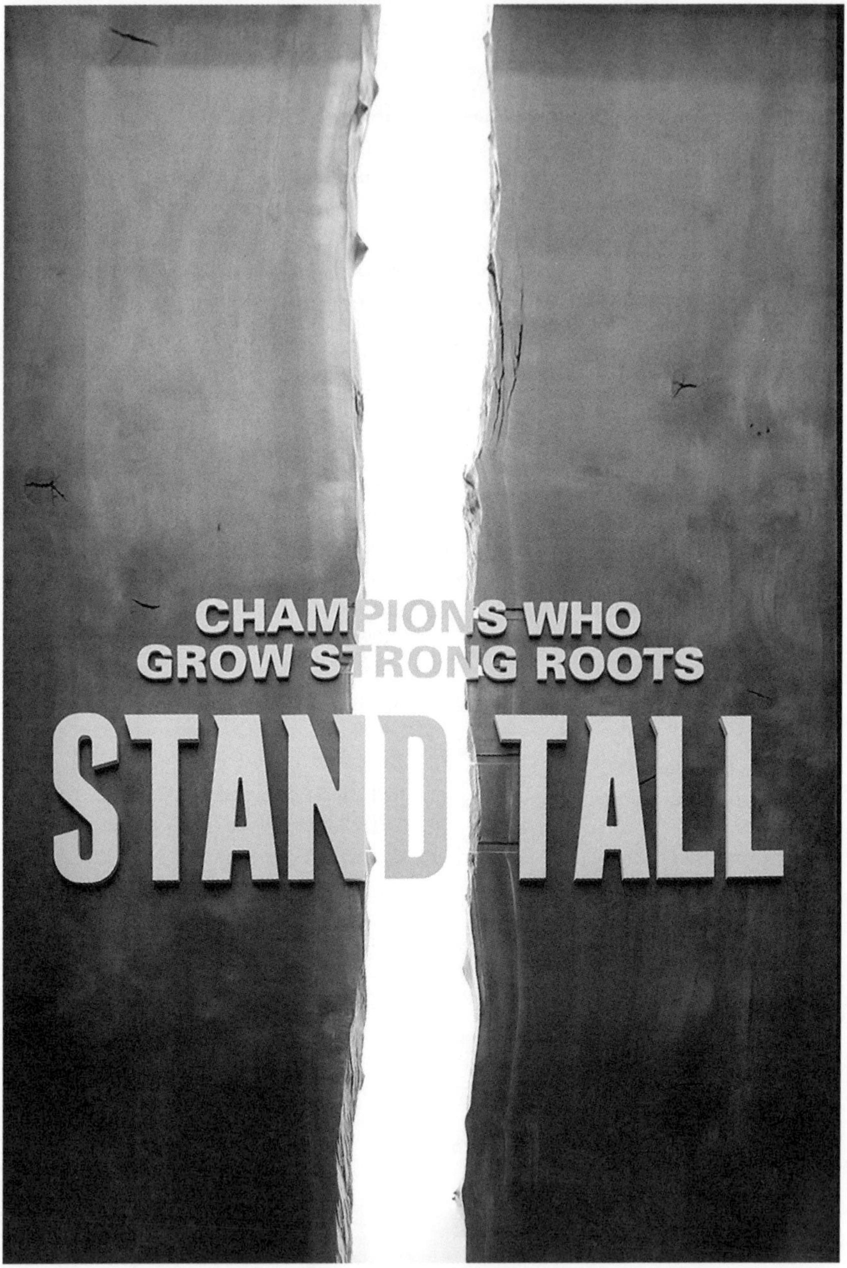

In the entrance to the Student-Athlete High Performance Center, photos of NAU greats such as Lopez Lomong and Angela Chalmers share space with a split wood display with these fitting words for Lumberjacks: CHAMPIONS WHO GROW STRONG ROOTS STAND TALL.

Photography Credits

Front cover

Photo montage designed by Dariusz Janczewski. Runners photo: © Colin Schultz. NAU men at the starting line of the 2021 NCAA Cross Country Championships, held in Tallahassee, Florida, on November 20, 2021. Mountain photo: Bob Blasi/Coconino National Forest.

Front matter

Pages iv–v (Bosley and Young leading): courtesy NAU Athletics/CourtneyVondracek.

Pages xiii–ix: Welcome to Flag! map by Dariusz Janczewski.

Page xv (L. Lomong): courtesy NAU Athletics.

Page xx (Dome): courtesy NAU.

Prologue

Pages 2 (NAU women at nationals, Molvin), 3 (Smith), and 5 (Beamish): all courtesy NAU Athletics.

Part I

Chapter 1

Page 16 (Haberlack): courtesy Shirley Haberlack

Chapter 3

Page 27 (Mills/Young): courtesy James T. O'Neil, M.D.

Page 30 (Ryun/O'Neil/Young): courtesy James T. O'Neil, M.D.

Pages 32–3 (Ryun/Daniels/Von Ruden): image by Rich Clarkson. Courtesy of the McGovern Historical Center, Texas Medical Center Library, IC 077 Medical World News Photograph Collection, IC077-6960-001. Personal permission granted to Jim and Anne Ryun by Rich Clarkson.

Chapter 4

Pages 40 (U of A and NAU runners) and 41 (Sliney): from the collection of Scott Giddings.

Pages 42–3 (1971 team): courtesy Ron Mann.

Page 44 (Harbster/Matthews/Mann/Selby): courtesy Jeff Matthews.

Chapter 5

Page 55: Skydome Construction as seen from the S. Milton Road/I-17 bridge. NAU.ARC.1976.2.47. Northern Arizona University Archives. Special Collections and Archives, Cline Library, Northern Arizona University

Page 59 (Louie on his side): Lumberjack Statue #1

Being Moved. NAU.ARC.1974.15.14. Northern Arizona University Archives. Special Collections and Archives, Cline Library, Northern Arizona University.

Page 59 (Louie standing): courtesy Zoe Schrag.

Chapter 6

Page 67 (1980 team): courtesy Ron Mann.

Part II

Chapter 7

Page 75 (Mann/Young/Haberlack/Murray): courtesy Ron Mann.

Page 79 (Chalmers): courtesy Ron Mann.

Chapter 8

Page 87 (1988 team): courtesy Gaines DuVall.

Page 88 (Mann with cigar): courtesy Ron Mann.

Page 90 (1991 team): courtesy Gaines DuVall.

Chapter 9

Page 95 (yearbook, scoreboard, 1995 team): all courtesy Ron Mann.

Page 101 (Ahnström and Sheikh/Smith): both photos courtesy Mike Leary.

Pages 103 (Mann/Kyte), 105 (Watkins/Weilacher), 106 (2003 team), and 107 (Mann with watch): all courtesy Ron Mann.

Chapter 10

Page 113 (Hardy): courtesy Traevin Hardy.

Pages 117 (2005 team) and 119 (J. Nilsson): both courtesy Cheryl Treworgy/Pretty Sporty Photos.

Chapter 11

Page 122 (Anthony/Gmitroski/Hennigar): courtesy Vicente Úbeda Pitarch.

Part III

Chapter 12

Page 134 (McNeill): courtesy NAU Athletics.

Page 137 (van): courtesy Ron Mann.

Pages 138–9 (Estrada), 141 (Zienasellassie/McElroy/Shrader), 142 (Shrader and McElroy), and 145 (Chipangama): all courtesy NAU Athletics.

Chapter 13

Page 155 (Heins): courtesy NAU Athletics.

Chapter 14

Page 159 (Baxter, Beamish, Day, Glines, Trouard, Weitz, Zeinasellassie): all seven photos courtesy NAU Athletics.

Page 165 (Zienasellassie/Heins/Weitz): courtesy NAU Athletics/ Dave Wegiel-Pinola.

Page 166 (Heins/Day): courtesy NAU Athletics/ Justin Casterline.

Chapter 15

Page 171 (Haberlack): courtesy Shirley Haberlack.

Pages 173 (Beamish), 174 (P. Lomong), 178 (Baxter/Day), and 181 (hat and 2017 team): all courtesy NAU Athletics/Justin Casterline.

Chapter 16

Pages 186–7 (Day and NAU runners) and 189 (2018 team): courtesy NAU Athletics/Ricky Bassman.

Page 192 (NAU and Japanese runners): courtesy NAU Athletics.

Part IV

Chapter 17

Page 199 (Bosley): courtesy NAU Athletics.

Chapter 19

Page 217 (Grijalva): courtesy NAU Athletics/Ricky Bassman.

Page 222 (Quax): courtesy NAU Athletics.

Chapter 20

Pages 229 (Young) and 231 (Raff): courtesy NAU Athletics/Adriana Candelaria.

Chapter 21

Pages 242 (NAU women at start and O'Neill), 244 (Young/Nur/Ferro/Grijalva), 245 (Hasty), 246 (Smith/Nur), and 247 (2021 team): all courtesy NAU Athletics/Adriana Candelaria.

Epilogue

Page 252 (Nur mid-race and Nur on podium): both photos courtesy NAU Athletics.

Page 258 (leaders emerge), 258 (team with microphone), 259 (Bosley with trophy): all courtesy NAU Athletics/Courtney Vondracek.

Back matter

Page 262 (2016 team): courtesy NAU Athletics.

Page 262 (alumni with 2022 champs): courtesy NAU Athletics/Courtney Vondracek.

Page 264 (Nilsson sisters): courtesy Cheryl Treworgy/Pretty Sporty Photos.

Page 266 (Grijalva/Young): courtesy NAU Athletics/Courtney Vondracek.

Page 268 (strong roots): courtesy NAU Athletics.

About the authors

Page 272 (Baxter): courtesy Matt Baxter.

Page 272 (Mann): courtesy Ron Mann.

Back page

Page 274 (team at White House): courtesy Jarred Cornfield.

Project Backers

These generous people backed the *Running Up the Mountain* book project through a crowdfunding campaign on Kickstarter and via other avenues. The names in bold ran extra laps to fund this project. Our gratitude goes out to the more than 200 backers who helped us reach the top.

Matt Baxter and Ron Mann

Andrea Bookout, *in memoriam*
Ben Rosario
Chris Gomez and Ryan Stevens
Christian Graham
Dean M. Hebert
The Deren Family
Douglas Mapel, MD
Elliot Gindi
James Murray Good
Jenny Marczynski
Jill Larson
Jim McCarthy
Julie Hammonds and Matt Anderson
Kit Wobeter, *Coe College XC/Track '06*
Marci Martinez and Doug Madsen
Michael Kallsen
Michael McManus
Myles Schrag
Monica Schrag
Neil and Diana Weintraub
Paul Ostapuk *'80*
Refugio Reyes
Rikke Ulslev Degn (Pedersen)
Rob Economy
Sam Lloyd-Perks
Sean Kerrigan
Sean Kennedy
The Shrader Family / Brian Shrader
Toby Gualter
The Van Arkel Family
Tommy Wheeler / The Wheeler Family
William B. Brancato

About the Authors

Matt Baxter

Matt Baxter was the runner-up at the 2017 NCAA Cross Country Championships and a scoring athlete for NAU's first three national team titles. He finished his college career as a five-time All-American with one individual conference title. He's now a professional runner for Flagstaff-based HOKA NAZ Elite, where he has been a New Zealand national champion and previous national record holder in the indoor 5000m and the road 5K. This is his second book. He also authored *Hurt Me If You Can: The Tales of a High School Runner,* a memoir of his formative years as an athlete in New Zealand. Baxter lives in Flagstaff with his partner, Emily, and son, Miles.

Ron Mann

Ron Mann is also an NAU alumnus and letter-winner who went on to coach his alma mater's cross country and track and field squads for 24 years, where he mentored 107 All-Americans, four NCAA individual national champions, and 16 teams that finished in the top 10. He coached USA men's national teams in international competitions and served on the coaching staff at the 2008 Beijing Olympics. Mann held many positions with the U.S. Track and Field and Cross Country Coaches Association, including the presidency from 2011–13. He coached 47 more All-Americans at the University of Louisville before retiring from collegiate coaching in 2013. Mann coached Wesley Korir, winner of the Los Angeles Marathon in 2010–11 and the Boston Marathon in 2012, and continues to coach elite runners. He has been inducted into nine halls of fame, including the prestigious USTFCCCA Hall of Fame in 2018. △

About the Publisher

Soulstice Publishing brings to life "books with soul" that inspire readers with stories of human potential realized and celebrate our unique position in the Southwest.

Soulstice took root in our mountain town of Flagstaff, Arizona, which sits at the base of the San Francisco Peaks, on homelands sacred to Native Americans throughout the region. We honor their past, present, and future generations, as well as their original and ongoing care for the lands we also hold dear.

Surrounded by ponderosa pines, enriched by diverse cultures, and inspired by the optimistic Western spirit, Flagstaff abounds with scientists, artists, athletes, and many other people who love the outdoors. It is quite an inspiring place to live. Considering the dearth of oxygen at our 7,000-foot elevation, you might say it leaves us breathless. △

Learn more at **soulsticepublishing.com**

Soulstice
PUBLISHING
books with *soul* • Flagstaff, AZ

The 2022 national champion cross country team was honored at the White House on June 12, 2023, to celebrate their victory. Front row, from left: Justin Keyes, George Kusche, Riley Human, Drew Bosley, Colin Sahlman, Brodey Hasty, Randy Espinoza, Theo Quax, Aidan Puffer. Back row, from left: Kang Nyoak, Caleb Easton, Corey Gorgas, Erik Le Roux, Cael Grotenhuis, Santiago Prosser, Jack Scherer, Ryan Raff, Aiden Barnhill, Nico Young.